Expectant Prayers for Expectant Mothers

A Daily Prayer Guide, Devotional, and Journal Through Pregnancy

Written By:
Jennifer J. Weiss

xulon PRESS

Expectant Prayers for Expectant Mothers
A Daily Prayer Guide, Devotional, and Journal Through Pregnancy
by Jennifer J. Weiss

Printed in the United States of America

ISBN 1-60034-498-4

www.xulonpress.com

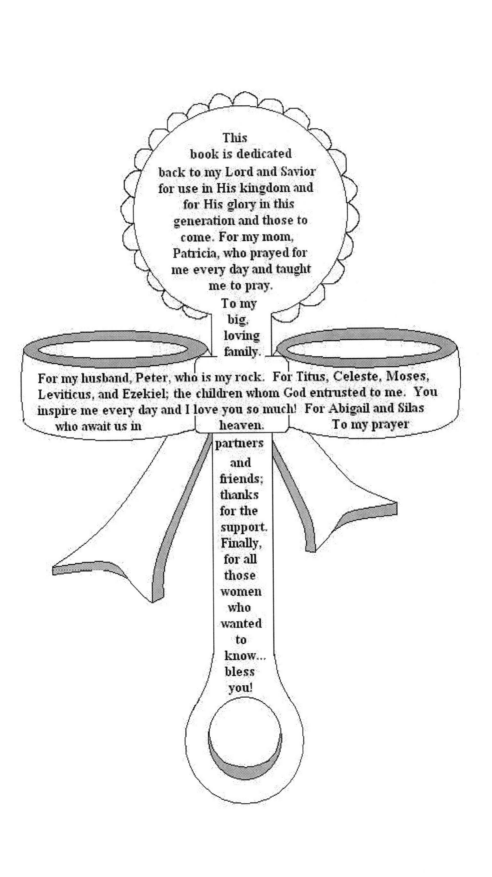

This book is dedicated back to my Lord and Savior for use in His kingdom and for His glory in this generation and those to come. For my mom, Patricia, who prayed for me every day and taught me to pray. To my big, loving family.

For my husband, Peter, who is my rock. For Titus, Celeste, Moses, Leviticus, and Ezekiel; the children whom God entrusted to me. You inspire me every day and I love you so much! For Abigail and Silas who await us in heaven. To my prayer partners and friends; thanks for the support. Finally, for all those women who wanted to know... bless you!

Table of Contents & Index

PART 1: BEFORE YOU FIND OUT (PLANNING TO WEEK 4)

PART 2: FIRST TRIMESTER (WEEKS 4-12)

TABLE OF CONTENTS & INDEX CONTINUED

TABLE OF CONTENTS & INDEX CONTINUED

PART 3: SECOND TRIMESTER (WEEKS 13-26)

TABLE OF CONTENTS & INDEX CONTINUED

TABLE OF CONTENTS & INDEX CONTINUED

PART 4: THIRD TRIMESTER (WEEKS 27-40+)

TABLE OF CONTENTS & INDEX CONTINUED

TABLE OF CONTENTS & INDEX CONTINUED

A Mother's Poem

In the quiet moments of the day,
I reflect on you and am filled with praise.
Hidden away from human eyes,
You're a miracle of God's design.

Expectantly I pray for you.
You're in my thoughts and in all I do.
What will you look like? What will you be?
What will you accomplish by age two or three?

You're like the morning, fresh and new,
Just as the roses kissed with dew.
I long for the day we're face to face,
Cradling you in my warm embrace.

My mother's heart is fully aware
Of all I'd like to teach and share.
I am immersed in joy and love
At God's blessed gift sent from above.

I pledge to parent with God's ways in mind
And leave a legacy of faith behind.
My life, in turn, will be blessed, too,
Through the life that God has given you!

.

Introduction

Congratulations! You're on an exciting journey to becoming a mother! Your life will never be the same. Let God show you what His plan and purposes are for you and your child/children. This journal will help you on your way to discovering what God wants for you and the child you are carrying.

As the mother of 5 children (plus two awaiting us in heaven due to miscarriage), I know that the time of pregnancy can be a rapturous time and sometimes a difficult one. The primary purposes of this Christian founded and Biblically based prayer journal is to recognize and celebrate that the baby you are carrying is being knit together and fashioned in your womb by the Creator Himself and to take an early pro-active approach to motherhood. It creates a venue to bond with your child, to begin nurturing those maternal instincts, and to begin praying for your baby - even in the womb! It is a personal journey written in an intimate way. There are many wonderful materials for expectant mothers out there, but few that are like this! I sensed a real need in the Christian community to step forth and begin recognizing and praying for our children even before they are born, as we know so many in this world don't even make it to birth. The enemy is targeting the unborn. We need to rise up with purpose and declare that the next generation will be a remnant of God fearing people with a God-planned destiny for them to fulfill.

The concept of a prayer and writing journal began as I went through my own pregnancies and childbirths. During my first pregnancy nearly twelve years ago, I started creating journals, blessings, and prayers for my oldest child and have continued to do so with each child (even for the children I miscarried). John 3:11 says, "We speak what we know and testify to what we have seen." The Lord has put mothers and children on my heart through teaching, intercession, and mentoring. This prayer journal is also a product of the vision the Lord birthed in my life many years ago to minister to women and children. If you are reading this now, you have already had many intercessory prayers going up for you and the baby/babies you are carrying.

Let me encourage you! We can begin praying for, blessing, and bonding with our children even before birth. What better time (in utero) when mother and child are so closely connected? God has a heart for mothers. He wants you to prepare yourself. We don't automatically become seasoned mothers just because we've given birth to a child. The forty weeks of pregnancy is a preparation time for you and your unborn baby. Praying lays a spiritual foundation that you can continue to build upon as your child grows. This prayer journal will introduce you to many concepts of parenting and help prepare you for the biggest ministry you will face in life...motherhood!

May God bless the pages you are about to read and inspire you to creatively write to and pray for the one who is being formed within your womb.

Jennifer J. Weiss, Mother and Author

"Let this be written for a future generation, that a people not yet created may praise the LORD."
Psalm 102:18

How to Use this Book

Expectant Prayers for Expectant Mothers is a book all about you and your pregnancy. What makes it unique is your interaction and additions through prayers and journaling. The book is not all inclusive. Adding your notes and thoughts is the goal.

When using this book, the following tips may help:

1.) Choose a time of day that works best for you. Select a time that is convenient and free from interruptions. Stay consistent. Each devotional is short and should take under ten minutes to read! Most of your time should be spent on journaling your personal thoughts and feelings.

2.) Pick a location that is comfortable and well lit. Environment is a key aspect for study.

3.) Start your devotional time with prayer. This helps prepare your heart for receiving what God has for you.

4.) Start reading the book wherever it applies to you. The sections are not only organized by trimester, but you will find a specific week referenced at the top of each page. Go back and read over the sections you may have missed if at all possible.

5.) Each day is formatted with a topic, verse, devotional, and journal tip. Read the verse and allow yourself a few moments to think about it before moving on.

6.) It is recommended that you use the space provided in the book to write down your thoughts. This will allow you to share not only what you wrote each day with your child, but also what you prayed and read about. Be sure to add any other thoughts for the day, information on doctor visits, etc. in your entries.

7.) Don't stop praying for your baby when you've finished the book. Keep it up!

8.) Share what you've written with your baby… in a few years!

If You are Planning a Pregnancy

"Before I formed you in the womb.... I knew you." Jeremiah 1:5

Isn't it an inspiring and thrilling thought that the God of the universe knew everything about us before we were even born? He knew what we would be like in utero, as children, as youth, as young adults, and even our last day on this earth! He knew the person you would marry, the job you would have, and how many children you would have. He has a plan for us and our children...and the generations to come. It makes perfect sense to add God to the equation of our decision making when it comes to this very important aspect of our family life.

If you are planning a pregnancy, now is a good time to begin praying with your spouse over your future family. Together, you can learn a lot about each other through agreement in prayer and understand your individual views about life issues that will affect your family. Amos 3:3 says, "Do two walk together unless they have agreed to do so?" Matthew 18:18 tells us, "... if two of you on earth agree about anything you ask for, it will be done for you by my Father in heaven."

I have met a lot of people who haven't had any children and already have in mind what they want their family to be like (big, small, all boys, all girls, a mix of all), but what is most important is what <u>God </u>wants for you. He knows the desires of your heart. He also knows what His perfect will is for your family. Only He can see into the future and knows what the outcome of our lives will be. Learn to place all your expectations in Christ. It's possible that You and He may have very different ideas about what your family will be. Jeremiah 10:23 says, "I know, O Lord, that a man's life is not his own; it is not for man to direct his steps."

Be open to the Lord's leading during times of prayer. If you need a lesson in how to pray, study the Lord's Prayer in Matthew 6. Too often we neglect this important aspect of preparation for pregnancy, but I can't tell you how important it is. God wants to move in every area of your life and having a family drastically changes life! God is the giver of life and all good things. It's wonderful that you are seeking His will and plans for you. I encourage you to keep doing so. 1 Thessalonians 5:17 says, "Pray continually, for this is God's will for you in Christ Jesus." Finally, Philippians 4:6 encourages us by saying, "Do not be anxious about anything, but in everything by prayer and petition, with thanksgiving, present your requests to God."

Lord,
I thank You for the desire that we have to have a baby. I know that You have a plan for us and we are seeking Your will. Let Your will be done on earth as it is in heaven. Let Your will be done in this family! Matthew 26:39 says "Not as I will, but as You will". I want whatever Your will may be. We accept Your plans and we are asking You to help us walk in obedience according to Your will.
If there is anything in me that would keep me/us from being a good parent, I pray that You would remove it from my life. If there are any spiritual issues that may need taken care of, Father I am asking You to bring them to my mind that they might be dealt with. If there are any relational issues or emotional issues, deal with those too, Lord. We want everything in our lives to line up with Your perfect will. Make our path clear to us. We want to know and walk in Your ways, not ours. A man's way seems right to Him, but the Lord shall direct his steps.
Prepare us for the days that lie ahead and go before us. All our days are numbered and known by You. We will seek You at all times, Father. We ask all these things in Your name. Amen.

Journal Tip: If you are trying to have a baby, write down your thoughts, prayers, and feelings about having a baby and what having he or she would mean to you. Have you already been praying about a baby? What are your dreams for your family?

Notes:

_____

_____

_____

_____

_____

_____

_____

_____

_____

_____

_____

_____

_____

_____

_____

_____

_____

_____

_____

_____

_____

If You are Contemplating Adoption for Your Baby

"The Spirit Himself testifies with our spirit that we are God's children." Romans 8:16
"A Father to the fatherless..." Psalm 68:5a   "God sets the lonely in families." Psalm 68:6a

You may be a mother who is embarking on a journey in life that can be scary and unsettling, especially when you are by yourself. No matter how your little one was conceived, you still have a wonderful opportunity to bond and pray for your child in the months that you are carrying your little one. The decision to adopt is something that must be approached prayerfully and carefully. But know that God has gone before you! If you do end up placing your child through adoption, knowing that you had the gestational months to pray over your baby will mean so much to you later on. Include your thoughts and feelings about the baby and pregnancy in this prayer journal and send it on with your child when you place them. It will be something that they will have from you forever. Tell the baby about yourself, who you are, your spiritual background, and more. They can know you and know that they were loved by you, even if you aren't there with them in a physical way.

What a heritage of blessing to give your little one. He/she will know that they were prayed for and cared for, even in your womb. You will always have a special part in the life of the baby. You chose to bring them into the world, under God's direction! That in itself is quite an accomplishment, considering the options that could have been chosen instead!! He <u>will</u> give you the strength to see your pregnancy through. Let God speak to your heart in this time. Although the road ahead might be difficult, God still has a plan for each soul created. He has a plan for you. He has a plan for your little baby. If you're placing this child, God has a family He wants your little one to be entrusted to. Let God take control of this situation and see Him work! With God, we are never alone.

God,

I thank You that with You, I am never alone. I pray that You would comfort me in the times when it seems the darkest. Direct my path in a clear way. Set my feet on solid ground and in a sure direction. When I need help or guidance, send Your Spirit to speak to me, to comfort me, to lead me. I thank You for this baby and for my part that I am about to play in his/her life. I know You have a special role for me. Bring me to a place with You so that I will feel Your presence near, like being wrapped in a blanket... a secure place. When I am sad, bring me joy. When I am weak, hold me up. When I am overwhelmed, lift me up. I am placing all my trust in You to bring about Your will. Take away all my guilt and shame. Lord, You haven't come to condemn me. You have come to set me free from my past and from all bondages. I accept the work you did on the cross to be a work you did for ME! Thank You for Your unconditional love. Help me to walk in Your ways. Today is a new day and an exciting day. You have come to bring life to me... abundant life... exciting life. You are also bringing life through me. Thank You for allowing this miracle to happen to me. If there is any unconfessed sin, I confess it now as being under the blood. If there is any repentance needed, I humbly bow at your feet and acknowledge that I need You and that only You can make me new.   Be with me every step of the way and put people in my path that can help me along this road. May Your will be done in this baby's life. If You are leading me to adopt him/her out, go before me and prepare a place for him/her. Place him/her in the family that You desire him/her to be raised. I love You, Lord, and trust in You. Amen.

Journal Tip: Write down your thoughts and feelings about adoption. What are your fears (if any)? What kind of parents would you like to see raise your baby? What has God done in your life to show you that adoption is the best option for you?

Notes:

_____

_____

_____

_____

_____

_____

_____

_____

_____

_____

_____

_____

_____

_____

_____

_____

_____

_____

_____

_____

This Journal Was Written For:

_____

Born on: _____

Time: _____

Where: _____

Size and Weight: _____

Written By:

_____

PART 1
Before You Find Out

PRAYING TO HAVE A BABY

"I prayed for this child, and the Lord has granted me what I asked of Him."
1 Samuel 1:27

When we think of a godly role model of a mother who prayed to conceive, we need not look any further than Hannah. Her prayers began long before conception. Year after year she prayed for a son (1 Samuel). Those around her began to make fun of her. They were doubtful onlookers who failed to see what God was doing. She pleaded with the Lord to not forget His servant in her misery! Eli told her one day after she was praying that she was to go in peace and that God of Israel was going to grant what she had asked of Him. Sure enough, little Samuel was born into the world. The name Samuel means "Because I asked the Lord for him". My own mother prayed thirteen years before conceiving. Now, that's diligence! You probably won't have to wait that long. Keep praying and God will answer.

Dear Lord,
I thank You for remembering Your servant this day. I ask that You would look upon me with favor and grant my request. You alone know the future my child would have. I want to raise him/her in the fear of the Lord, that they may serve You all of his/her days. I ask that You grant me peace in this hour while I quietly wait for You. Your Word says that when Eli spoke to Hannah, she arose and was no longer downcast. I ask for Your will to be done and my heart trusts in You. In Your name I ask it. Amen.

Journal Tip: How long have you wanted a child? Write down your thoughts today concerning the wait and how you have felt.

Notes:

_____

_____

_____

_____

_____

_____

_____

_____

_____

NOTHING IS TOO HARD FOR THE LORD

"Is anything too hard for the Lord?" Genesis 18:14a

Is anything too hard for the Lord? He created <u>all</u> things and breathed the breath of life into man. Nothing is too hard for him! This passage of scripture is delivered to Abraham from the three visitors who came to tell him that his wife would have a baby by the same time the next year. I have always loved this verse, but find it even more compelling that it is given to Abraham concerning pregnancy! Perhaps you are in the planning stages of pregnancy and think that you're never going to get pregnant. Don't allow desperation and stress to settle in! Let me assure you that God is in control of your life and nothing is too hard for Him to accomplish. In His time frame and according to His will for your life... it shall be done. Nothing is too hard for Him. Perhaps you are overwhelmed with other situations in your life at the moment. It doesn't matter what the need, there isn't anything that you face that God sits back at and says, "Well, I guess that's too hard for Me to fix!" On the contrary, whatever you are facing today, stand on Genesis 18:14a. Claim that verse and see what God does for you!

Dear God,
Your promises give me life and hope. I thank You for Genesis 18:14, which reminds me that nothing is too hard for You. Because You have created me, I know there is nothing that I face that is beyond Your control. I thank You for the peace that floods me by the assurance of Your omnipotence! You see all that I am going through and I trust that You are working all things out for my good. I will trust You in all areas of my life. Thank You, Lord, for sustaining me today and lifting up my countenance! Amen.

Journal Tip: Apply Genesis 18:14 to an area of your life today (such as praying to conceive). Write down what today's verse means to you.

Notes:

_____

_____

_____

_____

_____

_____

_____

_____

_____

_____

Before You Find Out

GOD'S WORKMANSHIP

"For we are God's workmanship, created in Christ Jesus to do good works, which God prepared in advance for us to do". Ephesians 2:10

When you think of the complex design of human life, you realize that there must have been a Creator. Ephesians 2:10 tells us that we are God's workmanship. I get very vivid mental pictures of babies being formed in the womb whenever I read this passage. Each cell and fiber within your baby is being exquisitely sewn together until they are fully formed. The verse goes on to explain that we are created in Christ Jesus (upon salvation) to go and do whatever it is He originally knit into our first fibers. Our minds can hardly comprehend it all. He has a "total" plan for us, created with purpose and design. He made it well in advance and doesn't just make it up as we go along in life. There are specifics attributes in our lives that no one else has. He chose our hair color, skin color, eye color, length of our fingers, formed our fingerprints, etc. Not only physical traits are determined by God, but also our personalities, character strengths, and interests. Each one has a purpose. What a God we serve!

Dear God,
I praise the work of Your hands today. I praise the wonder of life and the specific plans that You drew up well in advance for me and my baby. You know who he/she is at this moment and can see him/her in the future. You know every word he/she will utter; ever place his/her feet will take them, every work their hands will find to do. I pray that Your plans would go forth uninhibited. I ask that You would bless the work of Your hands and make this child a great blessing for Your Kingdom. I ask that You not allow me any expectations of him/her that does not line up with Your grand design. As this baby is being formed in secret, I know that You are overseeing all. Thank You, Lord, for remembering me and my little one today. Amen.

Journal Tip: Explain how you feel knowing you and your baby are God's workmanship.

Notes:

_____

_____

_____

_____

_____

_____

_____

_____

_____

WE'RE MADE IN GOD'S IMAGE

"So God created man in His own image, in the image of God He created them."
Genesis 1:27a

God created us in the image of Himself. What a magnificent thought. Many people in this day and time try to belittle the divine authority of God to make us believe that babies are just "embryos" or "fetuses". They portray our children as non-viable blobs of cells! We are people from the moment of conception. We contain everything we need to form into a human being, not to mention a spirit God has given us that will live forever. We were made in the likeness of the creator of the Universe. We are physical body, soul, and spirit.

God,
Thank You for the life that may be growing within me. I recognize this little one as being made in Your image. I acknowledge that this baby is already a person with a soul. I pray that You would continue to radiate Your image in my child even after delivery. Create them to be everything You intended him/her to be. Thank You for fashioning us in such a beautiful way. I pray that if I am expecting that You would oversee the implantation process. Make the uterine wall healthy and may this baby attach easily. Let me not fear about any cramping or spotting I may experience, as all can be normal in the implanting of my baby. Keep me safe from miscarriage and allow this pregnancy to progress without any complications. Amen.

Journal Tip: Write down your thoughts about your baby being a (developing) person. What would their little life mean to you?

Notes:

_____

_____

_____

_____

_____

_____

_____

_____

_____

_____

Before You Find Out

PRAYER-PARTNERS IN PREGNANCY

"Carry each other's burdens, and in this way you will fulfill the law of Christ."
Galatians 6:2

Have you considered enlisting the help of a trusted friend or close family member to help you pray during your pregnancy? Perhaps you already have someone you share prayer requests with on a daily basis. If you don't have anyone in mind, I suggest finding someone! Look at women in your church or let your Pastor know, as he might have someone to refer you to. God honors the prayers of His people and a cord of two or three is not easily broken. There is strength in numbers. If you are weak, a prayer partner can help encourage you and lift you up when you need it!

God,
I pray that You will show me someone that I could pray with concerning my pregnancy and baby. I know that when we bind together with two or three in prayer, You WILL be in our midst. The prayers of a righteous man are powerful and effective. As I grow and learn about You during this time, I pray that my prayer partner will grow and learn as well. I ask that the prayers brought forth for this baby will produce much spiritual fruit. In Your name, amen.

Journal Tip: Include some names of people who are helping you pray for your pregnancy and baby. How have they helped you during other times in your life?

Notes:

_____

_____

_____

_____

_____

_____

_____

_____

_____

_____

_____

_____

_____

FINDING OUT

"For there is nothing hidden that will not be disclosed, and nothing concealed that will not be known or brought out into the open." Luke 8:17

As you are waiting to find out if you are expecting or not, you may be feeling a flood of emotions. Isn't it wonderful that God can see everything that is going on within you, even when you don't know? Rest in Him. The wondering will be over soon.

God,
I know all things are in Your hands. During this secret time, I ask for Your peace and patience. If a baby is forming within my womb, I ask that You would begin to work in my life and in the life of my unborn baby. You are the ultimate head of this family and the head of my life. All authority is Yours. We acknowledge Your greatness and power. Your works are marvelous and my lips want to praise you continually. Thank You for the joy that floods my soul. Help me to be content in whatever state (pregnant or not) that I am in. I accept Your will fully, whatever that may be. Amen.

Journal Tip: By what date will you know if you're expecting (when would your cycle start)? How are you feeling about possibly being pregnant?

Notes:

_____

_____

_____

_____

_____

_____

_____

_____

_____

_____

_____

_____

Before You Find Out

PREGNANCY TEST

"Examine yourselves to see whether you are in the faith; test yourselves."
2 Corinthians 13:5

Have you taken a home pregnancy test yet? There are many test kits available to you over the counter and most work in a similar way. You don't have to buy the most expensive type to get a clear result. I recommend getting a two pack test just in case you want to test again (as most women do). Morning urine is the best to test, the first day you missed your period (or some brands you can buy offer results a little earlier). One you have your results, you will have proof to whether you are expecting or not. It is a good idea to schedule your first obstetric appointment as soon as you find out… and the sooner the better. In the same manner, God asks us to test our faith. We should examine our walk with Him daily to see if there be areas we are growing in or anything in us that should not be. Daily examination can come through prayer or meditating on Him and His Word.

Dear Lord,
Thank You for examining my heart and mind today. I pray that if there be any way in me that is not pleasing to You, that You would show me. I want to be walking with you every day.
Be with me as I take my pregnancy test. I pray that You would guard my mind and emotions during this time. Go before me. I know that You already see my womb and know whether or not there is a baby present. I ask that You be with me and strengthen me, no matter what the results are. I am asking for Your will to be done, no matter what that is. I am going to put my trust in You. You are the God who shares in my joys and my sorrows. I pray that no matter what happens that You will give me grace and peace today. This day will affect me for the rest of my life. Be with me now, Lord. Amen.

Journal Tip: Write down the account of getting your test and what the results were. Write down your feelings.

Notes:

_____

_____

_____

_____

_____

_____

_____

_____

_____

PART 2
The First Trimester

Week 4

CONGRATULATIONS, BEING THANKFUL

"Thanks be to God for His indescribable gift!" 2 Corinthians 9:15

Congratulations on your baby! By the time you find out you're expecting you're already 4 weeks along (2 weeks by conception). No matter how the baby was conceived, planned or unplanned, he/she is on the way. It's time to get to prayer! We should begin this journey by thanking the Lord and praying for the overall pregnancy.

Lord,
I thank You for this baby! I pray that You would bless this baby right now, even in my womb. I pray that he/ she would sense Your presence and that You would surround and protect us with Your angels. I know that You know him/her already. I pray that You would begin showing me what to pray and how to pray for this little one I am carrying. I pray that I would have a healthy pregnancy and delivery without any complications. If complications do arise, I pray that You will be with me during this entire process. I pray that during the days of my pregnancy, I will be able to rest in You and in the knowledge that You have everything under control. I want Your will for my life and for the life of my unborn child. I pray for a healthy baby to grow within me. Help me to nurture and care for myself, as in turn I am nurturing and caring for the well being of my baby. As a mother, my physical body will be the home for my growing baby during the next several months. I pray that You would help me to stay healthy and to eat nutritiously in order to be a good home for my little one(s). I pray that You would give me opportunities to physically rest and to pray each day for this baby. Thank You for this blessing, God! Amen.

Journal Tip: Be sure to write down how and when you found out about your baby and how you are feeling.

Notes:

_____

_____

_____

_____

_____

_____

_____

_____

_____

_____

JOURNALING

"At the Lord's command, Moses recorded the stages of their journey."
Numbers 33:2a

Journaling will be an important part of your journey through pregnancy. You may find it's one of the best parts. Throughout this book, you will find journal tips at the bottom of the daily devotion. I've often thought of this passage in scripture with amazement and all the written records that Moses wrote at the direction of the Lord. If he had not been diligent with his work, we would not have the Pentateuch (the first 5 books of the Bible)! Those first five books of the Bible teach us so much about creation, life, the Lord, History, etc.

Journaling not only provides a way to record the history you are making with your pregnancy, but it also allows your feelings to be expressed. You or your baby may enjoy going back and reading through all the things you experienced or felt during this special time. Perhaps it would be good reference for you with future pregnancies that you may have. It lets your child know what you were thinking about him/her before he/she was born. The journal is worth all the time and thought that you put into it. Enjoy the experience!

Dear Lord,
Help me to keep a written record of the things that I think, learn, and feel during my pregnancy. Open up time for me each day to contemplate the miracle that You are working within me. I praise You for Your goodness and for blessing me in the ways that You have. Grant me diligence to walk this path before me. Give me strength to finish the journey. Deal with me, as I write down my thoughts and feelings. Birth something new in my spirit as I am preparing to give birth in my physical body. Teach me new things each day and I pray that You would speak to me in a real, tangible way. Reveal Your goodness to me. Thank You, Lord. Amen.

Journal Tip: Do you like to write? Do you think a goal of making a journal for you and your baby will be easy or difficult? If you could describe/introduce yourself to your baby, what would you say?

Notes:

_____

_____

_____

_____

_____

_____

_____

_____

Week 4

BABY IS COMING FOR A REASON

"By faith Abraham, even though he was past age- and Sarah herself was barren- was enabled to become a father because he considered Him faithful who had made the promise."
Hebrews 11:11

If you have prayed for a long time to conceive, or even if a baby was be a complete surprise, God is in complete and total control. When you are expecting, God has allowed you to become pregnant for a reason. That little life budding inside you is a true miracle of God. He or she has a God given destiny to fulfill. Look at Abraham and Sarah. God told Abraham that he would have a son, but he and his wife were past the child bearing years. Whatever God says about your childbearing will happen, provided that you are obedient to Him. I also like the insight that He already sees our future as if it were done. This statement to Abraham wasn't a proposal of something, it was a declaration and God saw it (in the Spirit) as completed. Sometimes what He has declared for our lives seems totally against the flow. Sarah found it so amusing when she overheard the prophesy concerning her pregnancy that the Bible says she laughed! Later on, however, Sarah gave birth to a little baby boy, whom they named Isaac "meaning laughter". Let's judge the Lord faithful, just as Sarah of old did.

Father,
I thank You for this baby, whom You have given life to. Just as with Sarah of old, there may be things about this pregnancy that is not deemed as normal, but God I know You are faithful and have a perfect plan for this little one. You have called him/her by name. Please be with me during this pregnancy and with this baby. No matter if this body seems well equipped to handle a pregnancy or not, You are in control and I have nothing to fear. I am judging You faithful to complete this work that You have begun. I ask that just as in Isaac, this baby will be a baby of promise. I pray that he/she would bring great joy to me and this family all the days of his/her life. Let us never forget that You are the one that created him/her and entrusted him/her to me for safekeeping. Thank You for this baby! Amen.

Journal Tip: Can you relate in any way to the story of Sarah from the Old Testament? How has your pregnancy warranted judging God as faithful? Has God given you any promises concerning this baby?

Notes:

_____

_____

_____

_____

_____

_____

Week 4

GOOD HEALTH DURING PREGNANCY

"Dear friend, I pray that you may enjoy good health and that all may go well with you."
3 John 2

God is concerned with your health and the health of your unborn baby. It's important before and during pregnancy to maintain a healthy lifestyle as possible. You should be choosing and taking a good pre-natal vitamin every day. If you haven't started one yet, your doctor or midwife can recommend some and will probably provide you with samples. When you go to your first visit, the doctor or midwife will ask you for some family health history. It will be important to gather as much information as you can before you see your practitioner. They will also assess your general health. Be sure to get plenty of rest and drink plenty of fluids during the day.

Dear God,
I thank You for being concerned with my health during this pregnancy. I ask that You would keep me in Your hands during this entire pregnancy. Keep me in good health. Where there may be illness, I ask for healing. Please keep my baby safe and healthy during this entire pregnancy. Show me how to maintain a healthy lifestyle and to make positive food and life choices every day that will promote vitality and growth in my baby. Thank You for keeping me in Your hands. Amen.

Journal Tip: What are some of the things you are doing or planning to do during this pregnancy that will keep you healthy? Do you have good health hygiene and other habits? What could you do to enhance your healthy lifestyle?

Notes:

_____

_____

_____

_____

_____

_____

_____

_____

_____

_____

_____

HAVING A BABY IS A FAITH LESSON

"Now faith is being sure of what we hope for and certain of what we do not see."
Hebrews 11:1

Having a baby is a life lesson in faith. You are sure that baby is on the way. You are certain that this little one is growing steadily and will one day be born. The first trimester is basically one that doesn't display too much in your outward appearance of the life growing inside you. Regardless, you know he/she is there. Faith can start, as the Word says, as small as a mustard seed... not unlike your baby. In time, your faith will be built to bigger size where it will be apparent to all...not unlike your baby, either. You may need faith to trust that the Lord is going to supply all you have need of at this time. The need of faith applies to many different areas of our lives. Let God teach you about faith during your pregnancy. It's a lesson you will never forget.

Father,
I thank You for this perfect object lesson in faith. May I remember it always! Teach me about what true faith in You means and how I can apply it to my everyday life. During my pregnancy, help my faith in You to grow, just as this little one is growing inside me. You know what I hope for. You give me certainty for that which I cannot see. Even when our human eyes can't tell that You are working, YOU ARE! Help me to keep this hope within me. Your Word says that without faith it is impossible to please You (Hebrews 11:6). I have faith in You and what You are doing in the creation of this little child. I pray that You would grant him/her a measure of faith in double portions...faith that can move mountains...faith that the great men and women of the Bible possessed. Let it be a heritage to my child. Thank You, Lord. Amen.

Journal Tip: How does it feel knowing you are pregnant, yet no one can tell? How does the principle of faith apply to you personally while you're expecting?

Notes:

_____

_____

_____

_____

_____

_____

_____

_____

_____

Week 4

DEDICATE YOUR BABY TO THE LORD

"From birth I was cast upon You; from my mother's womb You have been my God."
Psalms 22:10

Even before your little one is born, you can dedicate them back to the Lord. Dedication is simply an act of the parent to will and determine to raise your child in the fear of the Lord.
Hannah dedicated Samuel to the Lord when she conceived. (1 Samuel 1:27-28)

Lord,
I pray that You will help me raise this child in the fear and admonition of You (the Lord). I want him/her to grow up to serve You, in whatever way You choose, all of his/her days. I declare that You are the Lord of this house just as Joshua declared, "As for me and my house we will serve the Lord!" I willfully commit him/her into your hands. I am the earthly parent, but this child is Yours, Lord. You created this baby and You have a plan for him/her. You have entrusted me to care for this little one and I will do my best to instill the Word into his/her heart and to teach them about You.
I see the Spiritual raising of this child as my most important priority in parenting. Teach me how to raise him/her in Your image. Amen.

Journal Tip: In your own words, write a short description of what you want your child to learn about the Lord.

Notes:

_____

_____

_____

_____

_____

_____

_____

_____

_____

_____

_____

_____

Week 4

JARS OF CLAY- ETERNAL SPIRITS

"But we have this treasure in jars of clay to show that this all-surpassing power is from God and not from us." 2 Corinthians 4:7

Life begins at conception. Life eternal comes from the saving power of Jesus Christ. God has made us (even the child you are carrying) with a physical body, a soul (our minds, emotions, and will) and spirit. Even upon death, our spirit will never pass away. They will continue to live forever and ever. Where we eternally live will depend on the choice we made in this life whether to accept Him as Savior or not. So, this gift (a spirit that will continue on and on) is our treasure that we possess in our jars of clay (our earthly bodies) when we believe on Him. The picture of the jar of clay as our human bodies is so appropriate. We are formed and fashioned by the hands of the Father into our physical form to hold our spirits. And just as jars of clay, our bodies can wear out. They are temporary. But no matter how old or young you are, the spirit within you will be forever. Read all of chapter 4 for a great devotional!

Dear God,
Your ways no one can fathom, but I thank You for creating life. I acknowledge that without You, there would be no life at all. You are the Creator of all things. The power of life is from You and not from man. You have given us an eternal treasure of life and have decided this day that You would create another life... my child. Bless this life You have given him/her. I pray that he/she will be grateful for this gift You have given to him/her. Make this baby a child of purpose and significance. I pray for all the babies of the world that are being considered for termination this day. Bring light into the lives of their mothers that they would know that life is a blessing and not a curse. Help mothers to choose life for their babies and not death. Protect the unborn today. In Your name, amen.

Journal Tip: Think about the fact that your child's spirit is going to go on forever. Write down your thoughts.

Notes:

_____

_____

_____

_____

_____

_____

_____

_____

_____

PRIORITIZE YOUR DAY WITH GOD

"In the morning, O Lord, You hear my voice; in the morning I lay my requests before You in expectation." Psalm 5:3

How do you start your morning? With breakfast? Reading the paper? With morning sickness? Seeking God? There is no better way to start your day then to devote time to prayer and reading His Word. It's also a good way to prioritize your day and set what you need before the Lord. He can and will bless your comings and your goings. Do you have an appointment with the doctor today? Pray that all goes well and for protection driving there. Do you have to go to the store today? Ask Him to direct your purchases, give you strength, and to meet the needs you have in your household. Pray for the baby you are expecting today, too. Expect great things from God!

Dear Lord,
Help me to prioritize my day in a way that is pleasing to You. I ask that You would bless my comings and my goings, especially in this time where I am expecting. Whatever time I meet with You in prayer during the day, please bless it. Any need or worry that I cannot meet, please meet it. My entire day is Yours and I pray that it would unfold as You have created it to. Help me to meet each new day with anticipation. Bless this baby within me. Help his/her growth to be normal and overseen by You! Thank You, Lord. Amen.

Journal Tip: Do you have a normal time for prayer and devotions? When is it? What kind of things do you do during that time?

Notes:

_____

_____

_____

_____

_____

_____

_____

_____

_____

_____

_____

Week 5

FINDING A DOCTOR OR MIDWIFE

"Our dear friend, Luke, the doctor..."   Colossians 4:14a

Can you imagine having a doctor or midwife that is considered a friend and is a Christian as well? Luke, the doctor turned disciple, was one! God has someone in mind that He would like to care for you during your pregnancy. Choosing a doctor or midwife is more than simply seeing whom your HMO will cover. Perhaps because of circumstances, you won't feel like you have much choice in the matter, but God knows all of the details surrounding your search for a physician. Even if your doctor or midwife is not a Christian, perhaps God wants to lead you to him/her to bring them revelation! Let's ask Him today to be in charge and to lead you to the doctor or midwife that you are supposed to have.

Dear Lord,
I thank You that all the details of my pregnancy are seen by You and known by You. You know our finances, our health insurance plans (if any), and the criteria we must meet. God, there is someone that You have in mind that will deliver my child. I pray that You would orchestrate the events in my life and bring them all together so that I may find the doctor/midwife of your choosing. Let me know without any doubt which one I need to use. An OB/GYN is an important part of a woman's life and I want one I can trust and rely upon. I ask for someone who is knowledgeable, willing to listen, and most of all who knows You. If they do not know You, help me be a light unto him/her. In all, I pray that You would give me peace about the doctor/midwife I am to have and to not worry about the financial end of things (either insurance wise or other). I place all these things in Your hands and ask for Your will to be accomplished today on earth as it is in heaven. Thank You, Lord. Amen.

Journal Tip: Have you contacted a doctor yet? Make a list of possible names or write down the one that you will be seeing. Remember to pray for your physician or midwife. They will have an important part in your life during the next few months.

Notes:

_____

_____

_____

_____

_____

_____

_____

_____

_____

44

Week 5

SCHEDULING YOUR FIRST DOCTOR/MIDWIFE VISIT

"Do not be anxious about anything; but in everything, by prayer and petition, with thanksgiving, present your requests to God. And the peace of God which transcends all understanding; will guard your hearts and your minds in Christ Jesus." Philippians 4:6-7

By now you will have scheduled or are about to schedule your first prenatal visit with your obstetrician, midwife, or whatever means of help you are going to enlist in the delivery of your baby. There are many choices when it comes to providers and delivery methods. God knows what method would be best for you and who you are to seek for assistance. Be sure to write down questions you may have to take to your care provider. The first months of pregnancy routinely call for a checkup once a month and then increase in frequency closer to delivery.

God,
I ask that You would direct my steps in planning for my pregnancy. I know that You have someone in mind that is going to help in the delivery of this baby. I pray that You would lead me to the doctor (or other person or persons) that I am supposed to use. Open the doors for me so that I won't have to spend a lot of time searching. Lead me to Your will in this area. I pray that You would bless my doctor (or other person or persons) with wisdom, patience, skill, and kindness. I pray that my life would glorify You so that when I go to my visits, there would be opportunities to bring honor to Your name. Let the knowledge and work experience as a healthcare professional bring blessing to me and my baby. Guide their hands, minds, and thoughts. Again, I pray for a healthy, uncomplicated pregnancy. Thank You for leading me in the direction You would have me to go. Amen.

Journal Tip: Write down the date of your first prenatal visit. What happened during your visit? Who is your doctor (or other person or persons) that will help you during pregnancy and delivery? Where is the doctor's or midwife's office located?

Notes:

_____

_____

_____

_____

_____

_____

_____

_____

_____

_____

Week 5

ASK GOD HOW TO RAISE YOUR BABY

"So Manoah asked him, "When your words are fulfilled, what is to be the rule for the boy's life and work?" Judges 13:12

In this scriptural account, the angel of the Lord had just come to tell Manoah's wife that they were going to have a son. She had been sterile and unable to have a child. She told Manoah what had happened and he immediately went to prayer to ask the Lord how they were to raise the boy. The angel of the Lord even returned to bring further clarity to Manoah! Who was that son? Samson. God is faithful to His promises. What a blessing to see that Samson's father cared immediately about what the Lord wanted this child to do! Let's pray that when it comes to seeking God's guidance in how to raise your baby that you will act with same fervency as Manoah.

Heavenly Father,
I thank You for this story about Manoah. I ask that You would rise up fervency in me to pray for and be concerned about the spiritual upbringing of this baby. May You and I be in unity concerning the raising of this baby. Let my will line up with Your will. I pray that I will be a godly woman and will teach this baby by example. May I walk an upright and righteous life before You and before others. Let me be salt and light in this home and with all those that I come into contact with. I pray that You would bless me today in body, soul, and spirit. Grant me the guidance that I am seeking for this little one. In Your name, amen.

Journal Tip: Write down some thoughts or feelings about how God would have you to raise your baby.

Notes:

_____

_____

_____

_____

_____

_____

_____

_____

_____

_____

Week 5

GOD SEES YOU DURING PREGNANCY

"Here I am and the children God gave me..." Isaiah 8:18

Sometimes during pregnancy, you wonder if anyone cares or sees what you are going through. You wonder what God was thinking when he blessed you with a child! You'll have times of sheer joy and others moments (especially close to delivery) of doubt and trepidation. Nonetheless, God sees where you are at on your journey at all times. He sees right where you are today... in this very moment...and He will meet you there.

God,
I thank You that You see where I am at all times. You know what I am going through and the challenges that I face even when no one else does. Let my mind rest on You today and think on all the wonders of your character and personality. Thank You for knowing my baby and being involved in every facet of his/her development. Thank You for giving me the opportunity to bring this baby into the world. Amen.

Journal Tip: Write down some of the feelings that you have about being pregnant today. What are some things that are going on in your life right now?

Notes:

_____

_____

_____

_____

_____

_____

_____

_____

_____

_____

_____

_____

_____

Week 5

TESTS DURING PREGNANCY

"because you know the testing of your faith develops perseverance."
James 1:3

Now that you are pregnant, you are just beginning to discover how many tests you must endure. You've probably already taken a home pregnancy test, possibly had blood work taken at the lab, and had a pelvic exam by your doctor or midwife. Later on during pregnancy, you can look forward to more tests such as Alpha Fetal Protein, Gestation Diabetes, a Strep culture, Ultrasound, or whatever else the doctor or care taker feels is necessary. For the first time mother, you may find all this poking and prodding to be a bit bothersome. The tests do serve a greater good, however. The tests will reveal if everything is progressing normally, or if there is something the doctor should be aware of. In the same way, the testing of our faith serves a purpose as well. When our faith is testing, God shows us areas that need our attention. Let's ask God to oversee our times of testing and to give us the strength to persevere.

Heavenly Father,
You see this pregnancy from beginning to end and already know the tests that I will face. I thank You that You are all knowing and present with me no matter what I have to endure. I ask that You give me strength, courage, and perseverance to face each test as it comes. I ask that all the tests would go well and that I would be an easy patient to deal with. Help me deal with pain when tests are painful and to face them with courage. I know You will be with me during each process. Let the tests results reveal normal results, I pray. If at any time there is a problem, I know that You will provide the solution. I place all these tests in Your hands. I give you all my fear, timidity, and weakness and ask in return that You give me courage, boldness, and strength. If there be any area in my spirit that needs attention today, I pray that You would reveal that to me and show me how to conquer it. Develop this perseverance in me. Thank You, Lord. Amen.

Journal Tip: What kinds of medical tests have you had so far? Be sure to record each one as you go through it.

Notes:

_____

_____

_____

_____

_____

_____

_____

_____

48

CHANGES IN YOUR BREASTS

"I am a wall, and my breasts are like towers." Song of Songs 8:10a

Have you noticed some changes in your breasts lately? No doubt, you can expect them to enlarge as your pregnancy progresses. They may also be tender and sore. This is normal due to hormones and the function that they were created for in motherhood. You may need to go out and get some bras that will fit better. It's normal to experience a change from 1-2 sizes during pregnancy. If you are planning on nursing, they will tend to increase as well as lactation begins. Nursing will also require a few good nursing bras. If you are unsure what to buy, talk to some moms that you know or simply choose a department store where a clerk can help you with measurements, etc.

Heavenly Father,
Your plans for me are perfect and You know them before I do. Your have purpose for these changes in my body. I pray that You would help me to adjust to these developments. Bring me wisdom and assistance in the areas where I need help. I pray that You would provide all that I need to clothe and care for myself. Give me a touch in my physical body today, especially when it comes to aches and pains. Apply healing to these areas, I ask. I pray that You would help me to be as comfortable as possible during this time of growth and expansion. In Your name, Amen.

Journal Tip: Have you noticed changes in your body since becoming pregnant? Have you purchased new clothing to help you adjust? What are the most noticeable changes you have experienced?

Notes:

_____

_____

_____

_____

_____

_____

_____

_____

_____

_____

_____

_____

_____

Week 6

ANXIOUS ABOUT PREGNANCY

"Do not be afraid for I am with you." Isaiah 43:5a

Are you feeling a little anxious about your pregnancy? It's normal for you to be thinking about the health of your baby and wondering what's going on inside you. Many women in early pregnancy begin to worry about miscarriage. Let me assure you that whatever happens, God is with you in all. You don't have to worry about the unexpected because to God, nothing is unexpected. He knows and sees all. God hasn't given you a spirit of fear, but of love, peace, and a sound mind (2 Timothy 1:7).

God,
Thank You for being with me even in the times I have fear or anxiety. I know that You are with me and won't allow anything to happen to me or the baby that isn't in Your perfect will. I will not fear the unexpected, but will put my trust in You alone. You are watching over me and this baby. You never sleep or slumber. I can rest in the peace of knowing that You are with me. I bind the enemy from trying to plague my mind and emotions with fear. I pray that my mind and emotions would be in perfect order. Amen.

Journal Tip: Write down the anxieties or worries that you might be having. Look them over and then turn them over to God.

Notes:

_____

_____

_____

_____

_____

_____

_____

_____

_____

_____

_____

_____

_____

_____

_____

CLEAN SPIRITUAL HOUSE FOR YOU & BABY

"You shall not bow down to them or worship them; for I the LORD your God, am a jealous God, punishing the children for the sin of the fathers to the third and fourth generation of those who hate me, but showing love to a thousand generations of those who love Me and keep My commandments." Exodus 20:5

Creating a clean spiritual house for your family will benefit your entire household. The Word says that the sins of the father can be revisited from generation to generation. Just like when the doctor takes your family history at your first prenatal visit (or consultation), you should also take a spiritual family history. Where there are illnesses prevalent in a family, it doesn't definitely mean that you will come down with heart disease, cancer, or whatever is prevalent. It may show or indicate, however where you might have trouble in the future. In the same way, if there have been "spiritual illnesses" in families, it may indicate weak areas that the enemy is fully aware of and would take any opportunity to pounce on if given the chance. Let's ask the Lord to clean out every nook and cranny of our families. Let's thwart off the enemy before he has a crack in our spiritual armor to penetrate.

Lord,
You know all the weaknesses in my family and where we have failed. I know the blood of Jesus covers all and was a complete work at the cross. I pray that You would redeem anything in this family the enemy would like to claim as his. If there are any weaknesses in this family due to the corrosion of sin, I pray that You would seal, strengthen, and rebuild that which the enemy has ruined. Search every nook and cranny of my spiritual house, Lord. Clean every closet. Remove anything that would hinder Your Spirit from moving in me. I know that as much as You have plans for our good, the devil has plans for our destruction. I cancel out any and all plans that the enemy has set forth and ask for Your healing to come to our spiritual household. Don't let the enemy have a foothold. I repent for my household and ask for You to rebuild anything that may have been damaged. Thank You, Lord, for restoration and redemption through Your name and Your blood. I pray that this baby will grow up in the confidence and knowledge that our foundation is sure and firm in You. Amen.

Journal Tip: You may want to list any "spiritual illnesses" that have plagued your family in the past. Then claim victory over those areas in the name of Jesus!

Notes:

_____

_____

_____

_____

_____

_____

_____

Week 6

A HOUSEHOLD SERVING THE LORD

"But as for me and my household, we will serve the Lord." Joshua 24:15

Have you ever declared that no matter what goes on in life, "As for me and my house, we will serve the Lord?" It's important for parents to rise up and decide what the spiritual course of action for your family will be. Either you will choose to serve the Lord or you will not. When Joshua made this declaration, he told the children of Israel that if they were going to serve the Lord that they should serve the Lord <u>wholeheartedly</u>. What is your plan for your family today? Are you going to serve the Lord and raise your child up in the admonition of the Lord or will you forsake the Lord and turn back to your "idols"?

God,
I declare today..."AS FOR ME AND MY HOUSE, WE WILL SERVE THE LORD!" I declare that my intention for this family is to please You in all we do and worship You wholeheartedly, putting You as the top priority in our lives. I declare that my child will be raised in Your ways and that this home will reflect the God whom we serve. I ask that as the generations turn into more generations that YOU will be our God and none other... not false Gods, not self, not material possessions, not wealth, or anything else. If anything has crept into this family that has kept us from serving You completely, please bring it to light and remove it. I repent of any area where I may have failed in serving You with all my soul, all my might, and all my strength. You are my God and I want You to be the God of my child's life. In Your name, so be it! Amen.

Journal Tip: Write down your commitment to raise your son/daughter in the ways of the Lord. What are some traits/characteristics of that commitment?

Notes:

_____

_____

_____

_____

_____

_____

_____

_____

_____

_____

_____

HONORING FATHERS

**"He will turn the hearts of the fathers to their children, and the hearts of the children
to their fathers; or else I will come and strike the land with a curse."
Malachi 4:6**

Today we are honoring fathers. No matter if you are married or not or how your child was conceived, fathers are very vital to children. Children need a godly male role model. It is said that girls receive their identity and worth from their fathers. Boys learn how to be a man and accomplish certain tasks from their fathers. It is important to pray for your spouse/baby's father during your pregnancy. Your child will need that strong assurance, protection, and love that only a male figure can bring. Be sure to communicate with your spouse what needs you have. He will want to play an active roll in the pregnancy, too. No, he is not carrying the baby, but there are things he can do to stay involved. Childbirth classes, doctor appointments, dinners out, time spent "talking to the baby", or simply rubbing your feet will keep him involved. Pray often for each other and your baby, too.

If you are unmarried for whatever reason, God can bring male support into your child's life to take that place. He says in His Word that He becomes a husband to the widow and a father to the fatherless. So, take heart if you are in a less than ideal situation. If your baby has come about as a result of violence (for some readers) God will bless you for sparing the life of your unborn. He will weave men into your little one's life in order to fulfill this parental roll. If you are adopting your child, pray for the father roll in your baby's life.

Dear God,
I thank You for (Father's Name) today. I ask that You would bless him abundantly and let him know what a special place he has in my life and in the life of our child. I pray that You would encourage my husband/baby's father to be the best dad he can possibly be. Grow in his heart today. Draw him closer and closer to You so that he can be a wonderful godly roll model to our child. Show him creative ways that he can feel involved in this pregnancy and childbirth. I want the perfect plan to unfold for my son/daughter. Let this baby have no lack in this area. I ask that You would make my husband a protector of his family and a defender of our beliefs and moral standards. I pray for strength to be bound around his neck and guard him against a wimpy attitude. Bring other men into my child's life that can spiritually build up his/her character and help strengthen his/her beliefs. Thank You, Lord, for the provisions You are making in this area of my baby's life. Amen.

Journal Tip: What kinds of characteristics make up a strong father? Why is that important to your child? What is your marital status? Do you need healing in that area? How does the father feel toward the baby? If possible, get him to write something briefly about his thoughts toward the baby and what he is doing to be a part of the pregnancy and childbirth.

Notes:

_____

_____

_____

_____

A YEAR OF BOUNTY

"You crown the year with your bounty, and your carts overflow with abundance."
Psalm 65:11

When you stop to think that a normal gestation takes nearly 100 days shy of a year, it's a sobering thought! Sometimes you will feel like it's been much longer than that, other times you will find yourself asking where the time went. Overall, you will probably come away remembering that your time of pregnancy and delivering your child/children into this world was a crowning point of your life. Crowns are reserved as a reward for victory or a mark of honor, a title, a symbol to impart splendor, or a finish to a task. During your pregnancy, trust God to bring bounty and abundance to you. He'll do this in the physical, emotional, and spiritual parts of your life.

Heavenly Father,
I thank You for marking this year as special for me. I trust that it is going to be a crowning point of my life. I ask that You would remind me often and give me a heart to understand the depths and heights of Your love for me, my baby, and my family. You want us to overflow in bounty and abundance. There is great harvest in the trials of childbearing and I want to see that fruit. I ask that You would apply these life changing lessons to my heart, soul, mind, and spirit. When You crown something, You give it high praise and honor. I thank You for making my pregnancy and childbirth such a tremendous time in my life. I ask that You continue to help my little one grow healthy and strong. Give him/her a strong mind and heart today and especially a heart that follows after You. Amen.

Journal Tip: What are your thoughts about God crowning this year for you? What does that imply about the life He is growing within you? Do you think God sees your baby as special? How are you feeling about your pregnancy and baby today?

Notes:

_____

_____

_____

_____

_____

_____

_____

_____

_____

_____

MEETING WITH OTHERS OFTEN

"Let us not give up meeting together, as some are in the habit of doing, but let us encourage one another- and all the more as you see the Day approaching." Hebrews 10:25

You may not think you do, but you <u>need</u> other people in your life! If you are married, your spouse will probably be your biggest support system in childbearing. Let your husband be the rock and protector that God designed him to be. God will also supply others into your life to help your spouse meet the needs you may have. If you are not married, outside sources will be the foundation of your support system. No matter if you meet with others by weekly church attendance, in your home for Bible study, at the café for coffee, or a simple conversation on the phone with a friend, you <u>need</u> to be encouraged right now. The closer and closer you get to your due date, you will find your connections with others to be of increasing value.

Dear Lord,
Thank You, God for the wonderful people in my life who encourage and challenge me. I ask that You would surround me with strong Christian friends and family who would pray for me and uplift me, especially during these last few months of pregnancy. I know there are others excited about my pregnancy and expecting this baby as much as I am. Let me lean on others when I need to and not be caught into pride. Strengthen me to ask for help when necessary. Keep those close to me from becoming overbearing or overly protective... keep all in balance, Lord. Show me who I can rely on and who I cannot. Refresh me in the times that I meet with my family and friends. Build up my spirit. Thank You, Lord. Amen.

Journal Tip: Do you get a chance to meet with others often? Who do you like to fellowship with? How does he/she encourage you or strengthen you? Who is your best friend? Is he/she going to have part in the birth of your baby?

Notes:

_____

_____

_____

_____

_____

_____

_____

_____

_____

_____

EYESIGHT

"And Elisha prayed, "O LORD, open his eyes so he may see." Then the LORD opened the servant's eyes, and he looked and saw the hills full of horses and chariots of fire all around Elisha." 2 Kings 6:17

Here in the 2 Kings, the Israelites were battling the people of Aram. One morning Elisha's servant awoke to find the city completely surrounded. That is when Elisha prayed that the servant's eyes be open so he could really see what was going on. When God opened the servant's eyes, he saw that there were more with them than against them. There were hills full of horses and chariots of fire surrounding them. God was protecting them with an angelic host!

By now, your little one's eyes are being formed. They will be a certain color, a certain shape, and will function in your child's body as one of his/her major senses. Just think of all sight means to you. You will see your baby for the first time and be filled with joy. You can appreciate creation. You can read a book, such as the one you're reading now. The list goes on and on! Now imagine if you didn't have your sight (as some mothers do not). Blindness can not only affect our physical body, but spiritual blindness can impair our Christian walk. You and your children will be engaged in spiritual warfare in the days we are living in. It's important for our spiritual eyes to be open to what God is doing or when and where the enemy would attack us. When we only focus on the physical nature (what we can see around us), we may just be missing the very thing that God is doing in our midst. Let's ask the Lord to sharpen our spiritual eyes so that we may see the truth in all things.

Dear God,
So many times in Scripture, Jesus touched and healed those who were blind. You not only care about what our physical eyes see, but also what our spiritual eyes see. I thank You for giving spiritual eyesight to the spiritually blind. I pray that You would open my eyes today that I may see the truth and reality of what is going on around me. I ask that You would keep the eyes of my child adjusted as he/she grows so that he/she would be able to see what You are doing in his/her midst. I thank You for reminding me today of all the reasons sight is important, physically and spiritually. I pray that You would keep my baby's eyes from any disease, complication, impairment, or degeneration of any kind. May there be health to his/her eyes today. I come against lazy eye, weak eyes, eyes with focusing problems, etc. I pray for eyes that can see clearly and function properly. Keep me in tune to his/her eyesight as he/she grows. May there be opportunity for routine eye exams and checks. Having poor eyesight can lead to many downfalls; from simple tasks to education. I ask that You give me the wisdom and ability to watch my child's eyesight carefully. Show me how to encourage him/her to see things in the spirit. Thank You, Lord. Amen.

Journal Tip: What color eyes do you have? What color of eyes does the baby's father have? Do you wear glasses or contacts? If so, when did you learn that you needed a vision correction? What does seeing things with spiritual eyes mean to you?

Notes:

_____

_____

_____

Week 7

LEARNING TO PRAY FOR YOUR CHILD

"This then is how you should pray; 'Our Father in heaven, hallowed be Your name, Your kingdom come, Your will be done on earth as it is in heaven. Give us today our daily bread. Forgive us our debts as we forgive our debtors. And lead us not into temptation, but deliver us from the evil one." Matthew 6:9-13

Maybe you are a regular prayer warrior, or perhaps this is one of the first times in your life that you have decided to pray for something on a regular basis. Prayer is simply talking to God. He tells us in His Word that we are to pray without ceasing! Prayer is the way we communicate with God, not only our needs, but also our praise for Him. During these next nine months, there will be many things you will face and feelings that you will experience that may be new and sometimes frightening to you. God can and will help you if you will seek Him. Use the Lords Prayer often as a guide when you do your daily devotional and journal time.

Remember the key points: 1.) Enter into prayer with praise. Don't just storm into the Lord's throne room and start demanding things. 2.) Ask for His will to be done here on earth as He sees it already done in heaven. He has a plan He wants you to follow and a plan for your baby as well. 3.) Trust Him to meet your needs every day. This may not be your *wants*, but He will supply what you have need of. 4.) Seek forgiveness when you've done wrong or done wrong to someone else. This also allows for daily examination of our hearts to see if there is any wicked way in us. 5.) Ask the Lord to keep you from evil and harm and to give you strength to overcome the attacks of the devil.

Following the pattern that Jesus taught will help you in your prayer time.

Dear Lord,

Thank You for this prayer example that You have given me through Your Word. Help me to remember the key points so that I can pray effectively. I want to be diligent in praying for my baby and pregnancy. I know that You can help me in areas that no one else can. Give me strength and persistence to travel this road ahead of me. My life is in Your hands, as well as my baby's life. I am dependent on You to see me through. May Your will be done in my life and this child's as You see it in heaven. May this pregnancy go as You have planned. During my gestation, I pray that You will provide all the many things that I will need. Keep me from harm and my little one from harm during the coming hours, days, and months. Yours is the kingdom, the power, and the glory forever. Amen.

Journal Tip: Is pregnancy your first experience in committed, continuous, long-term prayer? Ask the Lord to teach you more about prayer as you walk through this journey. Is there one part of the Lord's Prayer that sticks out to you? What is it and what does it mean to you specifically today?

Notes:

_____

_____

_____

_____

Week 7

POWERFUL AND EFFECTIVE PRAYERS

"The prayer of a righteous man is powerful and effective."
James 5:16b

"Effective" literally means "producing intended results". Consistently praying for your children not only brings them blessing, but also teaches the parent a daily discipline that will reap benefits for years to come. In all kinds of circumstances, our human words may wax eloquent, but let's face it, no words of man have ever called a universe into existence. It is only when we gain audience with the Almighty God that mountains start to move. No matter what you may face, if you learn to daily bring your prayers and petitions before the Lord, He will move on the behalf of your children. Little becomes much when God is involved. Our meager words, combined with the arm of the Mighty working for us, are both powerful and effective. Incredible!

Lord,
Even when I don't know what to pray for my child, I know that You have a master plan. I thank You that I can come to You and that Your Spirit can pray through me. No matter what obstacles or difficulties I might face during this pregnancy or in the years to come in raising this baby, I am confident that if I remain in You, there is hope. I believe in the power of the Almighty God to work and move on my behalf. I believe that as I act in obedience to pray, You will in turn make those prayers effective. Help me to incorporate this discipline of prayer into my daily life and into the life of my child. I thank You for the power of prayer. In Your name, amen.

Journal Tip: Write a simple prayer for your child to let him/her know how you prayed for them before birth.

Notes:

_____

_____

_____

_____

_____

_____

_____

_____

_____

_____

Week 7

NUMEROUS ACCOUNTS

"Jesus did many other things as well. If ever one of them were written down, I suppose that even the whole world would not have room for the books that would be written."
John 21:25

During your journey of pregnancy, it would be impossible for you to write down all the accounts of what God has done in your life during this time. This prayer journal is meant to be an aid in your memories; a proof of what God has done in you and through you during this time. It is not all inclusive. God will speak to you creatively and individually. This is all about what He is doing in YOU! God bless you on your journey.

Dear God,
Thank You for all You have done so far in my life. I am looking forward to this new road ahead of me. I pray that daily, as I seek Your face, that You would remind me of all the ways You are working in my heart and life. I pray that I would create wonderful memories for both me and my baby and a historical record for my baby that he/she could look back upon in the years to come. Bless him/her through this memoir that I am keeping. Relay to him/her that he/she has a wonderful Christian heritage to embrace and a faith to build life upon. Thank You, Lord. Amen.

Journal Tip: Why do you think it is important to keep memoirs of your pregnancy? What do you hope your child will think when he/she is older and could see what you prayed and thought every day of their pregnancy?

Notes:

_____

_____

_____

_____

_____

_____

_____

_____

_____

_____

_____

Week 7

DECISIONS

**"Whether you turn to the right or to the left, your ears will hear a voice behind you saying;
'This is the way; walk in it.'" Isaiah 30:21**

Decisions, decisions, decisions. Sometimes during pregnancy you are over-stimulated with choices. Which doctor will you choose? Which vitamins? Should I breast feed? Should I start a college fund? Whatever choices you are facing today, God wants to provide clarity and a sure footed path for you to walk on. Whatever you have need of, ask of Him and He will instruct you in the way you are to go. Choices don't have to be overwhelming. God can and will show you the way to go. Let's ask Him for some help.

God,
Today I am faced with _____. I'm not quite sure what to do, but I know that You are going to provide a way to walk. I hand this over to You fully and completely. I want what's best for me and my baby. You want Your perfect plan to unfold for our lives even more than I do. I trust You with this. Give me peace in this hour. May wisdom, knowledge, and discernment be granted to me in the areas of my life that need it. God, make corrections if corrections are needed. I ask for Your will to be done in this. When my child is older and in need of direction, I pray that he/she will seek You as well and hear Your voice clearly. In Your name I ask it. Amen.

Journal Tip: What decisions are you facing or going to be facing? Has God provided direction? Be sure to write it down when He does!

Notes:

_____

_____

_____

_____

_____

_____

_____

_____

_____

_____

_____

_____

LEADING YOU / GOD'S PRESENCE

**"The Lord replied, 'My presence will go with you, and I will give you rest.' Then
Moses said to him, 'If Your presence does not go with us, do not send us up from here.'"
Exodus 33:14**

In this passage, Moses had been called to lead the Children of Israel and was feeling a little anxious about
the daunting task in front of him. He already realized that God knew him by name and that he had found favor with Him (verse 12), but Moses realized that he needed more than that. He needed to know God's *ways*. Moses purposed in his heart that He was determined to pursue God. That meant more than a casual relationship with the Lord. He didn't want to go anywhere if the Lord wasn't there.

Moses actually says in verse 13, "teach me Your ways so that I may know You and continue to find favor with You". As an expectant mother, this story is very relevant to you. God knows you by name and you have found favor with Him as He has opened up your womb and blessed you with this baby. He has called you to take the hand of your little one and lead them into a life with Him. But how will you know how to do this? Our focus verse gives us the answer. You need the presence of God to go with you!

Heavenly Father,
I see the task ahead of me and know that You have prepared me for such a time as this. I thank You for this pregnancy and know that You have given me a huge task to accomplish. I ask, Lord, that Your presence will go with me. I want to know You and Your ways. I want to be a successful parent and that means I need to put a lot of effort into becoming closer and closer to You. I want everything I do to be blessed with Your presence. Help me to desire a closer walk with You because I know that it will not only bring me blessing, but my children as well. Help me to feel Your presence with me even now. Thank You, Lord. Amen.

Journal Tip: Do you feel like a leader? What are your thoughts about leading your child in life? Do you feel like the Lord's presence has been with you in life? Why or why not? Why will God's presence be important to you as a parent?

Notes:

_____

_____

_____

_____

_____

_____

_____

A SPIRITUAL HOUSE BEING BUILT

"Unless the Lord builds the house, its builders labor in vain." Psalm 127:1

A spiritual house is built much like a physical one is built. We build on the solid foundation of Christ, and add bricks of faith and righteousness. When we obey God and His word, the house gets stronger. God has a plan for how He wants your home (spiritually speaking and family speaking) to be constructed. When we get off track and try to do it in and of ourselves, it will end up in calamity every time. The Word says the foolish man built his house upon the sand. We all know what happened to that house. It fell when the rain came! We must build our house on the solid rock of Christ. Let's commit to let the Lord build our home piece by peace. Then all of our efforts will not be in vain.

Father,
I want my spiritual and family life to be built by You. You know the architect of each piece. You alone have a flawless design that will stand the storms of time and the tests of this life. I pray for a solid foundation on which to raise my child. I pray that this truth of building up a life in You would radiate through me and be passed on to this child's generation. I pray for a heritage of a strong spiritual house to be passed down through this family. Let us not rely on our own efforts, but solely rely upon You. For anything that our efforts construct are like the foolish man building on the sand. Help me to be wise and allow You to be my general contractor. Amen.

Journal Tip: Do you have a strong spiritual heritage in your family? If so, how did that strengthen you as you grew up? If not, start with you! What kinds of things have strengthened you and what are you hoping to begin passing down to your children?

Notes:

_____

_____

_____

_____

_____

_____

_____

_____

_____

_____

SEEK HIM NOW BEFORE THE TRIALS

"If you have raced with men on foot and they have worn you out, how can you compete with horses?" Jeremiah 12:5

Too many people wait until disaster strikes to seek the Lord! This is relevant to life as well as parenting. Let me assure you that God is concerned with every facet of your life, not just the big things. If He is counting the very hairs on your head, He cares about every aspect of our day! God admonishes us to examine ourselves daily and build up our endurance in Him. Our focus verse makes me think about this in terms of an athlete. A runner who has practiced and built up strength and stamina has the energy to see him through when it comes to race time. See what the verse says? If you have raced with men on foot and they have worn you out, how can you compete with horses? Spending the time now in prayer and seeking Him concerning parenting and raising your child can only benefit you later. You are in training for Godly parenting. Stretch those spiritual muscles today and work them! The strength will be there when You need it!

Dear Lord,
I thank You for Your Word that brings new light to my life every day. I thank You for instruction and wisdom in my life, especially during this new phase. I ask that You would help me gain Spiritual strength every day. Help train me as a parent. Show me how to grow and mature as a mother so that I can face challenges when they come with skill. I ask for Your strength and endurance. Give me the diligence and unction to train daily and to not give up. There is a goal in sight. Thank You, Lord. Amen.

Journal Tip: Do you feel like you are training yourself for parenting? Does it make you feel more confident in your abilities?

Notes:

_____

_____

_____

_____

_____

_____

_____

_____

_____

_____

Week 8

FORTY WEEKS OF PREGNANCY

"The Israelites had moved about the desert for forty years." Joshua 5:6a

Forty is a special number to the Lord. It is usually representative of tribulation or trial. God used the number forty many times in the Bible. During the flood in Noah's day, it rained for forty days and forty nights. Moses spent forty days on Mt. Sinai. Jesus was tempted in the wilderness forty days. The Israelites moved about for forty years in the desert! I especially enjoy the story of the children of Israel because we vividly see the transformation from the old to the new as Joshua brings them into the Promised Land! Is it any wonder that God would choose the normal gestation for pregnancy as forty weeks? On occasion, you may feel like you're going through a wilderness time during the next forty weeks. Just keep in mind that the Promised Land awaits you in your new little one. Let's pray for the endurance and strength to get through this pregnancy. There will be many things He wants to show you along the way. When you're done, you'll realize that your forty weeks were weeks of wonder and growth, not only for the baby, but for you, too.

Dear Lord,
What a wonder You are to have selected a gestation period of forty weeks! I know that pregnancy must be a special time to You. As I go through this time, I pray for strength, endurance, an open heart to learn, and ears to hear Your voice clearly. I want to enter into the Promise that You are giving to me through parenthood. Prepare me as I go along. Let me cling to You for direction, discernment, diligence, and determination. Show me new things along this journey. I place my life and the life of my little one into Your hands. Set encouragers into my path and connect me with the people that I need to be connected with (doctors, midwife, nurses, a hospital or birthing center, other mothers, mentors) whoever or whatever I need in my life at this time. Thank You, Lord, for allowing me the privilege to walk this spiritual journey with You. Amen.

Journal Tip: Does knowing that God designed pregnancy with a purpose in mind give you a new revelation about the process? How do you feel about facing forty weeks of pregnancy? What are some things you think God may want you to learn along the way?

Notes:

_____

_____

_____

_____

_____

_____

_____

_____

64

PREGNANCY SIGNS AND SYMPTOMS

"And the Lord worked with them and confirmed His Word by the signs that accompanied it". Mark 16:20b

Anywhere the Word of the Lord is confirmed, there will be signs that follow. Since discovering that you are expecting, there have been and will be signs that follow. Some of these may include morning sickness, a sensation of tugging in your groin area as your uterus expands, tender breasts, and of course the absence of a period. Although these are just some of the symptoms that can accompany early pregnancy, you can be assured that during pregnancy you will have multiple confirmations that your little one is on the way. The Lord is working to make all things according to His plan and design. Each little ache, pain, and tug has a purpose! Rest assured that He is solidifying His will in you today.

Lord,
I thank You today that where Your Word is confirmed, there will be definite signs that follow. I pray that You would keep me from fear, but allow me to rest in perfect peace that whatever is going on in my body has been ordained of You. I bind the enemy who would like to sow doubt and fear. You have not given me a mind to worry over every ache and pain. If there is something that I would need to bring attention to, help me to discern it and to seek help. I pray that this pregnancy would go according to Your divine plan and that none of the symptoms I am experiencing would overwhelm me. I place all things in Your divine hands. Thank You, Lord. Amen.

Journal Tip: What kinds of pregnancy symptoms have you been experiencing? How do these signs of pregnancy make you feel?

Notes:

_____

_____

_____

_____

_____

_____

_____

_____

_____

_____

Week 8

EMOTIONS

"I love the Lord, for He heard my voice; He heard my cry for mercy. Because He turned His ear to me, I will call on Him as long as I live." Psalm 116:1

Emotions can be a roller coaster ride when you are expecting. One day, you're as exuberant as the morning sun. The next day, the clouds and rain might roll in. Although these emotions are very normal, sometimes we can't seem to rise above them. This is especially difficult when you wake in the middle of the night feeling blue. Praise God that whenever we need Him, He is there to hear us. No matter when we call, He will hear our voice. This beautiful verse shows our loving God who hears and turns an ear toward us.   You can tell it all to Him. There's no care too small or too great. Let's ask Him to regulate your emotions during pregnancy and to provide guidance, comfort, or simply a listening ear when needed.

Father,
I turn all of my emotions over to You. I don't know how I can feel so many different things all in one day.   I understand that my body is going though quite a change and it's bound to effect me emotionally, but I ask You now to take my emotions into Your Hands. Where I have needs, fill them. When I shed tears, see them. When I cry out, hear me. Help me to understand that emotions aren't necessarily truth. Open my spiritual eyes to see the reality of it all. Give me peace today. In Your name, Amen.

Journal Tip: Have you been riding the emotional roller coaster this week?   Are there certain things that trigger specific moods?

Notes:

_____

_____

_____

_____

_____

_____

_____

_____

_____

_____

_____

HERITAGE AND GENERATIONS

**"I have been reminded of your sincere faith, which first lived in your grandmother
Lois and in your mother Eunice and, I am persuaded, now
lives in you also." 1 Timothy 1:5**

Are you a second, third, or possibly forth generation Christian? Has the faith of your family passed down from generation to generation? Even if you are the first generation of Christians in your family, you are soon to pass it on to another generation. God wants to perpetuate His saving grace into the historical annuals of your family! In this passage of scripture, Paul is conveying that he has watched as Timothy has been passed the spiritual torch from generation to generation. Isn't that a wonderful thought today? You are part of the passing of faith in your family.

Dear Lord,
Thank You for the spiritual heritage that I have been given in my family or my spiritual family. I ask that You help me keep with sound teaching, strong faith, and love. Help me to guard my life and doctrine closely and to reflect You to my baby. It is my desire that You continue to be gloried in this family from generation to generation. Give my child a strong sense of spiritual heritage and ownership of his/her position as a child in Your Kingdom. May he/she live a holy life and shun immorality and all the trappings that it brings. Give him/her an understanding of sin and that it has lasting consequences, not only on the person involved, but also to their children. Enable us to see Your saving grace grown in this family year after year. In Your name, Amen.

Journal Tip: What generation of Christian are you? How do you feel about being part of a spiritual heritage? What are you going to do to affect the historical annuals of your family?

Notes:

_____

_____

_____

_____

_____

_____

_____

_____

_____

_____

_____

Week 8

GOD'S BEST

"I am the LORD your God, who teaches you what is best for you, who directs you in the way you should go." Isaiah 48:17b

Families operate in different ways. What works best in one may not be the best thing in another. You need to consider what God would say is best for you when it comes to raising you child and running your household. It is He who will teach you and instruct you if you will simply ask Him to. There is a way that you should go and He will lead you. No two pregnancies are exactly alike. The experiences of your mother, sister, or friend may not particularly apply to your life or current situation. If in all things, by prayer and supplication, you make take your needs, frustrations, and goals to the Lord, He will be there with arms open ready to lead you. You know as a mother, you will want what is best for you child. You'll want him/her to have the best they possibly can in life and to be their best. God has a "best" for you and your children! It's up to you to allow Him to help you find it!

Heavenly Father,
I thank You that whatever I have need of, You have the power to meet it and can lead me on a peaceful path. I bring my family to You right now and ask that You direct us in the way we should go. You are my favorite teacher because I know that what I learn from You is life and light. I ask that I be taught of You. Teach me how to mother. Teach me how to parent and become a roll model for my son/daughter. Help me to love those around me with an unconditional love. I am comforted by the fact that You do everything according to my best interests. You have plans that are good for me and not harmful. Mold me and shape me into the person You want me to be. I pray that this family will be a blessing to this baby I am carrying. You know what he/she has need of and You have graciously allowed me to be a part of that plan for his/her life. I ask for Your direction and wisdom to rest upon me this day. Keep my body in health and give me strength for the days ahead. Thank You, Lord. Amen.

Journal Tip: Are you amazed that God has the best in mind for you? Have you discovered (at least in part) what that might mean for you or your baby? If you think of some specific examples concerning how God has lead you in the ways you should go, write them down.

Notes:

_____

_____

_____

_____

_____

_____

_____

GOD MADE LIFE AND BREATH

"And the Lord God formed the man from the dust of the ground and breathed into his nostrils the breath of life, and the man became a living being." Genesis 2:7

The breath of life came from God Himself! God made dust, formed man out of the dust, and literally breathed life into Adam. This was the beginning of all people. The breath of life comes from HIM! What an awesome thought. When your baby takes it first breath after delivery and you hear the cry, you will know what magnitude the breath of life holds. Sometimes following delivery, as you're waiting for the secretions to be suctioned away, those few moments of breathless silence can seem like an eternity. You long to hear the breath of life coming forth in strong, healthy, newborn cries. Let's praise the Lord for His life giving breath and giving us life!

Lord,
You are the giver and maker of life. I thank You for the life that You have breathed into my baby. Life is flowing through him/her at this very moment! One day, he/she will take his/her first breaths of their existence! How I long for the day to come! As for now, continue to form him/her into the living person that he/she is supposed to be. Fashion every part perfectly, just as You perfectly formed Adam from the dust of the ground. Life can be felt within me and I marvel at Your work! Praise Your name, Lord. Amen.

Journal Tip: Have you ever heard a newborns first cry as their little lungs inflate and they breathe their first gulps of air? How do think you'll feel when you hear the cry of your child for the first time?

Notes:

_____

_____

_____

_____

_____

_____

_____

_____

_____

_____

Week 8

ADVICE: GOOD AND BAD

"My sheep listen to My voice. I know them, and they follow Me." John 10:27

Advice. Some of it's good, some of it's bad. It seems when you're expecting (and even after the baby comes), everyone has some piece of advice that they need to share with you. Just remember that you DON'T have to follow what everyone else is saying. There is a still small voice that can guide and lead you in all truth, and that's the voice of our Lord. When you are in Christ, you will know His voice when you hear it. Beware of anything that makes you feel uneasy or seems to go against what you feel is right in your heart. Check everything with the Spirit to see if it's of Him or not.

God,
I pray that You would protect me from unhealthy advice! If someone attempts to offer advice that is contrary to Your will or that might be harmful to me, I pray that you would put a stumbling block in front of them. Close their mouths as You closed the lion's mouths for Daniel.
Let me strain all of what I hear through the discernment of the Holy Spirit. When there is helpful advice, let me turn my ear to wisdom and learn from it. Help me apply only that which is healthy and beneficial to my pregnancy. Incline me to make wise choices during my entire pregnancy. In Your name, Amen.

Journal Tip: Write down some good advice that you have been given over the past few months. Who gave you the advice? Has there been any advice that you have not taken? Why?

Notes:

_____

_____

_____

_____

_____

_____

_____

_____

_____

_____

_____

_____

_____

DOING WHAT IS BENEFICIAL

"Everything is permissible for me"- but not everything is beneficial."
1 Corinthians 6:12

There are many things during pregnancy that may be permissible, but not beneficial to you or your baby. Likewise, as your child grows, there may be things in life that seem permissible, but not exactly uplifting to their growth as a person or spiritually. You are responsible to lead your child, to guide and direct him/her in making good choices in life. That may be hard to do if you yourself haven't learned to make good choices. If you feel like you haven't made the best of life choices at times, learn from those mistakes and pray that God will redeem that which the devil would like to ruin in you. Choices are involved in every area of our lives and therefore it is very important to you to make healthy ones. Let God teach you how to make better choices through His Spirit, His Word, and in prayer.

Father,
I know there have been times that I have chosen things in life that have been permissible but not beneficial to my life. I pray where bad choices have been made that You would redeem what the enemy would desire to destroy. I pray for wisdom to make better choices in life and the wisdom to teach this baby how to make good choices. Let me receive wisdom, instruction, guidance, and ingenuity through Your Spirit, Your Word, and in times of prayer. Help us to reap a life of reward because of the good choices that we make through You. Thank You, Lord! Amen.

Journal Tip: What are some things that would not be beneficial to you during pregnancy? Have you been struggling with anything that seems alright to engage in, but isn't necessarily helpful to you? Why is it important to you that your son or daughter learn to make good choices?

Notes:

_____

_____

_____

_____

_____

_____

_____

_____

_____

_____

Week 9

FASHIONED BY THE LORD'S HANDS

"Your hands made me and formed me; give me understanding to learn Your commands."
Psalm 119:73

You baby is growing day and night in your womb at the Lord's direction. He set this process in motion and He is an integral part of the forming of your baby. I imagine His huge hands putting each little piece of your baby together as it is supposed to be. This figurative and imaginative picture reminds you that He is in charge of fashioning your child and is overseeing the developments. What a glorious thought today.

Dear God,
Praise Your marvelous works! I cannot fathom the intricacies of the development of my baby, but You see all. I know that You are attentively watching this baby form and already know her/him by name. My heart rejoices in You today. What joy! What blessing!
Plant within this child an ability to understand the things of the Lord. Write your commands upon his/her heart so that he/she may follow after You all of the days of his/her life. Amen.

Journal Tip: What do you visualize in your mind when you read this verse?

Notes:

_____

_____

_____

_____

_____

_____

_____

_____

_____

_____

_____

_____

_____

SPECIAL BLESSING

"Now be pleased to bless the house of your servant, hat it may continue forever in your sight; for you, O Sovereign LORD, have spoken, and with your blessing the house of your servant will be blessed forever." 2 Samuel 7:29

I believe that the Lord wants to specially bless you today:
"May God's blessing rest on you, on your baby, and on your household today. May He see His servant and remember her during pregnancy. Make today a day of remembrance to this mother. Look down upon this child, Lord, and bless him/her in body, soul, and spirit. Lift up this mother's countenance. Meet every need in this household, big or small. We ask for Your protection, Your strength, Your power, and Your authority to be displayed in this house today. Bless this mother with a light yolk of burden. Amen!"

Dear God,
Thank You for times of refreshing today. I accept the blessings You are pouring down on me. I ask that You would guard over every minute of this day and bring restoration to by body, mind, and spirit. Work in my sphere of relationships today. Repair anything that needs repairing and set me feet on a fresh path today. I ask for bold, new adventures in You and insight that only comes from Your Spirit. Make this pregnancy a blessing and reveal to me new truths that I would not have learned except through this life lesson. My heart, eyes, and ears are open to You. Bless this little baby within me today. Make him/her comfortable and resting secure. Thank You, Lord for Your goodness. Amen.

Journal Tip: Write a blessing for your household today. Do you feel the Lord's refreshing working in your life?

Notes:

_____

_____

_____

_____

_____

_____

_____

_____

_____

_____

Week 9

OLDER WOMEN MENTORS

"Is not wisdom found among the aged? Does not long life bring understanding?"
Job 12:12

For many of us, we are not experiencing pregnancy or childbirth the way our parents or grandparents did. In fact, if you ask many of them, they would tell you that now-a-days women like us have it easy! Advancements in pain medicines, the use of technology, and the increase of knowledge have made modern pregnancies and childbirths an entirely different ballgame. Let me stop right here and say, however, there is still great wisdom to be shared from those women who have walked this road before us. You need to realize: 1.) Some things will never change about pregnancy. Our feet still swell, as well as our middles! 2.) Some things will never change about childbirth. The baby still has to come out no matter what! 3.) Some things will never change about childrearing. The baby still has to be taught! So, don't just throw off your mom's advice like an old afghan with wild sixties colors. It may be a little "outdated" for your taste, but the truth is, if you're willing to take it, it still has a lot of good uses!
Here's a helpful tip. If you have women in your life that are close to you and you feel they need an "update", get them a subscription to a current baby magazine (or at least a few copies to see). You could also share with them the books you are reading or the other resources you found helpful. This includes them in your pregnancy and will also inform them of the current trends, methods, products, etc. of the day!

Dear Lord,
I want to thank You today for mothers or spiritual mothers You have placed in my life who have traveled this road before me. Help me to honor them and respect them for the jobs they have done raising children. Bridge this gap between the past and the present and help us both to meet somewhere in the middle. Check my spirit today and see if there be any wicked way in me. Where I am prideful, break it. Where I am stubborn, soften it. Allow my ears to hear the advice You may be sending me through others and to receive it as You intended. When advice given to me is not helpful, place graciousness and a humble spirit within me to respond to others in a kind, respectful fashion. Surround me with mentors that You have selected and keep me protected from meddlesome busybodies and controlling women. Thank You, Lord. Amen.

Journal Tip: Do you have a mother or others (like a mother to you) who are actively involved in your pregnancy? Who are they and how are they helping you?   What have you shared with them and what have they shared with you?

Notes:

_____

_____

_____

_____

_____

GOD TEACHES PARENTS

**"Call to Me and I will answer you and tell you great and unsearchable things
you do not know." Jeremiah 33:3**

Parenting is a process. God doesn't expect you to know everything about parenting the minute you bring your baby into the world. This time is a preparation time where you are learning about parenting and thinking on things that you may face in the future. Some of the biggest life skills that you are learning are how to call on God for wisdom, search His Word for knowledge, and pray for your children. Those three things will be the most invaluable tools you will possess as a parent. There isn't a parent alive that knows everything, but praise God… we know <u>Him</u> and He does know everything. When you call upon Him for your parenting needs, He will answer you. He'll give you creative answers to the most perplexing problems and best of all they will not be someone else's ideas. They will fit your family perfectly. So, when in doubt about anything concerning parenting, ask the Lord. He'll show you great and unsearchable things that you do not know!

Dear Lord,
I thank You for being my life line 24/7! I know I can come boldly to Your throne at any time of the day or night and You are always there to hear me. Remind me when the times get rough and tough that I should come to You seeking answers. Show me how to be the best parent I can be for the child you have given to me. Your advice is as unique as You have created us to be. You give answers that will specifically help me! I am in awe of Your knowledge, power, and splendor. Thank You for trusting me to parent this child. I place my direction, thoughts, and goals in Your hands today. In Your name, amen.

Journal Tip: How has God helped you so far during your pregnancy? What has He shown you about being a parent?

Notes:

_____

_____

_____

_____

_____

_____

_____

_____

_____

_____

Week 9

ROLL YOUR ANXIETY OFF ONTO HIM

"Cast all your anxiety on Him because He cares for you." 1 Peter 5:7

"Anxiety" means apprehensive uneasiness of mind, fearful concerns, or overwhelming sensations of fear. While you are expecting, anxiety may be caused by various factors that beforehand may have been of little or no concern to you whatsoever. Housing, bills, relationships, goals, finances, work, or expectations/certain aspects of your pregnancy may all play a part in making you anxious. Learn to roll of your anxiety on His shoulders. He cares so much about you today that He doesn't want you loaded down with the stresses of life, especially during pregnancy. Sometimes we think that God has blessed us so much with allowing us to conceive that we feel bad going to God over what our minds think of as trivial. Let me reassure you... He cares about every facet of your life. What's small to us is important to God. Don't be afraid to cast everything you can think of on His shoulders. His shoulders are broad enough to carry the load!

Dear God,
Thank You for caring for me and being concerned with every facet of my life, big or small. Today I resolve to cast all my anxiety on You because I know You never intended for me to have to carry burdens along with my baby. So, I bring everything to You and lay it at Your feet right now. I ask that You would take the heaviness from me and make my spirit light and alive in You. Help me not to get stressed out over situations that are beyond my control. I give everything to You. Form Your goodness in me and build a strong relationship between me and You so that I will eagerly bring my needs before You. Lead me on Your paths of righteousness I pray, not only for my sake, but also for the sake of my unborn baby.
As my baby grows, I want him/her to experience the freedom that comes in bringing all to You. Let me be an example in this area to him/her. Thank You, Lord, for loving me and carrying my burdens today. Amen.

Journal Tip: What are your biggest challenges that you are facing today? What seems small to you that you need to turn over to God?

Notes:

_____

_____

_____

_____

_____

_____

_____

_____

Week 9

NEW PERCEPTIONS

"Forget the former things; do not dwell on the past. See, I am doing a new thing! Now it springs up; do you not perceive it?" Isaiah 43:19

Have you watched television or looked at magazines lately and notice how the baby ads just seem to jump out at you? Have you been out shopping and noticing all the baby clothes, gear, and accessories, not to mention every mother with a child in tow? They've always been there, but before they were just another blip on your daily radar. Now that you are expecting, your perception of life will be rapidly changing. Your thoughts and your senses are gearing toward motherhood! Today you are embarking on a new frontier. New things are going to happening to you every day and you need to embrace them. God is taking you where you have never been before. You are blazing a new trail for your life. You will see during the course of your pregnancy that your energy will change, your emotions will change, your physical appearance will change, some of your opinions will change, your relationships will change, and life as you knew it will change. Don't be afraid to let go of the past to progress toward your future. Change may not be easy, but it is exciting. There will be a lot of change during parenthood as your child grows. Change will become familiar to you. Ask God today what He would have you learn during this process of pregnancy. You are in for quite an experience! Let's ask God to lead you during this time.

Dear God,
Thank You for the newness of life that You are bringing me during pregnancy. Help me to adapt to all the change that comes with it. I know that my life will never be the same since I found out that I am expecting. Help me to let go of the past wherever I need to. Help me to take a hold of and move in the new areas you are guiding me to. May I grow and be purified daily. I pray that through this process, You will teach me valuable spiritual and practical life lessons. Bless me as a mother and be with my little one today as he/she is growing. Give me peace and rest today as I go about my day. Thank You, Lord, for this new thing You are springing up within me! Amen.

Journal Tip: What kinds of new things are you experiencing? Have you had new experiences that have only come about because you are expecting?

Notes:

_____

_____

_____

_____

_____

_____

_____

PRAY FOR YOUR CHILD

"But in everything, by prayer and petition, with thanksgiving, present your requests to God." Philippians 4:6b

As a parent, the spiritual growth of your child will be a high priority. Developing the commitment to pray is a primary factor in this process. Unfortunately, just because we pray for our child doesn't mean that we are going to stave off all of the trials and tribulations of this life. When we pray, we establish a dependence on God. When the trials and tribulations come, it is much easier to face them when we have already created a foundation of stability. We need to pray for commitment to the daily discipline of bringing our children before the Lord through prayer.

Lord,
I pray that You would instill in me the deep desire and direction of how to pray for my child. Place a commitment and determination in me that the enemy will not be able to shake or undermine. I pray that I will be rooted and grounded in You so that whatever I face during this pregnancy and during my many years of parenthood, I will stand stable and firm.
Your ways are multifaceted. As my child grows, I will grow in spiritual maturity and strength as well. I pray that as I sow in the spirit, there will be a spiritual harvest reaped in my child. Teach me the importance of prayer and how to apply it to my daily living. Amen.

Journal Tip: Write down some things that you are praying for your baby today.

Notes:

_____

_____

_____

_____

_____

_____

_____

_____

_____

_____

_____

_____

_____

EVERY DAY IS PRECIOUS; LIMITED TIME

"Teach us to number our days aright, that we may gain a heart of wisdom."
Psalm 90:12

All life comes from God and every day we have is numbered by Him. Every minute of life counts. Just think of how rapidly your baby is growing inside and changing every day...every second. You will only have a certain number of days that you will carry this baby. In addition, most people don't think about the limited years they have to raise their kids until they are grown. Lord, teach us to number our days and to apply our hearts to wisdom! Don't waste any time! The best time to influence your child for Christ is the first tender years of his/her life. By the time he/she hits the teenage years, if a commitment to Christ hasn't been made, it will be more difficult. When we think about the time factor, we can understand a little clearly what Solomon meant when he wrote the verse "teach us to number our days...."

Lord,
You know exactly how many days, hours, and minutes that I will have to carry this child You have given to me. I pray that I will have a clear sense of the time frame You have given me to parent this child. I pray that I will enjoy this pregnancy as much as physically possible and to enjoy and utilize the time I have with my children. God, you have numbered our days. Give me a sense of the "big picture". Help me to never lose sight of the precious time You have granted to accomplish the tasks You have set before me. Amen.

Journal Tip: Try to imagine what the full scope of parenting will be like. Write down your thoughts.

Notes:

_____

_____

_____

_____

_____

_____

_____

_____

_____

_____

_____

MOUTHS FILLED WITH GOOD THINGS

"For out of the overflow of the heart, the mouth speaks." Matthew 12:34b

Our children need to have validation from us. One of the best ways to do that is verbally. We need to openly express to our children the love and admiration we have in our hearts for them. It's never too early to express what's abundant in your heart towards him/her. At the same time, what comes out of your child's mouth can be a real litmus test on what is going on in your home. Be assured what is in that heart will come out of the mouth sooner or later. Let's give this area over to the Lord and ask that He fill our hearts abundantly with good things.

Dear Lord,
I pray that You would open my mouth and let it speak praises today. First of all, I praise You for being a creative God who is personally concerned with Your creation. I thank You for my baby that You have blessed me with. I pray today that You would fill me with good things from Your storehouse. May the words and feelings that pour forth from me bring blessing to You and not dishonor. I want to say and do the right things in my home so that my children can model after those things. If there needs to be any correction in this area, I pray that You would bring it to light and help me to deal with it. I want to be filled with the goodness of the Lord and not of the destruction of the world. I pray that You will abundantly bless this child with all the fruits of the Spirit and fill his/her heart to overflowing. Bless this child today as he/she develops. Bless his/her physical mouth. I pray against any mouth deformities or difficulties. I pray that when he/she begins to speak that there would be no speech problems of any kind. Bless the words that will come from my little one. May they be words of life and not death. May his/her speech be used to glorify You and testify of Your good works. Amen.

Journal Tip: Consider the words of your mouth today. Can you think of at least three things that are praiseworthy? What are you feeling in the abundance of your heart concerning your baby?

Notes:

_____

_____

_____

_____

_____

_____

_____

_____

Week 10

SHINING LIKE STARS TO GOD

"Those who are wise shall shine like the brightness of the heavens, and those who lead many to righteousness, like the stars forever and ever." Daniel 12:3

Many parents, Christian or non-Christian, want their kids to be special and shine like a star! Sadly, for the most part, the focus isn't on what God created the child to be or how to truly be successful in God's eyes; it's all steeped in self-absorption and self satisfying desires. The fame of this world is fleeting. It is here one moment and gone the next. Names that are famous today in the eyes of the world will be remembered no longer if given enough time. God made us all to shine like stars, but that's not how the devil would like us to think. So how do we become like stars? This verse tells us that the *wise* will shine like the brightness of the firmament! What makes one wise? Those who listen to God's Word and obey it! This passage further describes those who turn many to righteousness will shine like the stars forever and ever. The scope of people our lives can touch can also be envisioned as endless as the stars! Let's ask the Lord to grant us this godly desire. Let's ask God to make your child shine like a star in this dark world and that their impact will reach as vast as the stars of heaven!

Dear Lord,
Thank You for this verse that shows us how our children can become stars by seeking after Your righteousness and walking in Your wisdom. This isn't the kind of star that will bring them fleeting fame or fortune. He/she will be a star to shine forth Your glory in a dark world and to lead others to You. You alone are great, God! You placed all the stars in the sky in the exact place that You desired it to be. I know You have a plan and purpose for this baby. I ask that he/she would live a life that would shine and would lead others to you. Let him/her impact others lives, so many that it would be as vast as the stars of the heavens. Thank You for this revelation to me today. I ask that You bless this little one. He/she is already a spark of light in my life. Thank You, Lord. Amen.

Journal Tip: Can you name anyone who has been a "star" in your life? Is there anyone who has made an impact on you and your spiritual walk? Why? Write down the things that impacted your life through others and ask the Lord to ingrain those same qualities into your child!

Notes:

_____

_____

_____

_____

_____

_____

_____

Week 10

AUTHORITY TO TRIUMPH

"I have given you authority to trample on snakes and scorpions and to overcome all the power of the enemy; nothing will harm you. However, do not rejoice that the spirits submit to you, but rejoice that your names are written in heaven." Luke 10:19

Have you ever heard the phrase, "Membership has its privileges."? When we have come to accept Jesus Christ as our Lord and Savior, His authority and power is available to work in and through us. No, it is not of our own power, but His. Are you facing something today that seems insurmountable in your own power? During this time of pregnancy, what are the "snakes and scorpions" you are facing? Are you worrying that harm is going to come to you? Rejoice that you are one of God's children and then be empowered through His Spirit. You have nothing to fear. He has enabled you to overcome.

Dear God,
I praise You today that my name is written in the Lamb's Book of Life. I know that no matter what I face, You have given me the power over the enemy. I do not have to be fearful or timid of the enemy. I give all that I am struggling with today over to You. I stand firmly on Your Word and will not let the enemy gain a foothold when it comes to my pregnancy or any other circumstance that is in my life. I pray protection over myself and my baby right now. Thank You, Lord. Amen.

Journal Tip: Why do you have power over the enemy? How does that make you feel in regard to your pregnancy? What are your thoughts on your baby today?

Notes:

_____

_____

_____

_____

_____

_____

_____

_____

_____

_____

_____

GOD'S LITTLE LAMBS

"He tends His flock like a shepherd. He gathers the lambs in his arms and carries them close to His heart; He gently leads those that have young." Isaiah 10:11

So often in the Word, God's children are referred to as lambs. Babies remind us of little lambs. They are pure and innocent. God is the great shepherd who oversees His flock of little lambs. He keeps them safe. The Word says, "He shall gather the lambs with his arms and carry them into His bosom." What a great picture of the protective nature of God and the sheltering He provides for us. We are close to His heart. This is also a promise to those who have young ones (babies)! This verse says He'll gently lead you! What a blessing!

Dear God,
Thank You for my little lamb, so precious, pure, and innocent. I thank You that Your loving arms are extended to him/her this day and that You are keeping him/her close to Your heart. I pray that he/she will always have ears to hear the protecting voice of the Shepherd, who keeps watch after him/her. Let him/her know Your voice and follow after You. I pray that he/she will never be a sheep that wanders away from the flock. Protect my little lamb from the enemy who would love to attack and devour him/her. May he/she love to dwell in the safe pastures of the Lord. Amen.

Journal Tip: What are your thoughts about Jesus being the Good Shepherd and your little one being like a little lamb? What else comes to mind when you think of lambs and Jesus?

Notes:

_____

_____

_____

_____

_____

_____

_____

_____

_____

_____

_____

Week 10

BABY PROOF YOUR HOME

"...Let the beloved of the LORD rest secure in Him, for He shields him all day long."
Deuteronomy 33:12

Have you started baby-proofing your house yet? It's never too early to begin thinking about making your home free from harm. A good way to do this may be to get down on your hands and knees and look at things from a baby's perspective. This might be most easily accomplished for you in your first trimester. Things that you may not have noticed before may seem very tempting to a little one crawling around. Look for things that might catch a little one's eye. Electrical cords and outlets should be made secure. There are all kinds of products you can buy to secure doors (like on kitchen cabinets) so that little ones can't open them. Move your medicines and cleaning supplies to a place where baby can't get to them or find a way to secure them from reach. Also, have some Syrup of Ipecac on hand and the numbers of your Pediatrician and local poison control readily available. Stairways may need to be gated so your little one won't fall. Cords on blinds should be put up, especially if they are around baby's crib. This would also be a good time to check the batteries on your smoke detectors or carbon monoxide detector. Have a plan for fire escape and perhaps get a fire extinguisher if you don't already have one. We are going to trust that God will keep you and your little one safe, but you also need to take measures to assure that he/she will be out of harm's way.

Dear Lord,
I thank You that You are my buckler and my shield. I know that You are actively involved in keeping me and my child from harm this day and in the days to come. Help me child-proof my home. Quicken my spirit to the things that need attention. I pray that I would find the resources I need to secure cabinets, fill electrical outlets, and block off stairs. I won't be given over to an unhealthy spirit of fear concerning the safety of my child. Show me what I can do to prevent unnecessary danger to my baby, but then I pray that I will rest in knowing You are keeping him/her from harm. Keep this home surrounded by angels day and night. Protect all who come and go from this place. In Your name, amen.

Journal Tip: What have you done or what are you planning to do to prepare for your baby?

Notes:

_____

_____

_____

_____

_____

_____

_____

_____

Week 11

FOOD CRAVINGS AND AVERSIONS

"Therefore, whatever you eat or drink, or whatever you do, do all to the glory of God."
1 Corinthians 10:31

Having any food cravings or aversions? Sometimes it's hard to eat like we should or stay active when you're expecting. Whatever you do, if you keep in mind that all is to glorify God, it gives you a new perspective on daily routines. Remember, your body is not only providing nourishment for you during this time, but for your baby as well.

Lord,
I pray that I will be able to nourish my body and this baby as You would have me to. I pray that I would have a desire to eat the right kinds of food, drink plenty of water, take my vitamins, and get plenty of rest while I am pregnant. Help me not to engage in any activity that might harm me or my baby. Let me do all during my daily activities to Your Glory. Amen.

Journal Tip: If you are struggling in this area, begin keeping a record of what you eat, when you take your vitamin, or what kind of exercise you are doing.

Notes:

_____

_____

_____

_____

_____

_____

_____

_____

_____

_____

_____

_____

_____

_____

Week 11

YOUR BABY'S NOSE

"All your robes are fragrant with myrrh and aloes and cassia" Psalm 45:8

What do you smell like? You may not think you smell like anything (with the exception of perfume you may wear), but your baby will be able to identify your scent as opposed to other mothers after birth. Around week eleven, your baby is developing the sense of smell. What a sense God has created in us. Imagine all the millions of things that smell, good or bad. That reminds me... get ready to use your sense of smell to tell when baby needs a diaper change. It will bring your sense of smell to an entirely new level!

Lord,
Thank You for all the senses that you are forming in my baby. Form everything as it is supposed to so that they will work and function as it should. You've given us our senses not only for our enjoyment, but for our protection. Our noses can detect fire, chemicals, or other things that might harm us. You had many purposes for our nose! Thank You for fashioning my baby's nose today with Your mighty hands.
Amen.

Journal Tip: Describe your nose and what you think your baby's nose might look like. Do you wear a certain type of perfume or have any allergies that bother your nose? What are some things you enjoy smelling?

Notes:

_____

_____

_____

_____

_____

_____

_____

_____

_____

_____

_____

_____

_____

CHURCH FAMILY

"I rejoiced with those who said to me, 'Let us go to the house of the LORD'."
Psalm 122:1

Are you plugged into a church family? If you're not, consider the benefits fellowshipping with other believers would have on you and your child. Church attendance promotes spiritual growth, especially in children. If you currently attend a church, now is a good time to go around and check out all the programs designed for kids. Start by taking look at your church nursery. Observe how they do things. What are their policies? Do they have background checks for workers? Is the environment safe and secure? Are parents required to work in the nursery? Is the area divided into sections for infants and toddlers? Is there a section where you could go nurse or feed your baby? Is there a problem with keeping your baby with you in the service if you wanted to? Are you are comfortable with those things? Talk to the workers, leaders/teachers who work with other kids in your church, and parents to get a better feel of what your church has to offer. If you are a first time parent, expect for your new arrival to be highly anticipated by your congregation.

Dear Lord,
Thank You for my church home and the support I find there. I pray that our church environment would be a positive place for the spiritual upbringing of my baby. Thank You for all of people surrounding my and my family who will help nurture and rear my baby. I ask that You would help me to be attentive to the surroundings that my child will be involved in. Show me what questions to ask, where to get involved, and how to trust others with my baby. Help me to never be forced into situations involving my child that I am uncomfortable with. When I need to assert myself into situations, give me boldness and the words I must utter. Let others around me respect me and my role as parent, even if I am a first time parent. I trust You to lead me in how to handle my child and raise him/her. I know that their raising and decisions concerning their upbringing is ultimately up to me. I want to make good choices for them. Thank You, Lord. Amen.

Journal Tip: What is your church home? If you do not attend a church, are you going to start attending a church? Why or why not?   Have you checked out the nursery? Who is in charge of the nursery program?

Notes:

_____

_____

_____

_____

_____

_____

_____

TALES AND FABLES

"There the birds make their nests; the stork has its home in the pine trees."
Psalm 104:17

Old wives tales and other fables can border on the ridiculous! I don't know who came up with the idea that babies were brought by the stork, but as we know that is far from the truth. It may make a nice movie scene, but that's not real life. We don't hear much about the stork today, do we? It's no wonder because it does seem so far fetched. During your pregnancy, you may hear not only unwise advice, but also fables that will border on the sublime. I'm amazed how many Christian women still toy with those ideas. I've heard of certain "tests" that can help you determine the gender of your baby (something with a weighted string), eating certain foods will effect how much hair your baby will have, and that if you carry one way or another (according to the perception of the viewer) you can tell whether your baby's a girl or a boy. I will say in jest that most of these will have a fifty percent chance of being right! Don't <u>rely</u> on fables, horoscopes, and old wives tales. Put your faith, trust, and hope in God.

Dear God,
I thank You that You are my source of hope, the foundation of my trust, and the building block of my faith. I will not trust in lies of the enemy or entertain them in any way. Please guard my heart and mind against anything that would erode your influence in my life. Help me to recognize what is beneficial to me and what is not. Set my mind on things above and not on silly notions of this world. You are doing something marvelous within me and I praise Your name for it. Help me to give You honor and glory in all I do during this pregnancy and to be a light to others around me. Thank You, Lord. Amen.

Journal Tip: What kinds of old wives tales or fables have you heard about pregnancy? How do you feel about those? Do you think they bring God glory and honor?

Notes:

_____

_____

_____

_____

_____

_____

_____

_____

_____

THIRST

"For I will pour water on the thirsty land, and streams on the dry ground; I will pour out my Spirit on your offspring and My blessing on your descendants." Isaiah 44:3

Pregnancy can bring thirst and hunger that is unimaginable. When I read this verse, I think about the pregnant woman who is thirsty. Just as our pregnant physical bodies long for refreshment, our spiritual beings long for the Lord. He is the living water. Those who partake of Him will never thirst again. He pours out Himself to us like water on the thirsty land. His Spirit quenches our dryness and billows out onto our children and our descendants. I also remember how He poured out His Spirit in the upper room in Acts, baptizing them in the Spirit. What a great picture of God's blessing as He pours our His Spirit on our children!

Dear Lord,
You quench my thirsty soul and refresh the dryness of my life today. I thank You for Your springs of living water. Replenish me today as only You can. Restore a fresh fervor in me today and cleanse my spirit. Rain on me. Reign in me. I claim Isaiah 44:3 for my baby today as a promise that You are going to pour out Your Spirit on him/her and bless all of our descendants. Fill this child to overflowing. Raise him/her up to be sensitive to Your Spirit and responsive to Your voice. In Your name, amen.

Journal Tip: Are you drinking enough water during the day? In the Spirit, do you feel replenished and refreshed? Write down a personal thought concerning your pregnancy or your baby today.

Notes:

_____

_____

_____

_____

_____

_____

_____

_____

_____

_____

_____

Week 11

JOHN'S BIRTH FORETOLD

"But the angel said to him: 'Do not be afraid, Zechariah; your prayer has been heard. Your wife Elizabeth will bear you a son, and you are to give him the name John. He will be a joy and delight to you, and many will rejoice cause of his birth, for he will be great in the sight of the Lord... he will be filled with the Holy Spirit even from birth.'" Luke 1:13-15

Zechariah had prayed for a child and God sent him an angel to confirm that his request was heard. Any time the Lord sent word that a child was going to be born, there was always a great destiny awaiting that child. John the Baptist was one of those prophesied births. John was not only the predecessor of Jesus, but was also one who prepared others for Jesus and His mission. He was a voice for the Lord and his strong voice to call the people back to repentance was heard. He baptized many, including Jesus, continually pointing to Christ as the fulfillment of all things. God had a specific name for the child... John. God knows your child by name and the great things he/she will accomplish for Him and His kingdom. He/she has a God given destiny to fulfill. Perhaps God has given you confirmations along the way that your pregnancy has been divinely ordered.

Heavenly Father,
You are great and awesome in all Your ways. You even know the name we will call our child even before it has crossed our minds or our lips. Grant me faith to believe that my prayers concerning this child are being answered. Show me the name that we are to choose for him/her. I pray that this verse will be real for my child as well, that he/she will be a delight to me and rejoicing will come because of him/her. This verse also gives me insight that our children can be full of the Spirit even from birth. I pray that the Holy Spirit will be in operation, even today in my little one. Bless him/her this day. Amen.

Journal Tip: Have you decided on a name yet? Have you had any confirmations about your pregnancy that show you that God is in total control of the entire event? What else comes to mind when reading today's verse, devotional, and prayer?

Notes:

_____
_____
_____
_____
_____
_____
_____
_____
_____

Week 11

RELATIVES OR FRIENDS EXPECTING

"When Elizabeth heard Mary's greeting, the baby leaped in her womb, and Elizabeth was filled with the Holy Spirit. In a loud voice she exclaimed: "Blessed are you among women, and blessed is the child you will bear!" Luke 1:41-42

Elizabeth and Mary were relatives. Mary had gone to visit Elizabeth who was already six months along in her pregnancy. The angel, Gabriel, who had visited Elizabeth, is the same messenger who went to tell Mary that she would be the mother of Jesus. The Holy Spirit came upon Elizabeth when Mary told her about her pregnancy. The baby (John) leaped in her womb. I have to stop and think that God works in mysterious ways. Of course, this must have further built Elizabeth's faith. She also had an unusual pregnancy; one God had granted to bring Him glory. Many things come to mind when I read the account of both of these extraordinary pregnancies. It makes us aware that God has ordained all things. No doubt that these two children were very special, but God has a special plan for your little one as well. Are you expecting at the same time relatives and friends are expecting? It fuels your joy to know that others are experiencing the same joy that you are. You also find a common bond in which you can draw strength.

Dear God,
You are continually amazing me with wonders during my pregnancy. I thank You for all the blessings You have given me thus far. I know that You have a special plan for the baby within my womb. I pray that Your plans would go forth uninhibited. May those around me who are expecting be a great blessing to me. Help us to encourage one another and share in each other's joy. At no time let competition or jealousy arise. We are all Your children and You give freely to all. Each of us has a specific role in the body of Christ. Let great joy arise as we share our news with family and friends. Thank You for blessing me this day! Amen.

Journal Tip: Are any of your relatives expecting a baby right now? How have your family and friends reacted to your pregnancy?

Notes:

_____

_____

_____

_____

_____

_____

_____

_____

_____

Week 12

BABY IS BEING KNIT TOGETHER

"Before I formed you in the womb I knew you, before you were born I set you apart; "
Jeremiah 1:5a

Every day the baby within you is growing at a tremendous rate! By twelve weeks, your baby will be fully formed. He/she will continue to develop and mature until he/she is ready for the outside world. No wonder God said it was like being "knit together". Every little piece, every vessel, every cell, every nerve is being fashioned by the creator Himself. He knows your little baby even before he/she will be born! He sees all that goes on day to day in your life and in the life of your baby. Praise His Name!

Lord,
I pray for the knitting together of this tiny baby within me. God, I can hardly fathom the flawless process that You set in order at creation. Babies are Your design; Your workmanship in the flesh. I ask that You let this baby grow and develop without any complications. I come against premature birth or any other condition that could affect the life of my little one. Help him/her to develop according to Your plan and to deliver in Your timing. Prepare him/her for life outside the womb. I pray that he/she would become everything that You are creating him/her to be. What a wonder to be a part of this magnificent process and to know that a tiny little one is developing life right inside me. Keep my body healthy as this little one continues to grow day by day. Amen.

Journal Tip: Write down your thoughts about God knitting together your baby. How does it make you feel?

Notes:

_____

_____

_____

_____

_____

_____

_____

_____

_____

_____

BABY HEARS WHAT YOU SAY

"May the words of my mouth and the meditation of my heart be pleasing in Your sight, O LORD, my Rock and my Redeemer." Psalm 19:14

As your baby is growing in your womb, they will have a first row seat to all that you have to say. True, it may be a little muffled, but baby is learning what your voice sounds like and becoming accustomed to your speech patterns.

When baby has been born, your words will have an impact on their development and sense of worth. Will you use words that will promote life or words that will promote death? Will your words uplift or tear down? Will you praise or curse? Start thinking about the power of your words and examine them against the grain of acceptability in Christ's eyes.

Lord,
I pray that my words will be healing, life giving, uplifting, faith building, and encouraging to my baby. Help me to examine my words before they leave my mouth... to think over what I have to say before I say it. I want my thoughts to be Your thoughts and my words to express the love I have for You, Lord.

Journal Tip: How do you see yourself in this area? Have you thought about what you say being heard by your baby even at this very moment? What kinds of words would you like to be known for as a parent? Do you think the way you act/think/talk now are acceptable in the Lord's sight?

Notes:

_____

_____

_____

_____

_____

_____

_____

_____

_____

_____

_____

_____

Week 12

BLESSING YOUR CHILD

"The Lord bless you and keep you; the Lord make His face to shine upon you and be gracious to you; the Lord turn his face toward you and give you peace." Numbers 6:24-26

This passage in Numbers was the blessing that the Lord gave Moses for the Israelites. You can use this verse or ones like it to speak blessings over your child. There are many examples to choose from! Who doesn't want the Lord to turn His face toward their child or for His face to shine upon them? As a parent, when you bless your child, you are asking God's hand to move upon him/her and to touch his/her life. You are showing dependence on God to bring forth good things from this life that He has created. Why not start today? Make blessing your child a habit. He/she will be grateful that you did.

Lord,
Today I want to bless my baby. I thank You for this spiritual tool that I can use in raising my child. Help me to do this often and in a heartfelt, genuine manner. I speak blessings over this baby now.
May the Lord bless you and keep you, little one. May the Lord make his face to shine upon you and be gracious unto you. May He turn His face toward you and give you peace today.
Thank You, Lord. Amen.

Journal Tip: Find other examples of blessings in scripture that you would like to speak over your child or simply write a blessing of your own.

Notes:

_____

_____

_____

_____

_____

_____

_____

_____

_____

_____

_____

_____

KNITTING

"For you created my inmost being, you knit me together in my mother's womb."
Psalm 139:13

God explains things in ways that we can understand them. Even if you haven't picked up knitting needles in your entire life, you can probably imagine watching someone knitting a sweater, a scarf, or perhaps a pair of baby booties. It's seems utterly amazing that skein of yarn that was just sitting there in its little paper wrapper could be fashioned into something useful. Picture the Almighty God knitting your baby together. He's creating each fiber, muscle, tissue, organ, brain, nervous system, respiratory system, digestive system, reproductive system, senses, and those little fingers and the toes of your baby. Doesn't it just amaze you? We have a wonderful designer and Creator!

Dear Lord,
As I sit and meditate on the wonder of You, I am in awe. My baby is growing and forming each intricate part of his/her makeup because of Your plan and design. Thank You for caring about each individual cell that makes up my child. I know he/she is being wonderfully made. I pray that all development would proceed normally and that there wouldn't be any complications with any of his/her organs. Even if complications do arise, Lord, I am glad that I know the one who fashions the body. There is nothing to fear because we are in the Creator's hands. I just sense a peace and contentment knowing that You are in control of this whole process. Bless this pregnancy, Lord. Amen.

Journal Tip: Do you have any hobbies? Knitting is a fun way to pass the time of pregnancy. Many women find making things for baby is a nice way to bond with your little one. Sewing or other crafts can help relieve stress, too. What do you enjoy doing for your baby?

Notes:

_____

_____

_____

_____

_____

_____

_____

_____

_____

Week 12

DON'T COMPARE TO OTHERS

"Do not judge, or you too will be judged. For in the same way you judge others, you will be judged, and with the measure you use, it will be measured to you." Matthew 7:1

When we look at others and judge, what we are really doing is making a comparison between them and us. That is the key we will focus on today. This is not to say that we are not to judge those in the body of Christ in relation to the fruit that they bear. Again, the focus is comparison. One of the most dangerous things to tear at the foundation of your pregnancy or parenting and how God wants you to do it is beginning to compare to others. Those things give way to other problems such as jealousy, envy, coveting, etc. All you should be concerned about is the standard of living set forth by God and that is revealed to us in His Word. What does it matter to you if you gained forty pounds during pregnancy, but your friend only gained twenty-five? What does it matter if your baby rolled over before so-and-so's? The truth is, that doesn't effect who you or who your child is at all. There is room enough in the house of God for all of us and we are all unique!

Dear Lord,
Thank You for making me and the baby I am having unique. I pray that You would guard me from feelings of inadequacy or low self worth when it comes to pregnancy or parenting. Show me who I am in You so that I walk in confidence. Give me understanding to my importance in life. Help me not to compare myself or my baby with others and to not give the enemy a foothold. Open my eyes to observe good character traits, methods of parenting, or other tidbits of information that I may glean benefit or wisdom from and not to look upon others with a critical eye. Help me to understand that we all have something to contribute to the body of Christ and that You see us all with equality.
Be with my baby today as he/she grows. Continue to fill my heart with love and wisdom, knowledge, and understanding. Amen.

Journal Tip: Do you have a problem with comparing yourself with others? Do you think others compare themselves with you? Why is comparing so dangerous? How does God see you?

Notes:

_____

_____

_____

_____

_____

_____

_____

_____

Week 12

THE SPIRIT BUILDS CHARACTER AND VIRTURES

"But the fruit of the Spirit is love, joy, peace, patience, kindness, goodness, faithfulness, gentleness, and self control. Against such things there is no law." Galatians 5:22

When we are God's and His Spirit dwells within us, the Holy Spirit will bear fruit in us. Our commitment, coupled with what the Spirit does in our lives, produces character and virtues. Outwardly, through our words and deeds, we are a reflection of what God has done on the inside. It seems that the Spirit's work in us and our character walk hand in hand.

Virtues are one of the most rewarding life tools you can instill in your child. The current trend of the world screams values of another kind, or possibly no restraints whatsoever. When you teach your children character building tools, you are giving them keys to unlock success in relationships of all kinds. Making virtues part of your daily commitment in parenting will have lasting rewards. Living a life that is one of character is a choice on our part. Teaching your child to desire good values sets a pattern that they will likely continue into adulthood. Values that are Godly resonate through us into a dark world and testify of the God we serve. The next few weeks will include devotionals on some of these virtues that you can instill in your child as he/she grows. Virtues are invaluable. May God hear our prayers and grant our requests!

Dear Lord,
Thank You for the fruit of Your Spirit. Help me to bear fruit in my life. Give me the desire to instill a godly belief system into my child. This includes virtues and character building. I know that these take time, consistency, and a disciplined pattern on my part. Help me to start when he/she is little. Show me through Your Spirit how I can raise a person of character. I know that these things will set a pattern for the rest of his/her life and have the potential to continue on from generation to generation. I pray that You would mark this family as one of godly principles, beliefs, virtues, and character. I pray that this family would be a reflection of You and Your ways. I cannot do this without the divine help and intervention of the Holy Spirit! May each of us rise up in these gifts and express them openly and freely. Amen.

Journal Tip: Begin writing down some of the godly virtues, beliefs, or character qualities you desire for God to bring out in your child. What kind of impact do you want your child to have on this world when he/she is an adult?

Notes:

_____

_____

_____

_____

_____

_____

Week 12

NOT HIDDEN FROM GOD & FIRST MOVEMENTS

**"My frame was not hidden from You when I was made in the secret place...Your eyes saw
my unformed body." Psalm 139:15-16a**

Even though you cannot physically see your child, you know they are there and can feel his/her
presence. God sees all the developmental stages of your baby. He can take a peek any time. How
wonderful!
In the next few weeks, the hands and feet of your baby will fully form and he/she can even been seen
sucking his/her thumb. Soon baby will become very active and around week fourteen, you'll
probably be able to feel the first movements. You are probably becoming very much aware of your
growing abdomen and the sensation of life within you.

Heavenly Father,
Thank You for this little life that is forming. His/her frame is not hidden from You and that brings me
great joy. I am excited and wait in anticipation to feel the first movements and sense the wonder of
life. Even though my womb is like a secret place, I am keenly aware of the baby. I pray that as the
baby develops that he/she would have a sense of awareness about who I am, even before birth. Bond
us together, Lord. I thank You for Your omniscience today, Lord. Amen.

Journal Tip: Have you felt any movements yet? Is your pregnancy starting to show? What kinds of
things is your body experiencing right now?

Notes:

_____

_____

_____

_____

_____

_____

_____

_____

_____

_____

_____

_____

PART 3
The Second Trimester

Week 13

TRAVELING DURING PREGNANCY

"So Joseph also went up from the town of Nazareth in Galilee to Judea, to Bethlehem the town of David, because he belonged to the house and the line of David. He went there to register with Mary, who was pledged to married to him and was expecting a child." Luke 2:4-5

Do you have any traveling planned during your pregnancy? Sometimes traveling can't be helped, but your doctor or midwife will probably recommend that you not travel during your last month. Just imagine how Mary must have felt traveling while expecting so close to her due date!

Trips may be a welcomed break from your normal schedule, but plan them with consideration of your health and baby's. If you travel long distances, make sure you get up and walk around to keep your circulation going. Also be sure to drink plenty of fluids while traveling so that you don't become dehydrated. The other concern will be taking plenty of bathroom stops. You will have to go more than normal since you are expecting, so keep that in mind. If you find that it's uncomfortable to sit for long periods of time, get a rubber ring or something to sit on to make the trip more pleasurable. Also pack some snacks because you never know when you might need them.

Dear God,
Thank You for seeing my comings and my goings. I pray that You would be with me during all the times that I may need to travel. I pray that You would go before me and prepare my way so that the trip would be as easy as it could be. Keep me safe while I am in transport. Keep me from accidents or delays. Help me to not become ill while I am gone. Watch over me at all times and this little one that I am carrying. Help me to relax and get sleep while I am away. Thank You, Lord. Amen.

Journal Tip: Do you have travel plans during your pregnancy or does your job require a lot of travel? Be sure to discuss your plans with your doctor to make sure that it's alright to travel. If you have been traveling, how do you do?

Notes:

_____

_____

_____

_____

_____

_____

_____

_____

_____

_____

Week 13

FORMED TO BE HIS SERVANT

"And now the LORD says- He who formed me in the womb to be his servant..." Isaiah 49:5

We all wonder what the future will hold for our children. What will they do? Where will God send them in life? He has fashioned us all from the time we were in the womb with a specific plan and design for our lives. This purpose compels us in life to fulfill its call. We have all been called to serve the Lord in whatever capacity God has built within us. Your job as a parent is to cultivate that which God has sewn into your child and hopefully see it to fruition in time. That task is sometimes easier said than done. We sometimes have preconceived ideas of what we would like our children to do, but this may not be what God has intended for them. We need to ask the Lord to line up our thoughts with His when it comes to our children. You may be asking yourself, "Why do I need to pray about this now? The baby isn't even born yet!" Even though he/she hasn't been born, God is forming them right now with the makeup to accomplish whatever it is He intends for them to do. Parents have so many choices of things they can get their children involved in, but if it isn't what the Lord wants for him/her, you shouldn't want it either. Kids in today's world are also becoming stressed out because they are expected to do too much! Asking God to lead you in decisions concerning your child's activities will assure that there will be a healthy balance in his/her life. Let's pray that God will direct you in helping you cultivate your child in the areas that he/she should grow in so that he/she can become an effective servant of the Lord!

Dear God,
Thank You for bringing clarity and direction to life when we need it. I thank You for the role I will play in my child's life to further them toward Your kingdom and Your purposes. I ask that You would lead me in making decisions that will effect what my son/daughter will do for You. I pray that You would open the doors to my child that need to be opened and close those that will need closing. Help me to make wise decisions when it comes to extra curricular activities such as sports or other team events, ministries that they may become involved with or other programs that could promote their calling in life. I pray that You would protect him/her and keep him steadily on the path that You have chosen for him/her. I don't want anything but Your perfect plan to unfold in his/her life. I ask that You go before him/her now and begin to work in me as the parent that I would make wise decisions concerning this child. I thank You for Your wisdom and direction, especially in the days ahead. In Your name, amen.

Journal Tip: What are some activities that you would like to see your child involved in (example: regular church attendance, Junior Bible Quiz, Kids Camp, sport, music, etc). Do you attend a church that offers other programs to kids? Become familiar with what these are and then make a list of possible programs/events that seem like they would be healthy for your child to do- then make those a matter of prayer. Trust God to show you what you need to get your children involved in and what you shouldn't!

Notes:

_____

_____

_____

HEART-PUMPING EVENT

"Oh, that their hearts would be inclined to fear me and keep all my commands always, so that it might go well with them and their children forever!" Deuteronomy 5:29

Today I am reminded of the little tiny heart that is pumping in your baby. The heart plays such a vital role in the sustaining of life. Stop the heart and you cannot live. The heart's function is to pump the blood throughout the body. As the main organ in the circulatory system, the heart has a big job. Blood is sent all through the body mainly in part because of the heart. If we observe what goes on in the physical as a metaphor for what happens in the spiritual, we can better understand such verses as Matt. 12:34, "As a man thinks in his heart, so is he." The emotional and spiritual heart controls what is in a person. Store things that are evil in your heart and evil will be circulated through the entire spiritual body. Store up those things that are good; things that are righteous, things that are holy... and those are what you'll become. The Word also talks about hardened hearts. Not only would a hard heart not pump blood well (if at all), but also a hard spiritual heart keeps us from incorporating the things of the Lord into our daily lives. Let's ask the great physician to work on our hearts today.

Lord,
As I know that my baby's heart is growing today, I pray that in time You would help his/her spiritual heart fill up with the fear of You and the keeping of Your commandments. Help me to raise him/her up in such a way that it would be easy to find You and honor You. I pray against any defects that would hinder this child's physical, emotional, or spiritual growth. I pray that You would examine my heart today and remove anything from it that might be hindering my walk with you. I pray that my child would grow up to give You his/her whole heart (Proverbs 23:26). Only You can make a perfect heart! Let the promise of giving our hearts to You follow generation after generation in this family. Amen.

Journal Tip: Have you viewed your child's heartbeat on an ultrasound? Have you had any hypertension during pregnancy? Do you have any heart problems that run in your family (physical or otherwise)? What kind of things do you hope your child will fill his/her heart with?

Notes:

_____

_____

_____

_____

_____

_____

_____

_____

SIGNIFICANCE IN GOD

**"I praise You because I am fearfully and wonderfully made; Your works are wonderful.
I know that full well." Psalm 139:14**

Everything that God makes has significance. There is not a single person of the face of this earth that He doesn't care about or have a life plan for. There is something wonderful about your life and something wonderful about the baby that you are carrying. Sometimes we don't feel so wonderful or special, but let me tell you today... it's a lie from the enemy! You are a prized treasure to the Lord. He sees you as a jewel. It may take some time in life to discover the paths that God would have us to follow, but the closer you walk to Him, the more He will let you know how very special you are to Him. Don't compare yourself to others. God didn't make us all the same, nor did He make us with the same gifts or callings. You are unique.

Dear Lord,
Even though I may not always feel like it, You have made me and my life has significance. I know that I have significance to my family and to this baby that I am carrying. I pray that I would walk in a way that is worthy of the sacrifice that You gave for me. I want to be secure in You; secure in my worth, secure in my place in this world, secure in the abilities that You have blessed me with, secure in my emotions, and secure in my calling as a mother. Help me to be a mother that encourages my child's sense of self value, but especially a godly view of who they are. I want to know full well the significance I have to You, Lord. Help me to sense Your presence today. Even let this precious baby feel Your presence as well. Amen.

Journal Tip: Why do you think you have value in this world? How does your child have worth, even though he/she hasn't even been born yet? Write down your thoughts, as well as any insecurity that you may feel about yourself. Let God give you the positive self-image that you need.

Notes:

_____

_____

_____

_____

_____

_____

_____

_____

SEEK GOD FIRST

"But seek first His kingdom and His righteousness, and all these things will be given to you as well. Therefore do not worry about tomorrow, for tomorrow will worry about itself."
Matthew 6:33-34a

Your Heavenly Father knows what you have need of today. As a Christian, we are admonished to follow hard after God and righteousness. When we do this, God will give you the things that you need. As your pregnancy progresses, you may be in need of many things. Maybe you need a crib, car seat, changing table, or baby clothes. Maybe you need a car to get you to and from doctor's appointments or a house to live in. Perhaps you need a miracle in your finances. Nothing is too big or small that God doesn't care about. He will supply your needs. Remember though, this doesn't mean that your every desire will be answered, but rest assured… you will have what you <u>need</u>!

Dear God,
Thank You for knowing my every need even before I express it to You. Today I bring _____ to You. I place the request at Your feet and ask that You would supply the answer.
I know that nothing is too big or too small that You wouldn't care about it. You are concerned with all things concerning my life. I ask that You would touch my baby in a special way today.
Even without asking, You are supplying what he/she needs for development. You are supplying nutrients to him/her. You are supplying a safe place for him/her to grow. In the same way, I know that You are going to supply the things I need because You are my Heavenly Father and You love me. Help me to be patient and to trust You for all things. I choose not to worry about tomorrow, but to put my hope and faith in You. In Your name, amen.

Journal: Have you come to Lord with needs today? Is there something that He has recently supplied you with that you could praise Him for?

Notes:

_____

_____

_____

_____

_____

_____

_____

_____

_____

Week 13

GLOWING

"Those who look to Him are radiant; their faces are never covered with shame."
Psalm 34:5

Has anyone told you that you are glowing? Pregnancy is a beautiful thing! When we are content with what the Lord is doing in us, our countenance will radiate how we feel inside. You will glow. It reminds me of the children's song "If You're Happy and You Know It". One verse says, "If you're happy and you know it, your face will surely show it!". The expressions we give on our faces show what we are feeling inside. You'll find this to be invaluable when you are first learning to "read" how your baby is feeling before he/she is able to communicate. Likewise, as they grow, children will look to our face to see initially see how to relate to the world. They will mimic their parent's facial expressions. Also, did you know that in studies babies preferred smiling faces to gloomy ones? Your child will also read your face to see how you feel in relation to him/her or their behavior. Remember when you were a kid and mom would give you "that look" that meant you'd better settle down? Our expressions have multiple purposes. Think about it.

Dear Lord,
I thank You for the love that You have placed inside me that radiates to others. I am especially thankful for this pregnancy and all that it means to me. I know that my countenance will show how I am feeling and I want the world to know that I am Yours and that there is something different about me and my pregnancy. I pray that I would radiate Your love to others and the peace that I feel inside. Help me to be conscious of the fact that my face is a window to my heart. I want my baby to mimic love and gentleness and not harshness and bitterness. If there be anything in me that would set my heart to fear, anger, or anything else that would effect how I in turn will relate to him/her, I pray that it would be dealt with right now. I want to glow with Your presence. I think of Moses when he ascended the mountain and spent time with You, the Word tells us, "he was not aware that his face was radiant because he had spoken with the Lord" (Ex. 34:29). I pray that I spend time with You that Your glory will fill me up and that it would shine to others, especially to those who are closest to me in my family. Thank You, Lord. Bless this child today. Amen.

Journal Tip: Write about your thoughts on facial expressions and how your countenance looks to others. Have you had any comments about "glowing" since you've been expecting? Do you think there are ways to improve in this area? If so, then how?

Notes:

_____

_____

_____

_____

_____

_____

Week 13

TAUGHT BY THE LORD

"All your sons will be taught by the LORD, and great will be your children's peace."
Isaiah 54:13

There is no greater teacher than the Lord himself! The things that <u>He</u> teaches you won't be easily forgotten. He is the best, most qualified teacher of every subject in life. What a joy to think that God has an integrated role into the developing of our minds, emotions, and spirits!

Lord,
I thank You that all my children will be taught of You. I pray that the things You teach them would be bound around his/her heart and mind. I pray that they would eagerly seek You for wisdom and instruction in all matters of life. When they are in need of answers, may they come quickly to You for aid. May Your instruction flow uninterrupted by selfish ways or schemes of the enemy! Teach me in Your ways, so that my instruction to my children would be an outflow of Your heart. Amen.

Journal Tip: What are some things that God has taught you over the years? What does the thought of God teaching your children mean to you?

Notes:

_____

_____

_____

_____

_____

_____

_____

_____

_____

_____

_____

_____

_____

_____

PURPOSE IN EVERY STEP

"Run in such a way as to get the prize." 1 Corinthians 9:24b

Your baby's feet are fully formed by week 14. By birth, you can expect him/her to wear size zero to one in baby shoes. You might be able to feel his/her kicks within a few weeks (if you haven't already). They feel like "bubbles". Those feet that are developing will someday enable your child to walk and run.

If you have ever done any type of running (marathons, track, cross country, etc.), you know that every step has a purpose. That purpose is to get you to the goal. In this case, the "goal" is a safe delivery for you and your baby. Every day is a step closer to the finish line. Your job is to complete the race as God has planned. It's a straight path. Childbirth is a **God-designed** process. This doesn't mean that there may not be hurdles to cross or other obstacles in your path, but with God's help you will reach your goal and receive the prize!

Dear Lord,
Thank You for helping me race toward the goal. I know that in this race, I might get tired, especially toward the end. Encourage me to keep running and to cross hurdles with confidence if they happen to be on my path. Bless the feet of my little one. May they always go where you would have them to go. Thank You for forming them with such care. I can't wait to feel their little kicks. Amen.

Journal Tip: Have you felt any kicks yet? What size feet do you have? Does the father have large feet? Have you bought any baby shoes yet?

Notes:

_____

_____

_____

_____

_____

_____

_____

_____

_____

_____

_____

Week 14

WORSHIPPING GOD THOUGH HOLY LIVING

"Therefore, I urge you, brother, in view of God's mercy, to offer your bodies as living sacrifices, holy and pleasing to God- this is your spiritual act of worship." Romans 12:1

According to the Word of God, we are not our own. Your child is not your own, either (regarding their spirits). We were all bought with a price. That price was the blood that Jesus shed on the cross for the remission of our sins. It is our duty to live a life that represents the work of the cross, worthy of the blood that was shed for us. Worship is not often related to how we live, but this verse tells us that when we live in a way pleasing to him, it is a spiritual act of worship. We should offer ourselves as a living sacrifice to Him. Are you worshiping God today with the way that you live?

Dear God,
I thank You for shedding Your blood on the cross for me today and for the sins of my baby, who does not yet comprehend his/her need for a Savior. Nonetheless, the price has already been paid by You for his/her salvation. I am amazed. I want my life to be holy and pleasing to You at all times- a spiritual act of worship. Help me to live that represents my gratitude for the price You paid. I want to be a glowing example to my baby. Help me to raise him/her in such a way that he/she would come to know You early in life. May he/she worship You with his/her life as well. Bless this baby today as he/she is forming in Your image. Help me to get proper rest and nourishment which will benefit me and my baby. Give my doctors wisdom and continue to go before me throughout this pregnancy. In Jesus' name, amen.

Journal Tip: Are you worshipping God today through the life you are living? How will that affect the life of your little one? How are you physically feeling today?

Notes:

_____

_____

_____

_____

_____

_____

_____

_____

_____

_____

BEARING THE YOLK

"It is good for a man to bear the yoke while he is young." Lamentations 3:27

Hard work is good for us…especially when we are young. Not only is it easier to bear, but we learn so many invaluable life lessons on our journey. That is a lot like pregnancy. The older you get, the harder it is for your body to bear the burden of pregnancy. That's not to say that you <u>can't</u> have children when you are older. The older you get and the more you grow in wisdom, the more you will comment, "If only I had known that when I was younger." Ours is not to look back in regret, but to go forward and learn from what we have experienced in our youth. God has allowed your pregnancy in the exact time He has ordained it, whether you are young or old. No matter what our maternal age is, we are all still growing and there's plenty of growing room left!

Dear Lord,
Thank You for growing in me today. I pray that through this journey of bearing a child that you would teach me valuable life lessons. I want to grow more and more in knowledge and wisdom. Teach me what I need to learn so that I can best be used in my ministry to my family and within the body of Christ. When I do make mistakes in life, help me to learn from those mistakes and to not repeat them. I pray that You would also go before my little one and teach him/her valuable spiritual and life lessons when he/she is young. Give him/her wisdom through the yolks that he/she will bear. I pray that he/she would be a light to all of those around him/her. Thank You, Lord. Amen.

Journal Tip: What have you learned so far from your yolk of pregnancy? How would that affect your opinions or actions during another pregnancy or if you helped mentor a friend during pregnancy? Are there things you wouldn't do over again?

Notes:

_____

_____

_____

_____

_____

_____

_____

_____

_____

ACCOUNTABILITY

"Do you not know that your body is a temple of the Holy Spirit, who is in you, whom you have received from God? You are not your own; you were bought at a price. Therefore honor God with your body." 1 Corinthians 6:19-20

Many things come to mind when reading this verse. First of all, we are not our own, neither is the baby we are carrying. The baby is not our possession to do with whatever we wish. He/she is a living, breathing, thinking, tiny little person. He/she will grow up to make decisions and choices on their own just like we make our choices. We as parents are there to guide them, not to control or "own" them.

This verse also reminds us that we are accountable to God for what we say, hear, think, and do. Our choices in raising our children should be made realizing that God has a plan for him/her. Children are not here to fulfill our desires, but the desires of one who created them. Finally, this verse reminds me of how as mothers we are continually called to honor God with our bodies. When your body is home for a baby for approximately forty weeks, you are continually making choices that will affect him/her. Likewise, when God comes into our lives, we should always be continually aware that His Spirit abides within us!

Dear Lord,
Thank You for the price You paid for my salvation. You paid the price and I want to honor You by living for You all the days of my life. Help me to remember that this child is not my own, but is ultimately Yours. Show me how to make decisions based upon Your plans for my baby and not my own. I also want to honor You in my body during this pregnancy. Even after I've had the baby, constantly remind me that there is one within me that I am accountable to... the Holy Spirit. Help accountability be something that comes easy to our family. Let my child learn it at a young age. Bless baby today! Amen.

Journal Tip: What are your thoughts about controlling children vs. healthy accountability? Use personal examples from your own life. Give some examples of how you were raised.

Notes:

_____

_____

_____

_____

_____

_____

_____

_____

VALUES

"What is highly valued among men is detestable in God's sight." Luke 16:15b

Trying to instill a sense of value in our children can be quite a challenge in this world. Our society seems to deem success in terms of popularity and money. God's Word is clear that a man is not successful in His eyes just because he has material wealth. Our materialism can become an idol, which we know is against God's Word. So what makes a person successful in God's eyes? His Word gives us clear insight into all the things he finds successful: having faith, living righteously, obedience, holiness, bearing His fruit, etc. We need to trust the Lord that He is going to give us all we need in our lives, whether that means a little or a lot. We need to learn to desire success in His eyes.

Heavenly Father,
I praise You that You are the giver of all things. I thank You for all the material possessions and blessings that You've allowed me to enjoy. I ask, Lord, that they do not become my focus, or the focus of my child. I ask that You would bring revelation to us in the area of "success". I want to be successful in Your eyes and I want the same for my little one. I pray that You would help me set a healthy balance in this home concerning material things (toys, clothes, etc) that would glorify You. I pray that my child would learn that he/she has value that cannot be measured in dollars and cents. You have made him/her priceless. Help us not to put our hope in money and things, but only in You, Almighty God. You alone are our source. Our confidence is totally and completely in You. Amen.

Journal Tip:
List some things that would make you or your child a success in God's eyes. What gives you a sense of value?

Notes:

_____

_____

_____

_____

_____

_____

_____

_____

_____

_____

Week 14

DAILY TRAINING AND RAISING OF CHILDREN

"Train a child in the way he should go, and when he is old he will not turn from it."
Proverbs 22:6

Training isn't something that happens overnight. It takes dedication, consistency, repetition, and a vision for the outcome. Have you ever played the piano or wanted to? When someone studies music, it can take many years to see any good come from it. You don't just sit down to the piano and plunk out Chopin. You start with a single note and then build upon that. With lots of repetition and practice, eventually beautiful music will be expressed. Once you realize that training your child is a process, your daily routine takes on a whole new meaning. What a difference a day makes! You're not looking for your little one to be able to baffle Biblical scholars at three or run off to become a missionary at ten. You are trying to instill a lifetime of dedication to the Lord and a stable Christian walk that will be maintained into adulthood and into generations to come. For example, there isn't any parent who would want to have their children taught music by someone who didn't know music themselves! Spiritually, <u>you</u> need to be up to par on your Christian walk in order to effectively train up your children!! No one said training was easy, but if you want to reach the goal you'll have to stick with it. Let's ask the Lord to guide us in this process.

Heavenly Father,
I realize that this role of parent is an ongoing process. I dedicate all my efforts into Your hands and ask that You would grant me wisdom, knowledge, and strength to raise up this child in You. Show me how to be the best parent I can be to my son/daughter. Give me the tools I will need just when I need them. Help me to not grow weary in the process of training or to give up. Help me to not to become lazy or lack when it concerns my children. If at any time I do, please bring me quickly back into correction so that their learning will not be hindered in any way. I thank You for this special promise in Your Word that if my son/daughter is trained in You, when he/she is old, he/she will not depart from it. I ask that You be in charge of his/her life's journey. Thank You Lord, for Your faithfulness. Amen.

Journal Tip: Have you thought about what kind of things you will do with your child to help them learn about the Lord? How do you feel about the task of training up a child in the way he/she should go? Do you have fears? Do you have anticipation?

Notes:

_____

_____

_____

_____

_____

_____

THE GIFT OF SALVATION

"For God so loved the world that He gave His one and only Son, that whoever believes in Him shall not perish, but have eternal life." John 3:16

What better gift could you possibly give your child than introducing him/her to Jesus? He is the gift that keeps on giving… throughout eternity! God so loved us that He gave His one and only Son to become the Savior of the world. Salvation is probably the most important lesson you will share with your child. Salvation is God's gift to all mankind. Do not take it lightly. Make it a daily goal to teach your child about the Lord through the reading of the Word. Explain salvation to him/her in an age appropriate manner so that he/she will understand what you are saying. If you are unsure of how to approach this, seek additional resources from your church or local Christian Bookstore. It's never too early to begin cultivating a relationship with the Lord. Hopefully, you will be the one to lead your child to Him at a very early age. Psalm 22:9-10 says "Yet you brought me out of my mother's womb; you made me trust in You even at my mother's breast. From birth I was cast on You; from my mother's womb You have been my God."

ABC's of Salvation:
A- Admit you are a sinner.
B- Believe that Christ died for you and your sins.
C- Confess your sins and accept Jesus into your heart.

God,
Thank You for giving Your Son for my redemption. May salvation come to my child at an early age. I claim Psalm 22:10 that states, "from my mother's womb You have been My God". Show me how to explain salvation to my little one in ways that he/she will understand. Lead him/her in the paths of righteousness. May he/she walk with You all the days of his/her life. Let this home operate in a manner that is worthy of Christ's name, which we bear. Thank You, God for Your amazing grace. Amen.

Journal Tip: When did you become saved? How old were you? Where were you? What difference did it make in your life? Why do you want your child to know Christ?

Notes:

_____

_____

_____

_____

_____

_____

_____

Week 15

RESPONSIBLE FOR OUR OWN ACTIONS

"For each one should carry his own load..." Galatians 6:5

So many times we would like to blame others for flaws in our own character. God's Word says that we are each responsible for our own conduct! That is also true for our children. We can train him/her in the ways of the Lord and they may still stumble at times. As this may or may not be a reflection of our parenting skills, it is vital to remember that they are responsible to God for what they do in life. They will have to answer to Him for the choices they have made and the things they have done. You cannot get your children into heaven, nor can you keep them out. God gave each of us the power to choose. Our conduct is our own responsibility.

Lord,
I thank You for the power You have given us as humans to choose what we will do in life and how we will conduct ourselves. I pray that I would understand for myself that everyone is responsible for his/her own conduct. This will be true of my child as well. I pray that You would place a desire within him/her to conduct himself/herself in a manner that would be pleasing and glorifying to You at all times.
May your Spirit lead him/her in taking responsibility for his/her actions good or bad. There are consequences to good choices and bad choices. Let me never feel guilty for any bad choice that my son or daughter may choose at any time. They will answer to me as a parent, but ultimately the authority is Yours. I pray that You raise them up in strength of character even from a young age. Amen.

Journal Tip: As a parent, how would you want your child to conduct themselves when they are apart from you? What can you do to help influence them to act in a Godlike manner at all times?

Notes:

_____

_____

_____

_____

_____

_____

_____

_____

_____

_____

BALANCED, STRESS-FREE HOMES

"Better a dry crust with peace and quiet than a house full of feasting with strife."
Proverbs 17:1

Have you ever been to someone's home that seems to be in utter chaos? It's a mess, the kids are a mess, there's lack of organization, and the children run around without any supervision! Our home environments should be harmonious and peaceful... a sanctuary from the outside world. If your home is chaotic, there is strife! Could it be that our physical environment may reflect our own spiritual condition? God is a God of order. Just look at his creation. He made everything with a specific, perfect order. This isn't a mandate to clean your house, but if you struggle in that area... why not ask God to show you why and to help you? There are many excuses that cover up the real issues that plague our lives! Do you have strife filling your home? God can do something about it. Do you need a stable routine? Do you need to regain control of your home life? God can show you how!

Dear Lord,
Thank You for this place I call home. Help me to do all I can to keep it clean, neat, and in proper working order. No matter if my home is big or little, I recognize that You have placed me as a steward over it and I ask that I would be a good steward. I know You have an order to all things. I pray that my home would be one of order, quietness, refreshing, renewing, peace, and restoration. If there is anything out of order in this home (spiritual, physical, or emotional), I pray that You would show me how to restore order in that area. Right now, I ask for wisdom in the area of _____. I struggle with this and I want to hand it over to You and ask for Your direction. I realize that my efforts without Your intervention are worthless. Help this home to be one of comfort for me and my family. I commit this place to You and ask for Your presence to be here. Thank You, Lord, for reigning in my heart and home today. In Jesus name, amen.

Journal Tip: Have you envisioned a home of peace and happiness when your baby arrives? How does adding someone to your home change the dynamics of your daily chores and responsibilities? Have you thought of how your schedule will change once your little one comes home?

Notes:

_____

_____

_____

_____

_____

_____

_____

Week 15

CONSISTENCY WITH YOUR CHILD

"But when he asks, he must believe and not doubt, because he who doubts is like a wave of the sea, blown and tossed by the wind. That man should not think he will receive anything from the Lord; he is a double-minded man, unstable in all he does." James 1:6-8

One area of parenting that we can stand to work on constantly is being consistent. Inconsistency tends to make a child (as a person) and the parental-child dynamic unstable. We must try our best to avoid sending mixed messages to our children. Changing your position on things, your stance on discipline, etc. will reap havoc and will undermine any good that was working in a child. Your child must know that what you think is what you think all the time. How you discipline is how you are going to discipline all the time. Of course, there are exceptions to this rule, but in those instances, it must be understood by the child why things have suddenly changed. Are you a person who is constantly being blown by the wind? Let's ask the Lord for His help in this area.

Dear God,
You are the God who never changes. You were, You are, and You will forever be. I thank You that I can depend on You one hundred percent of the time and You are one hundred percent accurate! Please help me in this area of consistency, Lord. I want to be a stable parent, who is sending proper signals to my child. I believe my positions on spiritual, life, and discipline matters must be worked out in my own life before I can effectively relate them to my child. Give me the understanding and wisdom I need to work out these things. Give me the boldness, strength, and diligence I will need to consistently parent my son/daughter. At any time when an inconsistency arises, help me to demonstrate the reason or be quick to set things right. In Your name, amen.

Journal Tip: What elements make the person in our focus verse unstable? Why are mixed messages harmful to our children? Does God ever change? Why is that important as our heavenly Father?

Notes:

_____

_____

_____

_____

_____

_____

_____

_____

PEER PRESSURE

"My son, if sinners entice you, do not give in to them." Proverbs 1:10

Peer pressure is something that we all have to face at some point in our lives. It may come in many forms, but the results are the same. It's one of satan's oldest tricks. When you're a child, it may be to steal, lie, or disobey your parents. When you're older, it may be to engage in certain activities like drugs or drinking. As an adult, it may be to go certain places with co-workers, to gossip, or to cheat on your taxes. No matter what the devil has planned for you, you have a choice whether or not go give into the pressures around you. You do not have to give in! Let's pray over your child to combat peer pressure in his/her future.

Dear God,
Thank You for the power to choose in life. I thank You for giving us the power we need to overcome the enemy. Please go before my child in this area of peer pressure. When temptation comes in like a flood, rise up a standard against it. Give him/her the desire to do what is right and at that moment of decision, bring to his/her memory all the precious scripture that he/she has been taught. Help me, as a parent, to instill Godly values in my little one so when the enemy comes in, he/she will recognize it and be able to stand strong against him and his plans. Keep him/her protected in this area. I know You always provide a way out. If he/she makes a poor choice, let him/her be swift to ask for forgiveness and make it right in the sight of men and You. May he/she be an example before his/her peers, even at an early age. Let him/her be an instrument for You to promote a positive, godly influence to others. In Your name I ask it. Amen.

Journal Tip: What are peer pressures that you faced when you were growing up? Do you think peer pressures have changed over the years? How did you handle peer pressure? What would you advise your child to do?

Notes:

_____

_____

_____

_____

_____

_____

_____

_____

_____

_____

DRESSING FOR A SPIRITUAL DAY

"Finally, be strong in the Lord and in His mighty power. Put on the full armor of God so that you can take your stand against the devil's schemes. For our struggle is not against flesh and blood..." Ephesians 6:10-12

When we are raising children, it is very important to teach them how to prepare for daily life. We wouldn't let them go out the door without dressing them and protecting them from the elements. Why would we spiritually let them go around naked? A quick study of Ephesians 6:10-20 tells us the things we need to do daily to protect ourselves out in the spiritual world. Study it and teach it to your child. It will equip him/her for battles that are sure to come.

Lord,
As I study Ephesians 6:10-20 today, show me how to apply this to life. Let it sink deep into my spirit and make it real to me so that I may someday teach it to my little one. It's much easier to teach something that I am living every day. Help me to realize that my child and I need all the pieces of armor that You have described in Your Word. Let salvation be my helmet. Let the Word be my sword. Let me have the belt of truth buckled around my waist and the breastplate of righteousness. Let my feet be fitted with the readiness that comes from the gospel of peace. Let faith be my shield and distinguish all the flaming arrows of the evil one. Help me to remain alert at all times to defend myself and my home. I want to daily absorb scriptural truth, trust in You, and share Your Word. In Your name, amen.

Journal Tip: Have you thought much about protecting your child in the spirit? Do you think the devil schemes and plots against children and babies?

Notes:

_____

_____

_____

_____

_____

_____

_____

_____

_____

_____

_____

120

INSTRUCTED BY PARENTS

"Listen, my son, to your father's instruction and do not forsake your mother's teaching."
Proverbs 1:8

Most of what your child learns in the first years of life will be greatly influenced by you. Feeding themselves, tying their own shoes, dressing themselves, and potty training are just a few lessons that come to mind. You would probably agree that it's not very easy to teach someone who doesn't want to listen to instruction. This may be true in part for a baby or toddler, who really can't help the short attention span that they seem to have. Let's pray that God will assist you and instruct you in how to teach your child effectively and that their hearts will be open to receiving instruction from you.

Heavenly Father,
I know there are many challenges facing me when it comes to teaching my baby new skills and tasks. I pray that You would grant me patience, diligence, and wisdom in those times. Give my little one a receptive heart to want to heed instruction from me. Show me creative, fun, interactive ways to introduce new things to him/her. Give me a teachable heart that would learn what You would have me to do with my child. Bless our precious times together and the milestones we cross, one at a time. Keep the communication lines of teaching and learning open, even as my little one grows. Thank You, Lord. Amen.

Journal Tip: What kinds of things can you imagine teaching your child?

Notes:

_____

_____

_____

_____

_____

_____

_____

_____

_____

_____

_____

_____

Week 15

THE VIRTUE OF GENEROSITY

"Command them to do good, to be rich in good deeds, and to be generous and willing to share." 1 Timothy 6:18

Character is built by what we teach and exemplify to our children. Paul tells us in this verse and in the ones preceding that we are not to put our faith in monetary riches (wealth), but in God who provides all things. No matter if you have much or little, generosity and a heart willing to share are characteristics we all can exhibit. We can all live righteously, provide good deeds unto others, and share in what we have (wealth, materials possessions, joy, kindness or whatever). This could be a motto character verse to live by!

Dear God,
Your ways are high and above all the ways of man. Even in our "greatness" You are far greater. I thank You for providing real ways to apply Your Word to our lives. Bless this child within me today and help me be rich toward him/her with goodness, generosity, and kindness. In turn, I pray that he/she will be raised to live a righteous life, and live a life full of generosity and willingness to share. Let this be demonstrated even when he/she is little and bless him/her all during his/her life. Raise him/her up to be a person of great character! Amen.

Journal Tip: What does generosity mean to you? Does this verse bring anything else to mind?

Notes:

_____

_____

_____

_____

_____

_____

_____

_____

_____

_____

_____

_____

_____

Week 16

THE VIRTUES OF INTEGRITY AND HONESTY

"May integrity and uprightness protect me, because my hope is in You." Psalm 25:21

Integrity and honesty are two virtues that the world is severely lacking in today. It's hard to find role models who emulate these morals to our children. We see many in the public eye who lie and skirt around the truth. I'm sure if you stop and think about it, many names would come to mind. God wants us to live lives of integrity and honesty. Even when it's difficult to tell the truth, it's important that we strive for honesty in our lives. Some think that lying is a way to get themselves out of a jam, but that is just the opposite of what happens. Lies come from the father of all lies, the devil. Lies actually bring death. Truth will be an important character trait in your child throughout his/her life. It is vital for you to have open, honest communication with your children in order to raise them. You don't want to feel like your child is lying every time you turn around or wonder if what comes out of their mouth is a big tall tale. Start young with this virtue. Stand your ground. Honesty and integrity will protect your family and child in many ways.

Dear God,
I pray that my son/daughter would rise up to the principles set forth in Your Word. I know that these virtues are impossible to accomplish without Your Spirit living in us and helping us. May my child walk close to You and know Your ways. May he/she strive to please You in all his/her ways. Help honesty and integrity be bound to him/her all the days of his/her life. When there is temptation to give into lies or deceit, may they feel Your presence near and be warned. Save him/her from the snare of the enemy. May others who know my child never question their integrity, but know him/her by the fruit that he/she bares. Let his/her integrity protect him/her. Help this character trait flow and accent every area of his/her life (personal, business, friendships, etc). May others see Christ radiating through the life of my child. Amen!

Journal Tip: Include a situation when you had to stand up in honesty or integrity. Why would honesty and integrity be something that you would desire in your child?

Notes:

_____

_____

_____

_____

_____

_____

_____

FANNING THE FLAME

"For this reason I remind you to fan into flame the gift of God, which is in you through the laying on of my hands, For God did not give us a spirit of timidity, but a spirit of power, of love and of self-discipline." 2 Timothy 1:6-7

God doesn't put a spark in our heart just to see it burn out in a few years. He intends for you to fan the flame. I envision a little match head burning as compared to a roaring bonfire. He wants the "bonfire" in our lives. Too many of us, for whatever reason, feel negatively toward ourselves and who we are in Christ. We go about our Christian walk and service in timidity rather than in boldness and power. As in the analogy, we spend all of our time trying to keep the wind from blowing out our little match head flame, rather than cultivating the fire. It takes persistence to get a fire going. You have to keep adding kindling and then fan the fire into flame. Friends of mine own a huge bellows that they have turned into a coffee table. When I first saw it, I thought it wasn't real because of the size (a bellows is what one would use to fan a flame). That assured me that it was real. What a fire that bellows could fan! When you fan a flame, you also must keep the fire in order so that the fire doesn't get out of control. It's meant to be contained to a certain extent and not run like a destructive wild fire. That's the gift of self-discipline. Keep fanning the flame of the deposit God has given you. It will catch, just like sparking the match head in others around you, including your children!

Dear God,
Thank You for the flame that You have given to my life. Help me to not be satisfied with a small experience when You desire to do something greater. Give me the energy, desire, and capabilities to fan what You have given and see it increase. I pray that I would be on fire for You. Where I have exhibited timidity, I pray that there would be boldness. Where I have been weak, grant me power. Where there has been doubt and rejection, I pray that there would be an overwhelming love. Where I have lacked in self-discipline, I pray that there would be order and organization. I want what You are doing to catch the wind of the Spirit and grow, spreading to others. Burn away all the impurities that are in my life and begin new, healthy growth. May the flame that You have given me spark in my child. Help him/her to be a "fanner of the flame" in this family and to those around him/her. I ask that he/she would burn with Your love and righteousness and that Your power through them would spread to others. I pray 2 Timothy 2:7 over my little one that you would give him/her a spirit of power, of love, and of self discipline. In Your name, amen.

Journal Tip: How do you view yourself? Are you the timid match head or the roaring bonfire? Write some reasons why you feel the way you do. Which one do you want your child to be?

Notes:

_____

_____

_____

_____

THE VIRTUE OF PURITY

"But there must not be even a hint of sexual immorality, or of any kind of impurity, or of greed, because these are improper for God's holy people." Ephesians 5:3

Doesn't this sound like an Old Testament command? Who would have thought that God would provide such a strict standard of living in the New Testament, let alone in our modern society! Well, He does. God demands purity and holiness in our lives, even if these are not concepts readily accepted by the world we live in today. Purity in mind, heart, and deed is extremely important to convey to your child in the world which we live. They will be receiving the opposite message of lust, greed, pride, and so on sooner than you think. Let's ask God to help you cultivate purity in your child.

Dear God,
Thank You for loving us enough to show us the way we are to live. I thank You that You are a God that only wants the best for us. In the culture of our modern society, it seems that purity is a word almost unrecognizable. I ask that You would help me teach purity to my children and live by example as well. Show me where he/she may be receiving a message that is contrary to what we believe. Allow me to intervene as his/her parent when it is according to Your will. I want my son/daughter to be holy and live a righteous life. I ask that he/she be determined to live a life pleasing to you all of his/her days, regardless of what pressures or messages might try to influence them otherwise. I ask that others would see that he/she is pure and never question it, especially when he/she is older. If they fall in this area, help me to be an agent of restoration in his/her life. I ask for wisdom and knowledge so that I can teach life building character skills to my child. Thank You, Lord. Amen.

Journal Tip: Why is purity important in the life of your child? What can you do as a parent to help assure that they will stay pure? Did you struggle with this area in your life? What would you change if you could?

Notes:

_____

_____

_____

_____

_____

_____

_____

Week 16

STAND AGAINST THE ENEMY

"No weapon formed against you will prevail, and you will refute every tongue that accuses you. This is the heritage of the servants of the LORD, and this is their vindication from me," declares the LORD." Isaiah 54:17

Bullies are a real problem in today's world. Mothers of young school age children often worry about this problem affecting their children while they are away at school. The ultimate bully could be considered as satan himself, as he sets himself up as accuser of the brethren. We often feel beat up and attacked by the enemy. If you're a Christian you can expect opposition. We are often targets of bullying, but we have an unmatched arsenal... God Himself. He fights for us when we cannot do anything about our situations around us. If you live long enough, you will eventually come into contact with someone that does not like you or agree with your views. Take Isaiah 54:17 to heart! Learn it and believe it! No weapon formed against you will prevail. You will have an answer for everyone who accuses you. It's a heritage of all those who serve God. So, if you are facing a situation where someone is bothering you today, or if you simply are looking toward the future when your son or daughter might face this, be encouraged. God will not let you down!

Dear God,
I declare Your Word to be true, Lord. I thank You for fighting for me at times when I am not strong. Protect me from those who would try to harm me in word or deed, especially during my pregnancy. I ask that Your Spirit would go forth and protect my child in the days to come. The enemy would like to accuse and bring condemnation down upon me and my children, but I will not stand for it today. I say no to the enemy. The Lord will be my vindication. I give you all my anxiety and fear today. Replace my fears with confidence in who You are. Thank You, Lord, for watching out for me and my child. Amen.

Journal Tip: Were you bullied as a kid or feel bullied as an adult? How would you feel if someone was trying to bully your child? What would you do?

Notes:

_____

_____

_____

_____

_____

_____

_____

_____

WORK ETHIC

**"For even when we were with you, we gave you this rule: 'If a man will not work,
he shall not eat.'" 2 Thessalonians 3:10**

American History attributes, "If a man will not work, he shall not eat!" as spoken from the mouth of Captain John Smith, leader of the Jamestown Colony. No doubt, its origins were from the Bible. Some in the colony were growing idle and reaping benefits from the hard working colonists. The rule was clear enough. If you didn't work, no food would be given. The rule was enforced, too. Captain Smith cared for the people too much to allow them to destroy themselves with idleness. We can all learn from this saying from the New Testament as Captain Smith did. Discipline provides perimeters and expectations that we need to live by. Yes, we all need boundaries! Also, idleness is not pleasing to the Lord. Yes, there are times in life where it is necessary to rest and God commanded a day to rest when giving the Ten Commandments. However, we do need to work in life. There are many reasons for this to be true, but most of all, we all need something to accomplish in life. Even a small child can be made to feel useful by accomplishing small tasks in the day. Getting your baby on a consistent routine will help you. As their learning and development increases, you will be able to do small things in the day that will encourage your child to increase in skills. Older children can be given small chores or tasks. Sometimes you can provide fun outings or allowance to reward jobs well done. Having tasks to do will teach children the values of a healthy work ethic, responsibility, dependability, helpfulness, and diligence. Whether it is finger painting or helping put toys away, God will show you how to incorporate helpful life building tasks into your daily routine.

Dear Heavenly Father,
Thank You for the knowledge, strength, and wisdom You have given me this day. Because of You, I am able to work at many things that I do in my day. I know that You have given me the strength and ability to do so. As I raise this baby, I pray that You will help me to display a strong work ethic to my child so that he/she will not gain an unhealthy view of work. I pray that he/she will be diligent and rewarded for a job well done. Show me even as he/she is little what things he/she can do that would encourage them to complete a task. Help me to build upon it little by little, precept by precept. Show me how to teach and reap a harvest of helpfulness, dependability, diligence, and consistency. Help my child to feel useful, but not to find their identity in their work. In Your name, amen.

Journal Tip: List some simple tasks that your child could do at an early age (beginning around 4-6 months). This isn't necessarily work, but anything that a child could do on his/her own that would give them a daily sense of responsibility…perhaps holding a spoon or cup, learning to hold a book while you read it, etc.

Notes:

_____

_____

_____

THE VIRTUE OF GIVING

"Give and it will be given to you. A good measure, pressed down, shaken together and running over, will be poured into your lap. For with the measure you use, it will be measured to you." Luke 6:38

What comes to mind when you think about little kids and their ability to give? Do you laugh? Most children tend to be selfish and have to be taught how to share. Giving is one of the key value characteristics that should be taught to your child. There are many times in life that we have to give. This is not only true for money, but of time, talent, energy, etc. This principle has a precept attached to it, as many of God's principles do. God says when we give; it will be given to us... good measure, pressed down, shaken together and running over. Like the parable of reaping and sowing, God instructs us that in what measure we give, it will be given back to us likewise. Let's pray that God will work this virtue of giving into the fiber of your child and that you, too, will be enabled to give generously of yourself when it comes to parenting.

Lord,
Thank You for this principle and precept about giving. I pray that You would enable me to give to overflowing when it comes to my child. Help me give my time, my love, my attention, my listening skills, my energy, my interaction, and my communication. I know in what measure I give, it will be returned to me in like manner. What a concept. Help me to give freely in spiritual matters, especially in my home where my child can learn giving by example. Freely You give and freely I have received. Show me and prompt me to freely give. Amen.

Journal Tip: What do you "give" to be a parent? Has anything changed in your life so far? What are some of the areas you may need to work on in giving?

Notes:

_____

_____

_____

_____

_____

_____

_____

_____

_____

_____

Week 16

THE VIRTUE OF HONOR

"Honor your father your mother." Exodus 20:12a

To honor someone is to hold them in high esteem. In today's world, children honoring their parents may seem impossible. It is God's plan for children to hold their parents in high esteem or honor. They should convey this in their attitude, thoughts, words, and actions. Do you see that honoring fathering and mother is also a foreshadowing of us honoring our heavenly Father? If we cannot respect the parents that God has given to us and they are physically among us, how can we revere God, who is unseen with the physical eye? God's precept is followed with a promise. If we honor our parents, then we will live a long, fruitful life. Let's ask for honor to adorn our children. It will not only bring them honor in our eyes and God's eyes, but also in the eyes of those in the world around them.

Dear God,
Thank You for this principle of honor that You have set forth in Your Word. Help me to perpetually honor those around me who You want me to honor, including my child. I pray that honor will adorn my child. May they respect and honor those in authority around them and revere those You have set over them. Bring blessing to his/her life because of obedience in this area. May he/she honor You as well. Let honor and respect pour forth from her/her life in attitude, thoughts, words, and actions. Show me how to cultivate this important characteristic in my child. Amen.

Journal Entry: How do you want your child to treat you? Would you feel hurt if they were disrespectful or rude? Is it important for you to honor your child?

Notes:

_____

_____

_____

_____

_____

_____

_____

_____

_____

_____

_____

THE VIRTUE OF RESPECT

"Show proper respect to everyone;   Love the brotherhood of believers, fear God, honor the King." 1 Peter 2:17

R-e-s-p-e-c-t. I know you've heard the song. What does true respect in Christ mean? Respect could be defined as to value another person and recognize their worth and their God given purpose. All life has value from the time of conception to the most elderly among us. God made all of us and we are to show proper respect for each other. We see a lack of this in our world today. Teachers, policemen, waiters, judges, even the President have very little respect among the people. Even the unborn are finding less respect for their very lives. We need to seek the Almighty God that He will come and raise up a generation who genuinely value others and not for selfish motivation or gain.

Dear Lord,
I pray that You would plant respect within my child. I know that he/she will learn this not only from Your Word, but also by my example. Help me to not talk of others or to others in a disrespectful manner. Let respect flow genuinely from all the members of this family to one another, to our extended family, and to the community in which we live. Show me how to teach my son/daughter how to have true respect, which comes from Your Spirit. When we desire to please You, respect is a natural result. Move the cycle of respect in full circle, bringing the gift of respect back to my child as he/she respects others.
I pray for this fruit of the Spirit to flow freely in this home. May it bring You glory. Amen.

Journal Tip: Who are some people that your child will need to respect from an early age? Why is it important for your child to respect you and for you to respect him/her?

Notes:

_____

_____

_____

_____

_____

_____

_____

_____

_____

Week 17

THE VIRTUE OF OBEDIENCE

"Children, obey your parents in the Lord, for this is right" Ephesians 6:1

What parent wouldn't love to have an obedient child? Unfortunately, obedience isn't a virtue children enter the world eager to fulfill. It's hard for a child's human nature to be tamed without the Lord. You must be in prayer over what will be beneficial and constructive to your child when dealing with obedience issues. God will help you gently teach your child perimeters for conduct that will fit your family. You are a unique family and God will do things differently in each one in ways that will work for them. Don't be tempted to compare your family to others. God desires for children to obey their parents. He says it is right. This is provided that parents are not requiring things of their children that would cause them to sin or go against God's Word. God desires for parents to be godly and to raise children who will fear Him. Parents are a foreshadowing of our relationship with God the Father. If we can learn to obey our parents whom we can see, we will be able to obey God whom we cannot physically see.

Dear Lord,
Thank You for a call to obedience in Your children. I pray that it will begin in me. Help me to listen to Your prompting when it comes to teaching my child how to obey. I pray that I will be gentle and loving at all times. I pray that I will be directed by Your Spirit. Help me to obey You so that my child will obey me. When the time comes when he/she has disobeyed, show me how to teach him/her effectively and bring him/her into correction. I pray that he/she would see good fruit from his/her obedience. I pray that he/she would be obedient to You and Your Word. Give him/her strength to make wise choices every day. Thank You, Lord. Amen.

Journal Tip: Can you think of a time when you were obedient or disobedient at a child? What were the results of your choice? Do you want your child to obey you and God?

Notes:

_____

_____

_____

_____

_____

_____

_____

_____

_____

_____

Week 17

TEMPTATION

"So, if you think you are standing firm, be careful that you don't fall! No temptation has seized you except what is common to man. And God is faithful; He will not let you be tempted beyond what you can bear. But when you are tempted, He will also provide a way out so that you can stand up under it." 1 Corinthians 10:12-13

At one time or another all of us face will face different temptations in life. What entices one person may have little to no effect on another. For one it might be spending too much money on baby or maternity clothes; for another, eating that third piece of cake when you're trying to eat a healthful diet while pregnant! Still others may have harmful habits such as smoking or drinking. Some days we may feel strong in the Lord, others as weak as a string of spaghetti. Whatever you may be tempted by today or tomorrow, know this: there is a hand reaching out to you at that very moment. God not only wants to see you overcome; He also made a sure way for you to overcome it. This verse tells us that He provides a way out so that we can stand underneath the pressures of temptation. Listen to what His still small voice is telling you today. He is not only wanting this principle to become alive in your mind, but He desires for your child to be an over comer as well.

Dear God,
Today I bring You all my heart and lay it before You. Who knows me better than You? You have not only seen what tempts me, but You have also equipped me with a line of defense. Help me in those times to see the way out that You have provided. I know that in life, we will continually be tempted. I ask that You build me up in strength, endurance, and discernment to recognize the enemy and stand up against him. This world is not a sin free world that my child is coming into. I ask for Your grace to surround him/her as he/she grows. There will be many temptations, even as a little child to do wrong. Help him/her to recognize Your ways out as well. I know there will be times when he/she will fail to make the correct choice. In those challenging time, I pray that You would use me to lead them into repentance and restoration with You. Solidify this concept in my mind so that I may effectively teach it to my child/children. Help me to know my child so that I will know the areas he/she struggles in. May he/she always be able to communicate openly with me even about temptations. I thank You, Lord for meeting all that we have need of. Amen.

Journal Tip: What are some of your biggest temptations? Have you seen God provide ways out for you in the past? How as a parent does this affect your ability to help your child through times of temptation?

Notes:

_____

_____

_____

_____

_____

Week 17

GOOD CHARACTER

"Do not be misled: "Bad company corrupts good character." 1 Corinthians 15:33

There are many debates whether children are who they are because of environment or are defined by genetics. Perhaps it is both. With that in mind, we have a responsibility as parents to create the best life environments for our kids that are possible. Here's an example. As a mother, you would probably say that if your child was on a play date and another child was hitting your child... that would be unacceptable. If the hitting was allowed to continue, your child would more than likely begin hitting back! Bad company corrupts good character. You have the right as a parent to determine what is healthy for your child and what isn't. Don't be wimpy! Even though it's not easy at times, taking stands for our children is part of being a parent. Standing up for our kids not only includes facing foes, but daring to set boundaries and limits for our kids and empowering them with good morals. We are given the law so that we know what is wrong. Too many parents fail to expect great things from their children. Some may even feel that having morals is a thing of the past or not "liberal"(not thinking outside of the box). Let me challenge you today to set moral goals and expectations from your child. It's never too early to begin training them up in the ways that they should go. There are standards that we should live by and they are found in the Word of God.

Heavenly Father,
I thank You that You have set a standard for man to live by in Your Word. I know that the law has been given to show us what is wrong. Help me to live acceptably in Your sight and to pass that example down to my child. Work it out in my heart that I would see clearly the good character traits that need to be built up and encouraged in my son/daughter. Give me the boldness to stand when I need to stand and the strength to endure when I need to endure. I pray that I would not allow any circumstance to infringe on the safety or godly upbringing that I am striving for in my child. Give me the words to say and the ability to clearly articulate what I am feeling and expect when it comes to my child or others. Show me how to promote healthy relationships in my child's life and to know what is going on in his/her environments. I want to play an active roll in leading them into life affirming relationships and not destructive ones.

Journal Tip: What kinds of morals and good character traits are you hoping to teach to your children?

Notes:

_____

_____

_____

_____

_____

_____

TRUTH

"This is good, and pleases God our Savior, who wants all men to be saved and to come to a knowledge of the truth." 1 Timothy 2:3-4

What <u>is</u> truth? Do you know it when you hear it? Who decides what truth is? These are all important, deep questions. Two things are for certain. <u>God</u> is truth and His <u>Word</u> is truth. Just as faith comes by hearing the Word of God, truth is distinguished through the faith we have obtained by the Word, as well as by His Spirit working within us. In the Word, we see a standard of living that God desires us to live by. Truth has absolutes! We hear so much about thinking outside the box, but don't be deceived. There are perimeters that God has set for us to follow! Godly perimeters are not ones that you want to get outside of. In the Old Testament, there were no fences to keep the sheep safe so shepherds were used. They were responsible to keep the sheep safe and away from dangers. Today we have fences. Fences mark perimeters in which sheep should stay. Parents are the shepherds of the children and the fences are the Word. It is our job to share the Word with our children so that our children can understand the standards of Christian living and we are to shepherd their Christian walk and watch over them as they grow. We should desire truth in our homes and truth in our children. This not only means a truth in their faith, but also truth in their words and deeds.

Dear Lord,
Thank You for giving us truth and showing us the way to live. I want to be a seeker of Your truth and that my son/daughter would be a seeker as well. You have given a standard of living in Your Word that I want to follow. Show me how to convey what is truth to my child and what is not. Even if the world is accepting and tolerant of false hoods, I pray that deception would not creep into this home in any fashion. Guard me as I am guarding over my child. I don't want to allow anything spiritually, physically, or emotionally dangerous into my home. Build up my faith and knowledge of the Word. I thank You for Your salvation, which saves me from sin, death, and destruction. You want all to be saved and to come to a knowledge of the truth (1 Timothy 2:4). I pray this for my child today. Amen.

Journal Tip: What are some truths from the Word that have building blocks in your spiritual life? Is there an example of when God led you in the way of truth when faced with something that could have deceived you? How will your child learn what truth is, especially when it comes to spiritual matters?

Notes:

_____

_____

_____

_____

_____

IMITATION

"Be imitators of God, therefore, as dearly loved children" Ephesians 1:5

All children go through the stage of wanting to imitate everything you or someone else does. This is true for both words and actions. In the beginning, it seems harmless enough, but after awhile, it may start to get a little annoying. Sometimes children don't always mock the nice things that we do, either. Perhaps it's time to examine the things we do or say that may not be worthy of repeating!

Babies learn facial responses and much of their speech concepts through imitation. Isn't it fitting that God our Father tells us to be imitators of Him? If we are trying our best to follow this advice, our lives are sure to influence our children in a positive way. Let's ask Him to help us be imitators of Him and that our children will follow!

Heavenly Father,
I praise You today for leaving me an example that I can follow! I pray that You would help me to be an imitator of You. Examine my heart and see if there be any thing in me that would not be worthy of imitating. If there is anything in me that should not be there, I pray that You would remove it from me and help me to change. I pray that I would be a good example that my child would follow after. Raise us both up in Your image. May my speech and actions be ones that would glorify You at all times. Help me to understand You and Your characteristics so that I can teach them to my child. Thank You, Lord. Amen.

Journal Tip: What kinds of things would make you an imitator of God? What does that mean to you? How will you express these things to your child so that he/she may be an imitator of God?

Notes:

_____

_____

_____

_____

_____

_____

_____

_____

_____

_____

Week 17

THE VIRTUE OF SELF-CONTROL

"But I tell you that anyone who is angry with his brother will be subject to judgment."
Matthew 5:22a

Think of someone that rubs you the wrong way. Would you like your comments and responses about that person to be imitated by your child? How do you deal with anger? Many people struggle tremendously in this area; if not in their own lives, in their relationships with other people who battle anger. Even when we get angry, it is important not to sin. We must deal with anger before it turns into bitterness. This is important to learn as a parent. The Bible tells us in Proverbs 15:1,"A gentle answer turns away wrath, but a harsh word stirs up anger." How do you think you will speak to your children when they push you to the limit? How do you want your child to speak to you or others? Teaching your child about self-control should start in the home. We must allow the Holy Spirit to work in us and let this fruit of self-control shine forth.

Dear Lord,
I ask that You would turn on a spotlight into my heart right now. I ask that You would examine me and my ways. If there be any wicked way in me, expose it so it can be dealt with. I pray in this particular area of anger that You would help me not to sin while I am angry. Help me to never let the sun set before I have dealt with issues. I want to put them to rest before I lay my head down to rest. In dealing with my child, help me to approach correction and discipline with a gentle answer and not with harshly spoken words. At those moments, put the words I am to speak in my mouth. Help me speak words that will bring life and not harm. I pray that my life will be a worthy example for my little one to follow. If there are any areas in my heart that need healing due to anger (on my part or someone else) be the balm of Gilead in those areas right now. I thank You for being Lord of all of my life. I want every single part of my life to reflect the God that I serve. Raise up my child to be a person of gentle answers. I pray that anger will never be a leech that will attach itself to my child's thoughts, heart, spirit, or mind. Don't allow him/her to give the devil a foothold into his/her life through bitterness. Keep him/her protected from flaming darts of anger and give him/her wisdom in times when dealing with others who battle anger. Thank You, Lord for helping in these areas. Amen.

Journal Tip: Write down some gentle discipline comments. (E.g.. How would you tell a child to stop hitting his brother?) Have you ever been corrected as a child in a poor way and remember how that felt? How do you want your child to feel after you have disciplined him/her? What is the goal of correction?

Notes:

_____

_____

_____

_____

_____

KEEP YOUR CHILD FROM EVIL

"'...and keep me from harm so that I will be free from pain.' And God granted his request."1 Chronicles 4:10b

In this world we live in, there are many kinds of evil facing us today. Crime, filth on television, and many other venues prove to us that we are in a raging spiritual battle. When the disciples asked Jesus to show them how to pray, he included ... "and keep us from evil". God can put a hedge of protection around you today and keep you from evil. This should also be our prayer for our children. We need God's protection over our children to keep them safe. We cannot protect them in our own flesh. We need to rely on the Lord to work for us in the heavenly realms.

Heavenly Father,
I thank You for desiring to keep me and my baby protected from the evil of this day. I know that the enemy is like a roaring lion seeking whom he may devour. I ask for Your divine protection in this hour to keep us from the evil one. Guard our physical bodies, our hearts, and our minds with a wall of fire that cannot be penetrated. I ask that You show me special grace during my pregnancy. Keep me safe from accidents, illnesses, diseases, and all other kinds of evil. I thank You that You keep an eye out for me at all times. In turn, keep this little one safe within me. I know that You have plans for good concerning me and my family. May all the days of this child's life be protected by You. Keep him/her safe under the umbrella of Your Spirit. You are like the hen covering it's chicks with its wings. I see my little one safe under the covering of the shadow of Your might and power. When the enemy comes in like a flood, raise up a standard against it! Thank You, Lord, for keeping us from evil. Amen.

Journal Tip: Write about the security you feel in knowing that God's protection will rest on you and your child in this present evil world. Do you have any fears about the present world we live in and what it will be like for your child growing up? List them and give your fears over to the one who will protect His children!

Notes:

_____

_____

_____

_____

_____

_____

_____

_____

DISCERNMENT

"Hear My words, you wise men; listen to me, you men of learning. For the ear tests words as the tongue tastes good food. Let us discern for ourselves what is right; let us learn together what is good." Job 34:2-4

Discernment is something that doesn't always come easy in life. It is the prompting of the Spirit of God within us telling us is something is from Him or not. I am always amazed at how some Christians think it is all right to digest whatever anyone tells them without questioning. There might be a hook in the apple! God prompts us to test things to see if they are from Him or not. Although we cannot teach discernment to our children (as it is a working of the Spirit of God within them) we can be there to encourage them and to pray for discernment. In these last days, there will be many who claim they are of Christ, but are not. These would draw our children away from the truth and pull them into human teachings and traditions. We must teach our children the Word so that they know God's ways and His plan for us. Two vital tools are the discernment of the Spirit and the Word!

Dear God,
I thank You that You never leave us alone in our time of need. You draw us to You when we are listening and when we pray. I ask for myself that You would give me discernment today. Discernment that will keep me from walking down the wrong paths in life, that would keep me from the teachings and traditions of men, and lead me to You. I pray that this discernment would show me what is right and what is good, what is of You and what is Not. I know we need Your Spirit in this hour like never before. Give me discernment as a parent to lead my child in Your ways and for daily guidance. I ask for discernment for my child. The enemy is out to deceive all who would believe on You, even targeting children. Guard my little one's mind as he/she grows. Show him/her how to rightly divide truth. I pray that You would keep him/her from evil and destructive influences. Speak to his/her mind, spirit, and soul from an early age.

Journal Tip: Why do you feel like discernment is important for you as a parent? Why does your child need discernment in light of the day that we are living in?

Notes:

_____

_____

_____

_____

_____

_____

_____

_____

138

CONFIDENCE IN HIM

"For the Lord will be your confidence." Proverbs 3:26a

Confidence is full trust or assurance. When I think of a confident person, I think of someone who holds their head high, knows who they are, knows where they are going, and shares that persona with others. What would compel a person to act in such a confident manner? That's a good question. People put their trust in many things; money, career, status, their own personal identity, but the word says for the LORD will be our confidence. After all, He really is the only one that is infallible in all things, knows all things, and sees all things. We may need confidence in various situations in life. Pregnancy can be one of those times. When we draw our trust and assurance from an infallible God, we are centered in Him. He's the core of our lives. Everything else flows as a result. Isn't it great to know the one who fashioned your body and created it to accomplish this task of pregnancy is the same one who is your assurance? Let Him show you how to rest in Him and to rely on Him as your confidence. He knows what He's doing, even if you don't,

Dear God,
At times when I doubt or struggle and feel like I am unable to handle this job you've called me to, assure me that You are my confidence. There is nothing that You do not understand or know about me, my baby, or the future. Help me rest in You today and know that all things are in Your hands, moving according to Your plan. I want to be confident in You and in this wonderful experience You are giving to me. Help this little one within me to know that You are his/her confidence in life. When all else seems to be against him/her in life, let him/her grab on to You as their confidence. You are the anchor and the rock of my soul. Thank You, God. Amen.

Journal Tip: Is God your confidence today in your pregnancy? Why or why not? Do you trust Him to fully take care of you and your baby?

Notes:

_____

_____

_____

_____

_____

_____

_____

_____

_____

_____

Week 18

PRAYING FOR YOUR CHILD AS AN EXAMPLE

"If you believe, you will receive whatever you ask for in prayer."
Matthew 21:22

Prayer is something that should be often seen and heard in our homes. It's important to teach your child how to pray through word and deed. The first prayers they utter will probably be a direct result of you teaching them how to talk to God. Consistency is a key to our prayer lives. You must teach him/her how to pray and cultivate this good habit into their lives. God wants a relationship with your child. Our relationships rely on open communication. God desires to have communication with all of His creation, including our children.

Lord,
I pray that You would instruct me in leading my child on a path of consistent prayer. You want open communication with my son/daughter (through prayer) and I want to be a part of opening that communication. Let it begin at an early age and continue throughout his/her life. I pray that in times of need that he/she will come to You. I pray in times of joy that he/she will come to You. I pray that he/she will come to You at ALL TIMES! Let him/her come to You will all matters, all subjects, all things! Honor his/her prayers and give him/her eyes to see that You work in response to our prayers. May this child experience great answers to the prayers that he/she brings forth to You... prayers that will build their faith and trust. Work through him/her as a prayer warrior . Help them come to the knowledge of what praying for others truly means and how it benefits the Body of Christ. Amen.

Journal Tip: Has God answered prayer for you lately? Convey a few ideas about why prayer is important to you or how God has used you to pray for someone else... especially your baby!

Notes:

_____

_____

_____

_____

_____

_____

_____

_____

_____

_____

TEN COMMANDMENTS / LAW

"When Moses finished reciting all these words to all Israel, he said to them, 'Take to heart all the words I have solemnly declared to you this day, so that you may command your children to obey carefully all the words of this law. They are not just idle words for you- they are life.'" Deuteronomy 32:45-47a

Some may argue that the Ten Commandments do not have any relevance to today's world, let alone the decrees that God shared with Moses throughout the Old Testament. God's laws are there to set boundaries and perimeters for us in life. Without boundaries, people live in chaos. Similarly, when we do not follow the plans that God has set forth for us, we are in spiritual chaos. The books of Biblical law encourage us to devote ourselves wholeheartedly to God and are still relevant to us today as Christians.

Rules aren't in place for our inconvenience, but are there primarily for our protection. God protects us from each other as well as pitfalls that satan might bring our way. Rebellion is a key defense the enemy has against God and His authority. God calls us to be obedient to Him and His Word and to pass down what we have learned to our children. Our focus verses for today tell us that we should command our children to obey all the words of the law. Let's make that our prayer today.

Dear God,
Thank You for Your Word and the law that we find within its books. They are life unto me and they will be life unto my children. I thank You for the protection that they bring! Where I have strayed from Your ways, I pray that You would bring me back into obedience. Help me to study Your Word in whole and not just in part. I pray that You would bring me understanding and illuminate the Word within my spirit so that I will be able to impart it with clarity to my children. I come against rebellion and any other method the enemy would use to keep me or my children from following You with all our minds, hearts, and strength. I pray that You would keep my child from the pattern and ways of the world and transform his/her mind as he/she grows in You and the knowledge of Your Word. Bind every Scripture that he/she may learn to his/her heart that they may follow them and seek after You all the days of his/her life. Amen.

Journal Tip: Write down the 10 Commandments and any other forms of Biblical law that you can think of that are relevant to today and that you would want your child to know. Refer to Exodus 20 if you need help.

Notes:

_____

_____

_____

_____

_____

Week 18

THE VIRTUES OF HUMILITY AND SERVITUDE

"Serve wholeheartedly, as if you were serving the Lord, not men."
Ephesians 6:6-7

No matter what we do in life, it will never be fulfilling unless we do it with a servant's heart and as unto the Lord. Let's pray for your child that whatever he/she does in life will be taken on wholeheartedly and with a spirit of humility. Humility is a virtue that seems to be of little regard in our modern world. We hear things like, "Every man for himself!" or "I am worth it!" What does the Bible say about it? The Bible says God loves those who are humble in spirit. Also, don't be afraid to give time to your church, your extended family, or various ministries when you are expecting. Some mothers have found that volunteering with children's ministries or nursery duty helps them to gain some valuable experience with children before they have their own. You can always take time to pray for others, send a note of encouragement to someone who needs it, or to make a quick call to uplift someone. Ask God today what you can do for Him today while you're expecting. If you are listening, He will use you for His service. Approach your pregnancy and motherhood with enthusiasm and in a way pleasing to Him!

God,
I ask that You would give my child a servant's heart. Jesus himself said that He didn't come to be served, but to serve. I know that You expect the same from us. I pray that my son/daughter will work at whatever they do with gusto. Let him/her work as unto You. Give him/her many opportunities in life to be Your hand extended. Season his/her servant's heart with gratitude and thanksgiving. Let no task, big or small elude my child because of a haughty spirit. Teach him/her by Your Spirit what it means to be a servant. Amen.

Journal Tip: During your life, what have you done with a servant's heart? Write down at least one example. Could pregnancy be one of those examples? How would having a servant's heart help the flow of your home?

Notes:

_____

_____

_____

_____

_____

_____

_____

_____

THE VIRTUE OF PRAISE

"From the lips of children and infants you have ordained praise."
Psalm 8:2a

Praise is something that everyone can do, young and old. God deserves our first fruits of praise. He is so worthy of our praise and created us to give Him praise and glory. Praise can radiate into every part of us; our families, finances, homes, and the beautiful country we live in. The possibilities are endless. Each time your child learns a new skill or can perform a new task, you'll give him /her praise. That's wonderful encouragement to him/her. Praise is an important part of our lives. Let's ask God to help praise flow freely in our lives and in the lives of our children.

Dear Lord,
I want to praise You for everything You are to me and for everything You have given me. You have blessed me spiritually, emotionally, and physically. I thank You for this little baby growing inside me. I pray that praise would flow from my mouth continually, not only to You, but to everyone around me. Let the words of my mouth be pleasing to You. In turn, let this little one's mouth praise You with pure praise. Your Word says that you have ordained praise even from the lips of children and infants. Help me to be a "praiser", which will show my little one how to praise You. There are many different ways to praise You. Whatever the method, I pray for a release of praise within me at this moment. Don't allow anything to come in the way of the flow of praise in this household. When I give praise to my child, let it bring life and blessing unto him/her. No matter what our circumstances, help us to understand that praise is something we can always do. In Your name, amen.

Journal Entry: What are some of the things that are praise worthy in your life? Write them down and verbally express your praise to the Lord!

Notes:

_____

_____

_____

_____

_____

_____

_____

_____

DO NOT EMBITTER YOUR CHILD

"Fathers, do not embitter your children, or they will become discouraged."
Colossians 3:21

The word "embitter" means to make bitter. In this sense it could mean that we have caused our children to become emotionally distressed, pained, or grieved. As an expectant mother, you are probably saying to yourself, "I can never imagine doing that to my child." Sadly enough, for too many parents, their good intentions give way over the course of parenting. So, how does a parent cause their child to become bitter? There could be many answers to that, but some explanations could include: being overly harsh in punishment, putting more demands on them than what should be expected, criticizing them or their behavior too often, not praising them enough for jobs well done, or simply from being inconsistent with our words and actions. Ephesians 6:4 says, "Fathers, do not exasperate your children; instead, bring them up in the training and instruction of the Lord." We should guard our minds and hearts from embittering our children and be aware of the affects of such actions. They will not learn or grow when the are in such a state.

Dear God,
Thank You for Your Word that continually leads us in the paths of righteousness. I thank You for reminding me that children can easily become discourage when they are embittered by his/her parents. I pray that You would set a guard over my mouth and mind, that I would not embitter my child. I ask that You would use me to build them up, rather than bring them down. At any time if I fail to do this, I pray that You would convict me of it immediately so that I can repent and make things right with my son/daughter. If there is ever a situation where others have embittered my child, I pray that you would help me to cultivate a heart of forgiveness and restoration and help them to not stay in unforgiveness, which breeds bitterness. I ask that You keep my child's heart pure and encouraged about You and Your teachings. Thank You, Lord. Amen.

Journal Tip: Have you been embitter in the past? If so, how did you deal with it? What can you do to guard against embittering your child?

Notes:

_____

_____

_____

_____

_____

_____

_____

_____

AGE AND PREGNANCY

"Then the Lord said to Abraham, 'I will surely return to you about this time next year, and Sarah your wife will have a son.'" Genesis 18:10

If you are familiar with this story, you will remember that Abraham was advanced in years and Sarah was well past the age of child bearing (verse 11). When the three visitors appeared at Abraham's camp site that day, little did he know exactly who he was entertaining. The Lord was in their midst! When the statement was made concerning the child, Sarah was listening at the entrance of the tent. She was so shocked by what she heard that she laughed to herself. In fact, when she later gave birth, they named the boy "Isaac", which means "laughter". Perhaps you would have been amused to if someone came to you last year and said that you were going to have a baby! Maybe you are wondering about your age today and giving birth. Maybe your child isn't coming along at everyone else's ideal time in life to have a baby. No matter if you are young, old, or somewhere in between, God has ordained this time just for you. He knew about it way before You did. Don't let your age bother you. God has everything orchestrated in His great plan.

Dear God,
I thank You that You know everything before it even happens. I have great trust, hope, and joy in knowing that my times are in Your hands. No matter what my age, You have ordained this child in my life. I pray against anyone who would come in and try to make me feel inadequate or unworthy of the task ahead of me. You know all my years and have seen fit to bring life into the world through me. Let great joy arise in my heart today; not a chuckle of doubt and disbelief. I pray that this baby will be a great blessing to me and my family just as Isaac was a great blessing to Abraham and Sarah. In Your name, amen.

Journal Tip: What is your current age? What are your thoughts about your age and having your baby?

Notes:

_____

_____

_____

_____

_____

_____

_____

_____

_____

_____

Week 19

HE WILL CARRY YOU

"You whom I have upheld since you were conceived, and have carried since your birth. Even to your old age and gray hairs I am He who will sustain you. I have made you and I will carry you." Isaiah 46: 3b- 4a

Have you ever read the poem "Footprints in the Sand"? In that poem, the author says he sees two sets of footprints on the sand, one his and the other the Lord's. Then times get rough, the author says there were only one set of footprints. This troubles the author, so he questions God about it. God assures him that when he only sees one set of footprints, those were the times that He carried him! How comforting. I think of that poem when I read this verse. This verse even takes it further than that. He says that He has upheld us since we were conceived and carried us since our birth. Even when we get old, he is still carrying us.

I think of what it means to be held and carried. To our children, it is not only comforting, but also at times necessary, especially when they do not have the skill to walk on their own. God uses three terms here to describe what He does in our lives 1.) Uphold 2.) Carry 3.) Sustain. Each variance of the word contains within its definition the idea of support. He supports us. He upholds us. He carries us. I like the definition of carrying: to move while supporting. He moves us while holding us close to His heart. According to this verse, He is even supporting your baby right now. Isn't that amazing? As a mother, you carry your baby constantly in your womb. The baby is created in you and that's where he/she will stay until delivery. Think of that in terms of the Lord. He created us and will continually carry us throughout our <u>entire lives</u>. Amazing!

Dear Lord,
Thank You for carrying me and supporting me through life even at times when I don't see you there with me. I know You are not only sustaining me, but this little one within me. You have made us and You are there with us at all times. Hold me close to You, especially during my pregnancy. I know that You not only uphold us physically, but emotionally and spiritually as well. Let me rest in Your arms today. Let my little one rest in Your arms today, too. As baby grows, give me creative ways to hold him/her and be affectionate toward them every day. Prepare me for the early stages of my baby's life after birth and give me the strength and stamina to carry the extra loads that I will bear. Amen.

Journal Tip: Write down your thoughts today about knowing that God is carrying your child through life even from conception. Also, have you thought about some of the ways to carry your baby around (car seat, stroller, baby sling, etc)? Have you purchased any of those items yet?

Notes:

_____

_____

_____

_____

Week 19

HOLIDAYS AND SEASONS

"He changes times and seasons..." Daniel 2:21

Holidays are fun when you are expecting. You begin to anticipate baby's first Christmas, first Thanksgiving, first Easter, and first birthday. Our perspective on things changes when we are expecting. We seem to look at the world in a whole new way. Just as the physical seasons, we go through seasons in life. Winter is a cold, dark, and dormant time. Spring is new birth and life. Summer is planting and abundance. Fall is the harvest. What season are you in today?

Lord,
I thank You that You change the times and seasons. Life doesn't stay the same. You are constantly bringing us through cycles that are developing character and depth to our spirits. I thank You for the season I am in right now. I also thank You for the weeks You have given me to enjoy during my pregnancy. I pray that I would see Your mighty hand at work during all seasons of my life. There is beauty in each one. Give me endurance to know that another season is just around the corner. Your timing is perfect and not one day passes without Your knowledge. I praise Your name today. God I ask that You care for my little one today. You are meeting the needs he/she has even as we speak. I see my baby growing like a tiny seed of spring. May he/she blossom this day into the child you are forming him/her into. Amen.

Journal Tip: What season are you going through right now in life? How does that affect your pregnancy? Write a special thought down about holidays concerning your baby- perhaps a family tradition you always celebrate or one you may start (for example, my family makes a new Christmas ornament every year for the tree!).

Notes:

_____

_____

_____

_____

_____

_____

_____

_____

_____

Week 19

TWINS; ULTRASOUND

"When it came time for her to give birth, there were twin boys in her womb."
Genesis 25:24

Could there be two in there? It's always fun to think about the prospect of having twins when you are expecting. You're probably getting ready to have your first (or perhaps second in some women) ultrasound around week twenty. Some things that may indicate that you are having twins would be a large-for–date uterus or more than one heart beat detected by your practitioner. No matter how many babies, you are carrying in your womb; God has planned this from the beginning. Is there one or multiples? You'll soon know.

Dear God,
Be with me as I am getting ready to have an ultrasound. I pray that the technician would be kind, pleasant, patient, and informative. Guide the technician to help me to see things that I normally wouldn't see with my own eyes. Give them skill and accuracy. I will be content with whatever You have given me! Thank You for this window into the womb through technology. Keep this child safe and protected while in my womb. Keep me from all harm and evil that might affect my baby as well. I praise You today for Your wonderful works. Amen!

Journal Entry: Have you dreamed about twins or your ultrasound? How are you feeling? What week are you in?

Notes:

_____

_____

_____

_____

_____

_____

_____

_____

_____

_____

_____

_____

_____

BIRTH ORDER

"But Jacob said, 'Swear to me first.', So he swore an oath to him, selling his birthright to Jacob." Genesis 25:33

The story of the twins, Jacob and Esau, pose some interesting questions to our modern day minds. What is the importance of birth order? Many studies have been conducted telling us that birth order affects how children act. Firstborns are said to have more dominant, leadership characteristics. Subsequent children act in more submissive or sub-dominant roles. God has planned for each baby you will have and already knows what their character and emotional dispositions will be. We must understand that our input as parents has a great role in our child's social and emotional development.

The most important birthright we possess is our spiritual birthright, through salvation. Back in the days of the Old Testament, birth order was important because it was the oldest who would receive the family inheritance and blessing. While some of that still may literally ring true today within our families, aren't we glad that we are spiritual heirs of Christ's salvation and His Kingdom? No one person is favored to God... all are equally important! So, let's pray that your child's God given abilities will shine through, but also that he/she will realize that we are all equal at the foot of the cross.

Dear Lord,
Thank You for the inheritance You have given to me and for this child I am blessed to carry! I praise You that he/she is growing in Your image and that he/she will grow to be an heir of Your Kingdom. I ask that You would raise up this child to be a leader and example to others, especially siblings. Raise him/her up in Your ways, Lord. Help me to recognize each talent and ability that he/she has and to cultivate those character traits that are unique to him/her. At the same time, I pray that You would instill in him/her the realization that we are all Your children and You love us all the same. You have given us all a great inheritance that we have not earned. We only have received it because we have been born again through Your Son. Thank You, Lord. Amen.

Journal Tip: Are you an oldest child, middle child, youngest child, or only child? How do you think that has affected your life, if at all? What are your thoughts about the birth order your child is in? How do you think that may affect him/her?

Notes:

_____

_____

_____

_____

_____

_____

Week 19

DEALING WITH SIBLINGS

"Now Cain said to his brother Abel, 'Let's go out to the field.' And while they were in the field, Cain attacked his brother Abel and killed him." Genesis 4:8

Jealousy and competition between family members isn't a new idea. Our first written record of such strife was attributed to the very first family. Adam and Eve had two sons, Cain and Abel. When jealousy entered the picture, coupled with pride and competition for attention, a horrible event occurred. Death entered the scene.

The families of today haven't strayed too much from that pattern set so long ago, but this should not be! God didn't intend for us to be at odds with each other in jealousy and competition, especially between family members. If this is your first pregnancy and there are no other siblings involved; consider this verse in regard to your nephews, nieces, neighbors, or even friends. Let's pray that God keep any root of jealousy or anger from entering your family equation in any way!

Dear Lord,

I recognize the tendency for jealousy and competition between people. Jealousy and competition ultimately bring death. For Abel, it was a physical death, but for many it is a spiritual death. Lord, I ask that You would be such an integral part of my son/daughters life that they would feel no need to compare themselves with others or be jealous of others. Let them come to realize at a very early age that You are the only critic in their life and Your opinion of them is the most important opinion. Where others might have a tendency to be jealous towards my child, bring resolve to the situations and healing. Bless him/her with the ability to remain humble and approachable all of his/her days. Where there are situations that cannot be resolved, keep him/her safely protected. At any time, if we add to our family, don't allow the spirit of jealousy to creep into this home. Let love, acceptance, worth, and value have a place with each family member. Let this home be a place that my son/daughter can feel secure in his/her feelings and importance. Let each child, no matter if there is one or more, to realize the vital role and place they have in this family and in the family of God. If there are struggles where they need parental guidance, help me to be there with healing words and instructions from You. Where there are areas of healthy competition (sports, etc), let my son/daughter learn valuable truths from You of how to treat others. I ask all of this in Your mighty name, Amen.

Journal Tip: Have you dealt with jealousy or competition in your life or seen it in others? Why do you feel that it is important for your child to have a Biblical view of jealousy and competition?

Notes:

_____

_____

_____

_____

_____

Week 20

THE GENDER OF YOUR BABY

"Male and Female He created them." Genesis 1:27b

Whether you're carrying a boy or girl has already been determined. Even though you don't know at the moment, God sees and knows all. With modern technological advances, there are now tests available to find out the gender of your child as early as five weeks! Around twenty weeks (and sometimes sooner), you might be offered an ultrasound, which may give you a sneak peak on who will be arriving on delivery day! An ultrasound is also a brilliant form of technology which allows you to see the reality of the baby inside your uterus! You can actually see the life within you. What was once an entirely "secret" process can be seen clearly through modern technology? Of course, God could see babies in utero all along!

Heavenly Father,
Thank You for this baby that You are creating. I pray that if I have an opportunity to view my baby on ultrasound that You would help me have an appreciation for what I am seeing. You have seen him/her all along. I pray that You would protect this baby and raise him/her up to be the man or woman You have created him/her to be. The enemy would like to strip men and women of all affiliations with their gender. God, I acknowledge that there are differences between male and females! I pray that You would develop a strong sense of godly gender identity in this baby. Thank You, Lord. Amen.

Journal Tip: Do you plan on having an ultrasound during your pregnancy? Are you hoping to find out if your baby is a boy or a girl? What would be nice about having a boy? What would be nice about having a girl?

Notes:

_____

_____

_____

_____

_____

_____

_____

_____

_____

_____

THE BODY IS ARRANGED BY HIM

"But in fact, God has arranged the parts in the body, every one of them, just as He wanted them to be." 1 Corinthians 12:18

Your baby is God's masterpiece. He has created him/her not only in His image, but has arranged every part of him/her. He is in control of everything. When I think about babies with Down syndrome or other conditions, I pause and think... are they any less than God's masterpiece just because they didn't come out the way we expected them to? I would say to you, NO! Just because the unforeseen may happen doesn't mean that God made certain babies "imperfect". We live in an imperfect world where unfair things happen. No matter what the mental or physical condition of a person, God can use <u>everyone</u> for His glory. Stop and think how you would feel if something were different about your child. Would this cause you to love him/her less? We have many tests today that give us knowledge and insight into the growth of our children in the womb. God doesn't want us to use the knowledge we gain through blood screens and various tests to begin weeding out the ideologically imperfect. Are we all not created in His image? Life is special to God and He is in control even when things appear to be out of our control. Perhaps a miracle in on the way today for someone who has been given a bad report today! Let's pray that all will go according to the Lord's will.

Dear God,
We pray for all the families today across the world who are facing challenges in their pregnancies. Lord, we know that You have fashioned each and every one of us in Your image, but that doesn't mean that we won't all be flawed in some way. We are all human and imperfect. I ask that You would touch each and every mother that has been given a bad report today. I ask that Your miraculous hand would stretch forth and touch their baby in the name of Jesus! Build them up in faith, trust, and assurance in You that You have a far greater purpose than what their physical eyes can see this day. I ask that You give me peace throughout my pregnancy that You are arranging every part of my baby just as You want them to be. I trust You with my joys and I trust You with my fears. Build my faith today. I bind the enemy from coming in and causing fear to grip me concerning the health of my baby. I ask that You would take away any and all fears and replace them with confidence and a sound mind. No matter what I am facing today or other mothers who may be entering the biggest challenges of their lives, I know You are going to see us through. My hope is found in You, Lord. Form this little one as You see fit today. Increase my love for this child daily. Amen.

Journal Tip: What kinds of fears, if any, have you had concerning the health of your baby? Have you had blood screens or tests to show you how baby is developing? What were the results? How did you feel about the results that you were given?

Notes:

_____

_____

_____

152

Week 20

ULTRASOUND

"Finally, brothers, whatever is true, whatever is noble, whatever is right, whatever is pure, whatever is lovely, whatever is admirable- if anything is excellent or praiseworthy think about such things." Philippians 4:8

An ultrasound can supply an amazing glimpse into the hidden world of your womb. Whether you are blessed to have this procedure or not, you can think about your little one who's growing within you and vividly imagine their likeness. Our focus verse summarizes what you may envision! Whatever things are lovely... aren't babies lovely? Pure? Oh, yes! Are babies admirable? Most Definitely! Of good report? It's a wonderful report to see your little one by ultrasound or to simply hear that you're expecting! If there be any virtue, if there's any praises going up to God thanking Him for this little one, think on these things!

God,
I am thinking on the premises set forth in Your Word concerning this baby. I can only imagine how lovely he/she is, how pure and honest. I pray that my mind will be set to think on these things. I pray that I would see this verse through Your Spirit and realize just what miraculous glory there is in it! You are worthy to be praised. Your creation is beyond words. I thank You for this bundle of love that is wrapped up within me. Blessed be Your name! Amen.

Journal Tip: Write down your feelings concerning your baby using the above verse as a guide. What things do you imagine are lovely about your baby? What is pure? (And so on).

Notes:

_____

_____

_____

_____

_____

_____

_____

_____

_____

_____

_____

Week 20

MATERNITY CLOTHING

"And why do you worry about clothes? See how the lilies of the field grow. They do not labor or spin. Yet I tell you that not even Solomon in all his splendor was dressed like one of these." Matthew 6:28-29

Have you started wearing maternity clothes yet? One of the highlights in first time mothers is the passage from normal sized clothes into the chic look of maternity wear. It seems that you can't wait to get into them, but by delivery... you can't wait to get out of them! Plan your wardrobe wisely. A few pieces to mix and match can go a long way. A simple solid pant or short (depending on the season) can go with just about anything. There are many ways to bargain buy or get the clothes you need without breaking the bank. Perhaps you'll find a friend willing to lend you some articles. In any case, know that this too shall pass and it's not worth worrying about what clothes you have and what you don't. You won't be in them forever!

The need for larger wear means that baby is growing. Now the outside world will notice your upcoming arrival as well. Be ready for the question "When are you due?", which will come frequently from now until you deliver. Enjoy your time during pregnancy, especially this new phase you are entering.

Dear Lord,
I thank You for the excitement and anticipation that I feel today. I know that my growing belly means that baby is getting bigger. Help him/her to grow at a healthy normal rate. I bless every organ and every cell in this baby today!   I ask that You make provision for me when it comes to maternity wear. Help me not to worry or spend too much time thinking about how I look. I know that You are going to provide me with what I need. As I adorn my new fashion statement, everyone will know that I am expecting. May I be a radiant example of Christ to those who will notice me. I pray that they will sense something different about me. If some inquire of me, help me always to be ready with a reply that would point them back to You, Lord. Thank You, Lord. Amen.

Journal Tip: Are you wearing maternity clothes yet or are you still in normal clothes? Are you excited about this new phase? Do you have anything that you have enjoyed wearing so far?

Notes:

_____

_____

_____

_____

_____

_____

Week 20

SPIRITUAL FATHERS & SONS

"Similarly, encourage the young men to be self-controlled. In everything set them an example by doing what is good. In your teaching, show integrity, seriousness, and soundness of speech that cannot be condemned, so those who oppose you may be ashamed because they have nothing bad to say about us." Titus 2:6-8

When I think of boys I think of strength and endurance. What a blessing for a boy to be strong in the Lord! They turn into godly men, who in turn become fathers. Whether or not you are having a boy, it's important for your children to have godly male influences in his/her life. Pray for your husband (or in some cases the baby's father) and other men you know who will have impact on the life of your child. Let's ask God to create strong, healthy growth in Him today.

Heavenly Father,
Thank You for the men that will be involved in my baby's life. I pray that You would design each relationship with a purpose and significance. I ask that if there be any unhealthy mentors/ influences in his/her life that You would change them or remove them. My desire is for my little one to be raised up strong in You, know You, and walk in Your ways. Help him/her to grow step by step. I pray that You would put a special bond between my baby and my husband (or the father). Do something in his relationship with You today that will draw him even closer to you. Give him a vision for what our family is to be like and drop in his spirit good things to think, say, pray, and do with our child. Help him to be an example of the mentor in Titus 2:6-8. Make him a man of self-control, integrity, seriousness, and sound speech. Draw us closer to You and closer to each other in order to raise this child in unity. I thank You for giving us a plan and design for families.

Journal Tip: List some of the men that are in your life at this moment (spouse, brothers, uncles, and friends). Consider if all of them are Godly influences or not. What are some of their special strengths or talents that could be taught to your child?

Notes:

_____

_____

_____

_____

_____

_____

_____

_____

SPIRITUAL MOTHERS & DAUGHTERS

"Then they can train the younger women to love their husbands and children, to be self-controlled and pure, to be busy at home, to be kind, and to be subject to their husbands, so that no one will malign the Word of God." Titus 2:4-5

Are you having a daughter? Whether you are or you aren't, at some point in your life you will be a spiritual mother to someone else. Spiritual mentors are vital to our Christian growth. I'm sure you can think of someone in the faith that has had a tremendous impact on your spiritual life. In Titus 2:4-5, Paul is admonishing the older women to instruct the younger women. There are many suggestions in this verse of what to address in these times of mentoring. Let's seek the Lord in this so that we many be good spiritual mothers to spiritual daughters.

Lord,
I thank You for this commission in Titus 2:4-5 that the older women are to teach the younger. I ask that You would use me in this way. Even if I never have a daughter born to me, You can use me to mentor others in the Spirit. I pray that I would have a heart that would instruct purity, kindness, self-control, a submissive spirit, busyness, and a love for You and Your Word. Likewise, as my child grows older, give him/her mentors and friends that would cultivate a strong relationship with You. Bring them forth to water what You have sown within the home and to reap a great spiritual harvest through my child. Open up opportunities for me to minister and likewise, allow my child to be a blessing to others as he/she grows. Thank You, Lord. Amen.

Journal Tip: Who has made a big difference in your life? What kinds of things did you learn from them? Is it important for you child to be trained up by Godly mentors?

Notes:

_____

_____

_____

_____

_____

_____

_____

_____

_____

_____

_____

BABY NAMES

"A good name is more desirable than great riches; to be esteemed is better than silver or gold." Proverbs 22:1

Have you been thinking about baby names? Do you know what the name you are considering means? What you name your child will be a legacy for him/her!   There are many resources on baby names out there that can help you find the meanings of names and give plenty of ideas for names. God told Elizabeth and her husband that their son was to be named "John", who later turned out to be John the Baptist. The angel told Mary that she was to name God's Son (whom she was carrying) "Jesus".   Let's ask the Lord to assist you in your efforts! Your decision will last a lifetime!

Lord,
There are times in Your Word where You declared what a baby would be named. I want to know what name You would have this child to be called! Only You know what this child will become and what destiny You have for them to fulfill in this life. I pray that You would supply a good name for him/her and that it would bring blessing and not rebuke to them all the days of his/her life. I know that You can bring forth Your will for this name we are seeking. Plant it within my heart and mind so that I would clearly know what You are saying. Thank You for this baby, whom You already call by name. Amen.

Journal Tip: What are some names that you are considering? What is the meaning of the name? Why did you choose the name you have for your baby?

Notes:

_____

_____

_____

_____

_____

_____

_____

_____

_____

_____

Week 21

SPEAKING OF WHAT WE KNOW

"I tell you the truth, we speak of what we know, and we testify to what we have seen..."
John 3:11

Women are almost always excited to talk about their babies, pregnancy, and delivery experiences. There will be times in the days ahead when <u>you</u> will be able to minister to those around you concerning pregnancy and motherhood. Someone will ask you one day to let them know what your pregnancy was like. Sometimes, you'll be in a group of women all sitting around and sharing what your pregnancy or birthing experience was like. I believe that God can do miraculous and supernatural things for you while you are pregnant. You have a wonderful opportunity to share God's love and grace to someone else through a common bond of mothering. No matter if birth experiences are similar or vastly different, God can use you to speak of what you know and testify to what you have seen. Perhaps you'll be the only light that someone has ever seen.

Dear God,
I thank You for the testimony that You are forming in me even at this moment. I pray that my entire birth, pregnancy, and motherhood process would bring You glory and allow me to share what You have done in my life with others. Even the challenges of pregnancy can be a testimony because I know You are with me through everything I endure. I ask that You would bring me divine encounters with other women as I grow or others whom I can share the pregnancy journey with. Others have ministered to me and I know it's just a matter of time before I am called upon to share what I have experienced. Put Your praises on my tongue! Help me be a light to all those around me. Thank You, Lord. Amen.

Journal Tip: Have you had anyone share with you that has been uplifting? Have you been able to share your experiences with others yet? If you have, share your encounter. If you haven't, what could you say about your pregnancy experience so far that would bring God glory? Write down a brief testimony.

Notes:

_____

_____

_____

_____

_____

_____

_____

_____

158

QUIVER; CHILDREN ARE A BLESSING

"Children are a reward from Him...like arrows....blessed is the man whose quiver is full of them." Psalm 127:3b-5

A quiver is simply a devise for holding arrows. The word likens the quiver to the family. I've often enjoyed this verse in Psalms when thinking about children. So many times people think of children as a burden. How opposite of the way God thinks! His Word says that they are a reward, not a punishment. You are blessed if your quiver is full of them. So, arrows in your quiver shouldn't make you quiver! No matter how many arrows you will end up with in your quiver, you are blessed indeed!

Lord,
Thank You for my little one. I see him/her as a great blessing to me. Your Word says that children are a reward. I don't know if I am deserving of a reward, but You must think I am. Thank You, God. I pray that You will always keep my children safe within the quiver. You have placed him/her in my hands to care for and that is a big responsibility. When I think of arrows, I think of great skill. Give me the skills I will need to shoot my arrows in the direction that they need to go. Sharpen my skills, O, Lord. Bless this baby within me today. In Your name, amen.

Journal Tip: What kind of fears do you have about raising your child? Do you worry about the skills you may or may not have? Do you see your baby as a blessing?

Notes:

_____

_____

_____

_____

_____

_____

_____

_____

_____

_____

_____

Week 21

RELATIONSHIPS AND YOUR CHILD

"Live in peace with each other." 1 Thessalonians 5:13

Relationships are the most difficult and rewarding bonds of life. People can build us up or tear us down. In families, relationships may be a strained at times, especially if some family members are away from the Lord. God wants us to guard our relationships closely. We should consider what types of friends the Lord would desire for us. We need to be willing to reconcile with others when it's needed or to cut off relationships when they are unhealthy. We must pray that God would be Lord over this area of our lives. Close, personal relationships not only affect you, they affect others around you including your baby. Ask God today what He would seek in your relationships… both yours and baby's.

God,
I pray for my relationships with others and for the relationships that my baby will develop over his/her life. Lord, I ask for him/her to be knit together in love and friendship with those whom You would wish to be in his/her life. I ask for true, loyal, compassionate relationships with others who have a like mind in You. Let those You bring in his/her life be encouraging and up-lifting, building one another up in Your love. I pray You would protect him/her from relationships that are unhealthy, harmful, or that would not glorify You. If anyone comes into their life that shouldn't be there, pluck them out immediately. I pray that the relationships You allow would be fulfilling and bring great joy to my son/daughter. May I find joy in them, too. Bring healing in my life where there may have been damaged relationships or hard feelings toward others. Amen.

Journal Tip: Is there a relationship that God has given you that has been a great joy to you? Have there been any that you have seen that were not good? What do you feel would be the kind of characteristics would you want in a person that would have any relationship with your son or daughter?

Notes:

_____

_____

_____

_____

_____

_____

_____

_____

_____

160

PLAN FOR A FUTURE SPOUSE

"For this reason a man will leave his father and mother and be united to his wife, and they will become one flesh." Genesis 2:24-25

A marital relationship is the one of the most intimate human relationship that we can have. God may choose for your child to remain without a spouse, but it's never too early to begin praying for this important aspect of your child's future. If you are married, there is nothing greater you can give your child than assuring them a stable relationship between you and your spouse. He/she will learn about relationships from you! Let's ask the Lord's will to be done in your marital relationship and the future relationship in the life of your baby.

God,
I place my baby's future in Your hands. If this future involves a spouse for my child, I pray that You would raise up that special someone in his/her life in Your time. I pray that the spouse would come from a Christian home and love You will all of his/her heart, soul, mind, and strength. Let your perfect will be accomplished in his/her life in this area. I pray against any attacks of the enemy that would like to tear down my home. Bind my family close together. Help us to give a loving legacy to our children for long, lasting, committed marriage. Make this household a place that love and affection flow freely. Help us show our children what dating relationships should be like and what to look for in a spouse. I pray for purity to adorn him/her. I come against lust, pornography, and all the wiles and tricks of the enemy that would work to tear down relationships in their lives and cause additions. Grant him/her wisdom to avoid all appearances of evil. Give them patience and endurance as they wait on Your perfect will. In Your name, amen.

Journal Tip: What are some important aspects to teach your children about love and dating? What kinds of things should they look for in a spouse? Write them down and pray over them.

Notes:

_____

_____

_____

_____

_____

_____

_____

_____

_____

IN-LAWS & GRANDPARENTS

**"When Esau was forty years old, he married Judith daughter or Beeri the Hittite, and also Basemath daughter of Elon the Hittite. They were a source of grief to Isaac and Rebekah."
Genesis 26:34-35**

It is often said that when you marry someone, you marry their entire family! These verses in Genesis 26:34-35 often remind me of in-laws and the important relationships with them. It is said that Esau's wives were a cause of <u>grief</u> to Esau's mother and father. What a sad statement! In-laws become grandparents to our children. What kind of grandparents will your child have? God knows what kind of situation you are in today, good or bad. He wants you to be a source of great joy for your extended family! He wants the baby's grandparents to be a blessing and not a curse to you and the baby. Perhaps you fall into a third category where relationships are broken. God wants to mend the hurts and pain that you have suffered.

Dear God,
Thank You for your hand that is upon me today. I thank You that You care about all the people who will be involved in the life of my baby. I pray that as this child's mother, I would be a blessing and a source of light to all in my family and extended family. In turn, I pray that You would give my child favor with his/her grandparents. Give them an open relationship, one that he/she can learn from. Help him/her to grow through the wisdom and knowledge of his/her grandparent's life experiences. Where there might be brokenness or hard feelings, I pray that You would mend and give wisdom. Restore and repair areas that have been shattered. Show me what I can do to help provide the best family environment that I can for my little one. Let your grace and peace cover the family dynamics in my life. I want You to write the story of my life. I don't want my life to be defined by circumstances that may have affected it over time. I pray for a healthy home life. In Your name, amen.

Journal Tip: What kind of family life do you have now? Do you have any concerns about your family? What things are you taking to God? If the circumstances permit, write down the names of your baby's Grandparents, maternal and paternal. Pray for them. Also include and thoughts, comments, or reactions they have had to your pregnancy.

Notes:

_____

_____

_____

_____

_____

_____

Week 21

SUCCESSORS

"No one will be able to stand up against you all the days of your life. As I was with Moses, so I will be with you; I will never leave you nor forsake you. Be strong and courageous, because you will lead these people to inherit the eland I swore to their forefathers to give them. Be strong and very courageous. Be careful to obey all the law my servant Moses gave you; not nor turn from it to the right or to the left, that you may be successful wherever you go. Do not let this Book of the Law depart from your mouth; meditate on it day and night, so that you may be careful to do everything written in it. Then you will be prosperous and successful. Have I not commanded you? Be strong and courageous. Do not be terrified; do not be discouraged, for the Lord your God will be with you wherever you go."
Joshua 1: 5-9

When Moses was taken away, God gave a command to Joshua, the successor of Moses. In a sense, our children will be our successors. We want them go on to accomplish greater things than we have done. We desire for our children to possess the promises that God had given to us and our family. Reading the verses gives us a good sense of God's assuredness that He is always with us, even in subsequent generations.

Dear God,
Thank You for commanding us to go forward with strength and courage. I ask that You would bless my children and my children's children. I pray that You would encourage my child to go forth in the spiritual heritage that he/she grew up in. May he/she go forth to do greater exploits than I have accomplished. May You give them increase in all areas of life and fulfill the promises that You have given to me concerning them. Bring them success and prosperity in Your eyes. Help him/her know that You will be with them wherever he/she goes!

Journal Tip: What kind of blessing would you pass down to your children? What are the promises of God that will pass down to your children?

Notes:

_____

_____

_____

_____

_____

_____

_____

_____

_____

Week 21

BLESSED TO BE A BLESSING

"You still the hunger of those You cherish; their sons have plenty, and they store up wealth for their children." Psalm 17:14b

Blessings from the Lord allow you to bless others. It works like a cycle. When God gives to you, you have the <u>ability</u> to bless others. Of course, it is your choice if you will bless others or not. The best area I can relate this to is our children. When God gives to us, we in turn can give to our children. We have all heard the verse that says, "... (You) know how to give good gifts to your children, how much more will your Father in Heaven give (the Holy Spirit to) those who ask him!" We have an innate nature that compels us to give to our children. How much more the Heavenly Father wants to give to us! Why? Because we are His children and that's just what parents do!

Dear Lord,
Thank You for Your blessings today that You give so freely and often unwarranted. Today I am praying that the blessings of God would pour out on me and my family. When You bless me, You give abundance so that I may give my children. I desire abundance in all areas of life and freedom from bondages that may be keeping me from God's best. I pray that I would flourish financially, spiritually, emotionally, physically, and relationally. Help me to walk in obedience in regard to Your blessings. Show me where to store up, where to give, and to what extent. I pray that my family and I will walk in accordance to Your will that You would prosper us even as our souls prosper! Thank You, Lord. Amen.

Journal Tip: Can you count some of your blessings today? What blessings will you be able to give to your children because of what God has already accomplished in your life?

Notes:

_____

_____

_____

_____

_____

_____

_____

_____

_____

_____

STRENGTHEN YOUR SPIRIT

"A man's spirit sustains him in sickness, but a crushed spirit who can bear?"
Proverbs 18:14

In times like pregnancy when we deal with a prolonged physical change to our bodies, we rely on the Spirit of God and what He has done in our spirit to sustain us. Daily prayer and reading of the Word are vital to strengthening your spirit and will revitalize you for the road ahead. No, this doesn't mean that we won't face challenges during pregnancy. Your morning sickness, fatigue, expanding waistline, or headaches may or may not disappear because you are praying. It does, however, mean that God will be with us and strengthening us through all. His Word tells us that He will never give us more than we can bear. He is concerned with every facet of your pregnancy, whether or not He answers in the way you want Him to. He <u>will</u> sustain you throughout your pregnancy.

If for whatever reason you are operating with a crushed spirit today, let God heal your spirit and restore you unto wholeness. It may be that a friend, parent, spouse, or acquaintance has wronged you or spoken a cruel word to you. Maybe you are overwhelmed. Let God's mighty hand touch you today.

Heavenly Father,
Thank You for knowing what I have need of even before I express it. I thank You for sustaining me during my pregnancy and teaching along the journey. Let Your mighty hand touch me today and strengthen my spirit. I ask that if I am weak in any area that You would bring it into restoration. Help me to grow in my time with You, my Bible reading, and prayer time. As my spiritual foundation becomes stronger and stronger, I know that I will be able to face any obstacle that might come my way without wavering. I know that You have been with me during my gestation so far and that You will continue to uphold me.
You are my Rock and my Shield. Touch this baby inside me today. Let him/her sense Your presence and Your spirit as he/she grows within my womb. Thank You, Lord. Amen.

Journal Tip: How does today's verse apply to you? Can you tell that as you grow in Christ, He is able to sustain you even in your physical body? Have you been operating with a crushed spirit?

Notes:

_____

_____

_____

_____

_____

_____

_____

BUILDING UP A SPIRITUAL FOUNDATION

**"The wise woman builds her house, but with her own hands the foolish one
tears hers down." Proverbs 14:1**

Have you ever seen a building being imploded? That's where a demolition crew uses an explosive (like dynamite) to blow a building up. Demolition normally takes a few seconds when the explosive is detonated. It's amazing that such huge structures that took such a long time to build could come down so quickly. Such is life. We take so much time building up emotions, careers, relationships, projects, houses... and in minutes they can all come crumbling down! This verse in Proverbs admonishes us to be wise and build up our house. In this case we are talking about our children. It's hard to think that destruction can come so easily to our children, but it is a fact that needs to be within our grasp of understanding. Things that take years to build up such as trust, faithfulness, security, self esteem, or loyalty can quickly be dashed to the ground. The devil comes to steal, kill, and destroy, but God comes to give life and abundance! We need to be wise and prudent in building up our children.

Lord,
Brick upon brick, line upon line, You write Your precepts on our hearts. I thank You that You are the master builder who crafts us so articulately and with such skill. I also understand that the enemy of our souls would prowl around like a roaring lion seeking whom he may devour! I am asking today that You would help me to be wise in the parenting of my child. Help me to build up and encourage and not to tear down. The enemy would like to use many "tearing down" tactics on my child. Anger, lack of self control, doubt, bitterness... these are all schemes of the enemy. I pray that You would keep us from evil. Keep my child from evil in the days ahead. Build this baby up on solid foundation so when the storms of life come, he/she will have a shelter where he/she can run to. You are the cornerstone that I want in this baby's life. Even now, begin building a life of strength in this baby. Help me to nurture and protect this baby at all times. Amen.

Journal Tip: What kinds of things will build a strong spiritual foundation for your baby? Do you struggle in any area that might threaten the building up of your child? Ask God to help you in those areas.

Notes:

_____

_____

_____

_____

_____

_____

_____

166

IN THE FAMILY OF GOD

"I will receive you, I will be a Father to you, and you shall be My sons and daughters, says the Lord Almighty." 2 Corinthians 6:17-18

The family of God is a wonderful habitation! If we have accepted Christ as our Savior, we are part of His family. His Word tells us that God will be a Father to us and we shall be His sons and daughters. You are a daughter of the Lord's and your child is a son/daughter to the Lord. The thought almost boggles our minds. We are all <u>His</u> children. Being a child comes with its privileges as well. We can ask our heavenly Father anything we have need of. We can tell Him our problems. He is our protector and defender. He IS everything a Father should be... AND so much MORE!

Dear Lord,
Thank You for calling me Your daughter. I sit in awe at the thought that I have a Father in heaven who surpasses all of my expectations of what a Father should be. I praise You today and thank You that You didn't create us in a subservient way but as "family". We are heirs of Your righteousness and partakers of all that You have made and ordained. I pray that my son/daughter would be called Your child as well and come to know You at an early age. Help him/her to grow in the knowledge that he/she is part of the Your family. Your Word says that the Spirit Himself bears witness with our spirit that we are the children of God (Romans 8:15-16). Thank You for Your family, Lord. Amen.

Journal Tip: Why is it important to be called a child of God? What does that mean to you? What kind of heritage does that give you?

Notes:

_____

_____

_____

_____

_____

_____

_____

_____

_____

_____

_____

ANIMALS IN THE HOME

"Now the Lord God had formed all the beasts of the field and all the birds of the air. He brought them to the man to see what he would name them; and whatever the man called each living creature, that was it's name." Genesis 2:19

Pets can be a wonderful addition to any family. Many couples who do not have children have learned some of their nurturing values by having pets. The animal's dependency to be fed, kept clean, and safe cultivates a wonderful sense of responsibility and care on the part of the owner. If you already have indoor pets, such as cats or dogs, you may wish to begin thinking about how you could introduce your new little one to the family. Some animals are very territorial, so if you have an aggressive breed of dog, you may wish to seek outside guidance from your vet. In any regard, a veterinarian's advice on introducing your pet to your new baby could prove helpful. Also asking the vet about harmful effects of certain pets on pregnancy would be appropriate, too. For example, some types of pets (such as reptiles) could potentially be harmful to your children. Pets can be a great learning experience for both parents and children. God created animals for many reasons. One benefit is our enjoyment.

Heavenly Father,
I thank You for the creation of animals and their place in our world. I pray that You would guide and direct my family in regard to pets. Please show me how to welcome my pet to my new baby and to make wise decisions regarding my animals. If we get a pet during the childhood of my son/daughter, I pray that You would use that experience as a valuable teaching tool. Help him/her to cultivate an appreciation for all of the things that You have created and to treat animals with a heart of mercy and kindness. I pray that even if we don't have any pets that you would not allow my child to be afraid of dogs or cats or any other domestic animal. Help him/her to have positive experiences with animals. Keep our family from the harmful effects of allergies to animals or their dander. If there needs to be medical assistance for allergies, send us to the proper people so we can manage those effects. In Your name, amen.

Journal Tip: Do you have or ever had pets? What did they teach you? Do you have fond memories about pets? Do you have pet allergies? Do you plan on having pets after the birth of your child?

Notes:

_____

_____

_____

_____

_____

_____

168

YOUR HOUSE WILL CHANGE

"'The glory of this present house will be greater than the glory of the former house', says the Lord Almighty, 'And in this place I will grant peace', declares the Lord Almighty."
Haggai 2:9

Have you ever heard the saying, "Having a baby changes everything"? It is true, but perhaps not as "negatively" as some might paint it. Flashes from television come to mind with half clothed babies needing diaper changes or others being disobedient and refusing to listen! That isn't it at all. Having a baby isn't about what you give up: finances, sleep, time, energy, or your sanity... it's about what you <u>gain</u>! No, you will never be the same after having a baby. Your body is never the same, your relationships are never the same, and your life is never the same. What joy! You will have the privilege of raising a son or daughter. You'll have moments of laughter, tears, memories for a lifetime, and love unending. Praise the Lord today that the present family you are creating will be greater than what you were experiencing before.

Dear Lord,
I thank You for this promise that this present house will be greater than the former. You have given me such a precious gift. My heart leaps with the expectation of this being fulfilled in my life. You knew exactly what You were doing when You gave me this baby. I pray that You would continually show me the joys of parenting, even in the times when it may not be pleasant. Help me to offer this child a parent and a home that is greater than the former because of You bringing him/her into my life. Let this child grow to appreciate the home environment that You have orchestrated. According to Haggai 2:9, You will grant peace in our home. Thank You, Lord! Amen.

Journal Tip: What was your life like before you were expecting? What do you think life will be like after you have the baby? List some things you are looking forward to in parenting.

Notes:

_____

_____

_____

_____

_____

_____

_____

_____

_____

Week 22

SLEEP

"I will lie down and sleep in peace, for You alone, O LORD, make me dwell in safety."
Psalm 4:8

As your pregnancy progresses, it may become harder and harder to get a good night's rest. The baby's position and increasing weight keep you from being comfortable. Likewise, when baby is born, most every parent worries about SIDS. Let's just ask the Lord to watch over the times of sleep; for you and your baby.

God,
I pray that You would bless me with a deep, restful sleep from this time forward in my pregnancy. No matter what is going on in my life or in the world around me, I pray that when I lie my head down on the pillow that I would do so in perfect peace. I pray for deep and rejuvenating sleep. Give me the rest and relaxation that I need for myself and baby. If I have to get up in the night for any reason, help me to return to sleep quickly and not interrupt the sleep cycle. Help me find ways that would allow me to have a better night's rest (a shower before bed, a body pillow, no liquids after 8pm, etc).
When baby comes, I pray that there would be no complications with his/her resting patterns, nap times, or sleep cycle. I bind the enemy from putting fear into my heart concerning SIDS or any other complication. I know nothing will happen to my baby that isn't under Your control, Lord. I pray that my baby will quickly settle into a sleep pattern that I can identify and keep consistent with. I pray that the crib, playpen, swing, car seat, or anywhere my baby sleeps would be a safe, comfortable, and secure place for my baby. Help me to recognize when my baby is tired and needs to rest, even as the sleep cycles change as he/she grows. May he/she get the rest that he/she needs every day. Protect us while we rest, Lord, and allow Your mighty angels to watch over us. Amen.

Journal Tip: How are you sleeping? Is there anything that helps you sleep better at night or during naps? Have you planned for where baby will sleep after delivery? Do you have bedding picked out?

Notes:

_____

_____

_____

_____

_____

_____

_____

_____

Week 22

WHEN YOU NEED HELP OR ASSISTANCE

"When Moses' hands grew tired, they took a stone and put it under him and he sat on it. Aaron and Hur held his hands up- one on one side, one on the other- so that his hands remained steady till sunset." Exodus 17:12

You cannot go through pregnancy alone. You may think you can, but sooner or later you are going to face the reality that you need the assistance of others to complete your journey. The verses in Exodus 17 talk about the time when the Israelites were battling the Amalekites. While Moses' hands were raised, the Israelites were winning, but when his hands began to lower, they would begin to be defeated. Noticing this fact, Aaron and Hur came alongside Moses and lifted up his hands and ultimately the victory belonged to the Israelites. This truth becomes vibrant when dealing with intercession and praying for others. Sometimes we need others to come alongside of us and give us the strength to finish the battle. God has or will bring people into your life during this time of pregnancy. Don't be afraid to let others lift you up; in a spiritual sense, or for emotional or physical assistance.

Dear God,
Thank You for bringing people in my life to help me during this pregnancy. Bring those alongside me who need to help me to stand. Remove those from my life who might be toxic or unhealthy to me. I ask that I will be accepting of the help of others when I need it and the ability to say "no" truthfully and kindly when I do not. Knit me together with those whom my spirit bears witness to. Raise up prayer warriors and intercessors that would bring me and my child before You in prayer on a regular basis. I thank You for the ministry that others provide. Help me to be gracious and grateful. Amen.

Journal Tip: List some names of the people that have been helping you during your pregnancy.

Notes:

_____

_____

_____

_____

_____

_____

_____

_____

_____

_____

ENTERTAINMENT

"Have nothing to do with the fruitless deeds of darkness, but rather expose them. For it is shameful even to mention what the disobedient do in secret. But everything exposed by the light becomes visible." Ephesians 5:11-13

Have you considered what forms of entertainment you are going to choose for you children? It's important to give this some thought before the baby comes. You can't undo what you might expose them to once the damage has been done. There are three questions you can ask yourself when choosing entertainment for yourself or you family 1.) Would God approve? 2.) What kinds of values is it teaching? 3.) Does it go against anything in God's Word? If any of your answers make you question whether you should be engaged in certain kind of entertainment, then err on the side of caution. It's much easier to loosen the reigns than it is to stop a run away horse! Consider what you are feeding into your mind today through entertainment. You'll be glad you thought of it now rather than after the baby comes.

Dear God,
I thank You that You are ever near me giving me guidance and discernment at all times. Guide me in all truth and wisdom when it comes to entertainment. I pray that You would fashion in my mind the criteria that entertainment should meet before allowing it in my home. I come against the enemy who would like to use this as a target of attack in my family. Help me to keep diligent watch over the television broadcasts, books, magazines, music, games, DVD's, videos, and other forms of entertainment that would enter my home. I ask that You would give me discernment to deal with potential hazards when they arise and to not be passive about what is going into the mind and heart of my little one. Help me to guard my own actions as well, as to set a good example before my child. In Your name, amen.

Journal Tip: What are some good forms of entertainments that you will encourage your child to engage in?

Notes:

_____

_____

_____

_____

_____

_____

_____

_____

Week 23

EXAMPLES FOR YOUR CHILD

"...but set an example for the believers in speech, in life, in love, in faith, and in purity."
1 Timothy 4:12b

Have you ever thought about what kind of example you are going to be to your child? The old cliché, "Do what I say, not what I do.", will not work for your child! Your life is the primary teaching example for your son/daughter. What you think and feel on the inside comes out in your actions. Don't live a double standard. It's time to begin thinking about your actions and see if they are lining up with the Word of God. Examine yourself today. There are probably many areas of your life which are glowing examples to your child, but what about those areas which are not? Consider your example today.

Dear God,
Thank You that Your Word shows us the way and that You never stop instructing us in life, no matter how old we become. Teach me Your ways today so that I may become a glowing example of You. My life will be a reflection of You and the first impression of Christ that my child will receive. I ask that You direct me in Your paths. Let Your will be done not only in thought, but in my words and deeds also. In the times where I feel like I may have failed, I pray that I would come to a quick repentance. Let healing and life building words flow in those times. As Your Word says, I declare that I will be a positive example for my child in speech, in life, in love, in faith, and in purity. May these examples that I exhibit bring glory to You. In Your name, amen.

Journal Tip: Using the verse from today, begin making a short list of godly examples that you want to show forth in your life. Then make a short list of areas in your life that you need to work on. You know yourself better than anyone else, so be honest. Allow God to work in those areas and make them a matter of prayer.

Notes:

_____

_____

_____

_____

_____

_____

_____

_____

_____

Week 23

MONEY LESSONS

"Keep your lives free from the love of money and be content with what you have, because God has said, "Never will I leave you, never will I forsake you." Hebrews 13:5

It's very easy to get caught up in wealth and materialism. Teaching your children the value of money, tithing, and giving is an important task. Train them up at an early age to save and show them how to spend. Take the time to teach them about credit, borrowing, and how to balance a checkbook. Teach him/her that our worth is not measured in dollars and cents. We need to have a healthy view of money and its purpose. Our money habits say a lot about our character and who we are. God calls us to be good stewards of our money. Equipping your child through proper teaching about money will benefit them the rest of their lives.

Dear God,
I acknowledge that all money comes from You. You are the one who gives us the ability to earn and we are responsible to You for our finances. I ask that You would bless this household with abundance in this area so that we are never short. You give and bless how You see fit. Help us to be faithfully consistent in our giving of tithes and offerings. I pray that there would never be any grumbling in this household about what You have given us. Your Word says that we are to be content with what we have. I pray for contentment to arise within me and within the life of my child as he/she is growing up. I ask that You would help me reason out a godly view about money so that I can pass it on to my child. I pray that he/she would be generous at all times and never stingy or hoarding. Show me how to pass on good advice about money to my child. I pray that he/she would always look to You for provision and not his/her own efforts or accomplishments. In Your name, amen.

Journal Tip: Write down some of your views about money. What kinds of things are you planning on teaching your child about money?

Notes:

_____

_____

_____

_____

_____

_____

_____

_____

_____

DISCIPLINE

"Moreover, we have all had human fathers... no discipline seems pleasant at the time, but painful..." Hebrews 12:9-11a

Discipline may seem like an ugly word in today's world. Discipline is simply correction in a loving manner, when applied as God intended. As a child of God, you may have experienced the correction of the Lord in your life. It doesn't seem pleasant at the time, does it? As a parent, you will need to correct your children on occasion as he/she learns and grows. Without perimeters in life, you are not providing the necessary guidelines that a child needs to develop properly. Little children are not able to reason or think through what consequences might come from their actions. Discipline does **not**, however, give a parent freedom to abuse! That is not consistent with God's Word at all. You should strive to approach discipline in a constructive manner and not a negative one. God can help you in this area.

Heavenly Father,
I pray for guidance when it comes to discipline. I pray that You would lead me in ways to correct my precious little one in a manner that would please You. I want to act in a loving way toward my son/daughter at all times. I bind any forms of physical or verbal abuse from my children, not only from me, but from all forms of authority in his/her life. May the discipline he/she receives be used for growth and not his/her detriment. I pray for healthy ways to correct my child in order for him/her to learn and grow. Correction can also be for our safety. I pray that he/she will heed correction and not rebel against it. I pray for the boldness to be firm in leading my children. I pray for consistency in discipline. Let me not waiver in my opinions and send confusing messages to my child. I ask for Your will to be accomplished in this area so that my child will become the person You intended him/her to be. Strengthen him/her in character. In Your name, amen.

Journal Tip: Have you thought about this aspect of parenting? Seek God about what kinds of discipline you should consider during the raising of your child. What is acceptable to you and what isn't? How would you want to be disciplined by you if you were the child?

Notes:

_____

_____

_____

_____

_____

_____

_____

Week 23

FAVOR FOR YOUR CHILD

"the Lord was with him; He showed him kindness and granted him favor..."
Genesis 39:21a

The story of Joseph in the Bible is highly interesting. Here we find a boy, favored of his father, whom the Lord spoke to in dreams at a very young age. His brothers became jealous and sold him into captivity, where Joseph was later imprisoned. There Joseph grew older and eventually found favor with Pharaoh and became overseer of all Egypt. What a supernatural turn of events! What stands out significantly in this story is the fact that God had a plan and purpose for Joseph and continually showed him <u>favor</u>. Sometimes our circumstances may seem the same as the plight of Joseph. The situation may seem dim or bleak, but in due time, God will exalt His children to a place of honor. May God show you and your child favor this day.

Heavenly Father,
I pray that Your favor would rest on me and my baby today. May his/her life be one that You continually bless. No matter what unforeseen circumstances he/she (or I) may face, continually be present; working everything out for Your good and purposes. We may not understand the reasons behind everything, but Lord, help us to put our trust in You. In due time, You will exalt him/her (me) to a place of honor. I ask that Your hand of protection continually be upon him/her (me). May his/her (my) life be used by You like Joseph was used; to minister to many people, including those of his/her own family. Thank You, Lord, for Your favor. Amen.

Journal Tip: What does God's favor resting on you and your baby mean? What kinds of things would His favor involve?

Notes:

_____

_____

_____

_____

_____

_____

_____

_____

_____

_____

_____

HE KNOWS ALL OF YOUR DAYS

"This is the day that the Lord has made; let us rejoice and be glad in it."
Psalm 118:24

This IS the day that the Lord has made. He knows all of your days and those of your baby.
He knew what this day would hold for you and what it would be like. Has your day been good,
bad, or so-so? When we start thinking that each day has been made by the Lord then we can
recognize that whatever it holds is in His authority and control! That's why the psalmist wrote...
let us rejoice and be glad in it. No matter what happens... this is the day that the Lord has
MADE!

Father,
Thank You for all the days You have given the baby and me and that they are under Your
authority and control. Help me to rejoice in knowing that nothing can happen, harm, or hurt us
that isn't in Your daily design. Likewise, any joy, peace, or praise that You have chosen for this
day has already been ordered. I acknowledge this day is from You and ask that it will unfold just
as You want it to. Let Your plans come forth unhindered Let this baby experience the day You
have made for him/her. I praise You for Your goodness in all things. Amen.

Journal Tip: What has your day been like today? What has been good about today?

Notes:

_____

_____

_____

_____

_____

_____

_____

_____

_____

_____

_____

_____

Week 23

FIND QUIET TIME WHEN STRESSED

"But I have stilled and quieted my soul; like a weaned child with its mother; like a weaned a child is my soul within me." Psalm 131:2

You might feel a bit over stressed from the demands of life combined with pregnancy. Quiet time is so important for you and your unborn baby. Any opportunity you have to relax and take a load off of your feet and mind should be savored. Letting your mind and spirit rest may be a key to your rejuvenation during this time. Learning to rest in Him and making an effort to quiet your soul will do you and your baby much good.

God,
Thank You for the understanding that I will need much rest and quiet while I am expecting. I pray that You would open up frequent opportunities for me to rest and to ease my mind. I know that this is Your desire for me that I rest in You. That's something that I want to learn and continue in as a discipline even after pregnancy. I pray that as I am quiet that my little one will rest as well. Less stress on me means a better growing environment for my precious child. Thank You for the desire to quiet myself. Amen.

Journal Tip: What are some of the ways you have found to relax during pregnancy? Is there a favorite quiet time that you can remember? What does the baby seem to do when you relax?

Notes:

_____

_____

_____

_____

_____

_____

_____

_____

_____

_____

_____

_____

_____

GOD WORKS EVERYTHING TOGETHER FOR GOOD

"And we know that in all things God works for the good of those who love him, who have been called according to his purpose." Romans 8:28

Sometimes bad things happen to God's people. Our minds can't always understand why God has allowed certain things to occur in our lives, but there is one thing for certain. He has said that in all things, God will work for the good of those that love him. I think back on some of the most trying times in my life and realize that I grew so much in the Lord during those times. Everything you have gone through in life so far has made you who you are today! The trying of our faith really makes us aware of what we are made of. Whatever you are facing today, don't forget that God is still working in your midst to bring about good. The baby you are carrying is going to be such a blessing to you, the nations, and to the Lord!

Dear Lord,
I thank You for always being in my midst, working in things for my good. I ask that in the areas where I am struggling today, I would realize that You have a greater picture in my mind. In the times where I would like to give up, remind me that it is worth it. No matter how much pain, discomfort, or doubt that I may go through, You are going to see me through. I place myself and my child in Your hands today and ask that You would supply all that we have need of, physically, spiritually, or emotionally. Help me learn this truth so that I can teach it effectively to my child. No matter what things look like, Your plan and purposes for us are; to prosper, for a future, and for hope. Thank You, Lord. Amen.

Journal Tip: Has your pregnancy been difficult or easy so far? Do you find this verse to be helpful in understanding that all you are going through is worth it?

Notes:

_____

_____

_____

_____

_____

_____

_____

_____

_____

_____

Week 24

MOVING DURING PREGNANCY

"He led them by a straight way to a city where they could settle." Psalm 107:7

Are you planning a move during your pregnancy? If you are moving from house to house within the same city, moving to a different state, or relocating to a foreign country for missions work, God will be with you wherever you go. If you aren't moving, there are still changes to your household that are probably taking place. You might be preparing a baby's room or having to adjust the setup of your home to accommodate your baby. Let's ask the Lord to oversee during this time.

Dear God,
Thank Your for Your provision and overseeing me at all times. I pray over my household that all things might run smoothly. If I am to move during my pregnancy, I pray that You would lead me on a straight path to the place that I am to be. Help me during this time, even if it simply means moving things around in my current home. Provide the resources and help that I need. I pray for strength and endurance during this time. Protect me and my baby from physical injury. Keep us safe from all harm and dangers. Place people within our paths to make this transition time easier. If You plant us in a new place, help us to connect immediately with people. Position my family right where You would have us to go. Give direction, discernment and wisdom for the days ahead. In Your name, amen.

Journal Tip: Are you moving during pregnancy? If so, write down a brief summary of where you are going and why you are going there. If you are not moving, what things are you doing to the place you live in order to prepare for baby?

Notes:

_____

_____

_____

_____

_____

_____

_____

_____

_____

_____

VOCATION CHOSEN

"Do you see a man skilled in his work?" Proverbs 22:29a

God sees the vocation that your child will have later on in life. As you consider the future job of your son/daughter, it comes to mind that we would desire our children to be successful in whatever God has called them to do. In the same respect, children of all ages have "work" to do. School, chores, and other tasks that are part of day to day living require focus, dedication, and diligence! Let's pray that God will go before your child when it comes time for him/her to enter into work.

Lord,
I pray that my son/daughter will excel in whatever work their hand finds to do and that he/she would do it with all his/her might. I pray that good habits would develop early in life that would set the standard for a strong work ethic later on. May whatever they do, tasks big or small, be done in a manner that would bring You glory. I pray that they would be found faithful to accomplish goals and jobs that would bring larger blessings later on. I desire that Your perfect will be accomplished in my child's future vocations. May he/she learn to seek You for direction before taking any job he/she might be considering. I pray that he/she would be paid well for the job that he/she does. All things are from You, Lord, including the strength to work and the opportunities that we are given. May my child find some way to minister through the job he/she will have. In Your name, amen.

Journal Tip: What are some of the tasks, chores, or vocations that you feel helped shape you into the person you are today? What did those opportunities teach you? Has God ever answered prayer in your life or in the life of someone close to you concerning a job?

Notes:

_____

_____

_____

_____

_____

_____

_____

_____

_____

_____

Week 24

HEAVEN

"And if I go and prepare a place for you, I will come back and take you to be with me that you also may be where I am. You know the way to the place that I am going."
John 14:3

When I think of all the different things that a person could teach children about the Bible, one of the most fascinating is the concept of heaven. Kids love to hear about heaven! When you teach your child that there is a heaven to gain and a hell to shun, you are teaching them the essence of salvation. What are we saved from essentially? We are saved from our sin. Where do all who are in sin spend eternity? Hell and eventually the Lake of Fire after the final judgment (neither of which sound very appealing). Children are fascinated with heaven and want to talk about it often. What are your thoughts about heaven? Who is in heaven and how do you get there? Why would you want to go there? Another important lesson heaven teaches us is the reality that there is a spiritual life existing that a person can't see with the human eye! This also teaches children about death and what happens to us after we die... a reality we all have to face at some point, either with loved ones, pets, etc.

Jesus tells us in this passage that heaven is a place he is preparing for us. He said we know how to get there (through salvation). One day, He will come back to take us there so that we can be with Him for eternity. We all have a beginning to life, which is our conception and birth, but we are spiritually beings that will have no end. Even death is not the end. Our spirits continue on. What a significant role you have played in bringing a life into the world... someone who will continue on forever. Teach your child about heaven.

Dear God,
Thank You for preparing a place for us. I am in awe at the thought of heaven and all that it means. Even if I do not understand it all, help me to teach this concept to my child, even at a young age. Give me the understanding I need and the creativity required to convey such a teaching. I ask that the reality of heaven would weigh on my thoughts as I go about my day. There is a heaven existing right now that I cannot see, but believe is there. Build faith in me and in my family so that we can believe in You, Your Word, and Your promises unwavering. Help my child to understand these faith concepts easily and protect his/her mind from the enemy who would like to come in and sow doubt. I thank You for the hope of heaven and the gift of eternal life. Amen.

Journal Tip: What do you know about heaven? What does it look like? Who is there? How do we get there? Why should your child know about heaven?

Notes:

_____

_____

_____

_____

182

Week 24

HEAVEN TO GAIN

"Then I saw a new heaven and a new earth, for the first heaven and the first earth had passed away, and there was no longer any sea." Revelation 21:1

Our goal in life is not this present body or earth that we live in. Heaven is not the consolation prize. Heaven IS the prize! Too many people get caught up in our lives here on earth and forget that there is life beyond this world. This life is preparation for the next. God has made us with the power of choice. We decide whether or not we will believe in Him or reject him. There are only two choices. Choosing to accept the Lord is the most important decision that your child will ever make. It's getting harder and harder to instill Christian values into our children in this modern day world. There are many coming in to uproot what you have planted in your child calling it "not thinking outside the box" or referring to Christian beliefs as "discriminating" or "non-tolerant". The Bible is very clear on how we are to live life and conduct ourselves. Don't be drawn away from the truth out of fear of persecution or pressure to conform to a secular society. There is a heaven to gain!

Dear God,
I thank You that You have already gone to prepare a place for me. I believe that You are coming again to take us to heaven. I pray for a boldness and steadfastness to rise up within me as a parent. I want to be determined and fixed to raise my child in the fear and admonition of the Lord. I come against fear that would keep me from presenting the entire gospel to my child. No matter what the secular system says, I want to stand firm in You. Help me to have a sure footing, to raise my child to understand Your Word, Your Will, and Your Ways. I ask that he/she would receive You at a young age. Open his/her heart for instruction. I come against the attacks of the enemy and ways that he will try to come in and undermine Your truth. I pray that all deception would be rejected by my son/daughter. May he/she develop a clear understanding of the truth so that he/she will not be moved when opposition comes. In Your name, amen.

Journal Tip: Why do you feel it's important to teach your son/daughter about heaven and hell? What are your thoughts about the times we are living in right now?

Notes:

_____

_____

_____

_____

_____

_____

_____

NATURE AND CREATION

"In the beginning God created the heavens and the earth." Genesis 1:1

What will you teach your child when it comes to creation? God the creator has made all things in this world. A reading of Genesis 1 will give you the list of all that was made. How did He fashion something out of nothing? If there is as design, there must be a designer. How will you explain this to your child, especially in light of the fact that the world is trying to slowly remove God and His influence from everything. Secondly, take time to enjoy nature with your child. Go outside and enjoy the beauty all around. Nature itself testifies that there is a Creator. Going to the ocean, seeing a mountain for the first time, watching birds migrate for the winter, watching apple trees bear fruit year after year, planting a seed and watching it grow, taking a walk in the woods, observing wildlife, climbing rocks on a river bed, or simply watching the stars at night can be God-affirming events in the life of your child.

Dear God,
Remind me to take time out of my busy schedule just to reflect on You. Help me to get away from all the hustle and bustle of my daily routine and do something that will feed my spirit today. I thank You for Your creation and the wonder and majesty of it all. From the misty mornings of the Mountain Regions to the beautiful sunsets over the Pacific, the towering trees of Yellowstone and other National Parks, the mighty rushing rivers of the Mississippi, the Great Plains rolling with crop, the distinct seasons of the Northeast, the sun kissed South, or the deserts of the West, You have created all. I can walk outside today and notice Your beauty all around me. Help me to develop a appreciation of Your creation and to pass that on to my child. I pray that I will instruct him/her to respect Your world and to care for it. Show me ways that I can teach esthetics in a godly way. I come against any physical conditions (allergies, lupus, etc.) that might inhibit him/her from being able to enjoy being outside. In Your name, amen.

Journal Tip: Do you enjoy nature and being outside? If you don't enjoy the outdoors now, did you as a kid? What did you enjoy? What kinds of things would you like your child to enjoy when it comes to Creation?

Notes:

_____

_____

_____

_____

_____

_____

_____

_____

Week 24

BEAUTY AND GOD'S VIEW OF US

"Man looks at the outward appearance, but God looks at the heart"
1 Samuel 16:7b

I don't know any mother who has ever gazed upon her child without declaring that he/she is beautiful. What does the Word say about true beauty? It doesn't matter how beautiful the outside of a person looks if they are not pleasing to the Lord on the inside. God knows our thoughts, the very desires of our hearts and that is what He looks upon, not our earthen vessels. As your body begins to change with pregnancy, you may start to question the beauty of what is happening. Don't fall into the trap of vain or worldly thinking. What is going on in your body is a true marvel of the Lord! You are beautiful in the Lord's eyes. In the same regard, it will be important to teach your son/daughter the simplicity of being beautiful in God's eyes. Who they are in character, morals, and righteous living is more important than what the outside conveys.

Dear Lord,
I thank You for the marvel that is happening within me. Let me see myself through Your eyes. Let me at no time regard myself with a harsh eye in relation to my weight or how others might view my physical appearance.
In the same manner, I pray that I will effectively teach my child that it's the purity of the heart that matters and not the outward appearance. At no time will they fall into the trap of vain thinking or over emphasis of the outward appearance. Don't let their confidence be in the way they look, but let him/her find confidence in You. I pray that he or she would also learn the truth to look at others the way You do. Help them appreciate others for how You have made them. Help my little one to keep a clean heart before You so that he/she will always be beautiful in your eyes. Amen.

Journal Tip: How has your appearance changed as your pregnancy progressed? Write down some personal thoughts on what makes someone beautiful.

Notes:

_____

_____

_____

_____

_____

_____

_____

Week 24

BED PRAISE

"Let the saints rejoice in this honor and sing for joy on their beds."
Psalms 149:5

Rejoice in the honor that you are carrying a special little someone today. No doubt when you are expecting, you will be spending a considerable amount of time resting in bed. Sometimes moms are even confined to bed for a time near the end of pregnancy. Let nothing that happens during your pregnancy alarm you. If you believe that God has a plan for you, one to prosper you and to bring you a sure future and a hope, then you have nothing to fear. You can rejoice in whatever situation you are in...even praising him upon your bed! Perhaps God will use that as an opportunity to learn more about Him, His character, and His ways. Your bed may become a cherished place where you can quietly reflect on God's goodness and where you can openly communicate with Him.

Dear God,
Even when I rest upon my bed, my heart wants to rejoice and sing of your goodness. I thank You for speaking to me at times when I am at rest. Let my bed be a place of sanctuary from the world and a place where I can meet You in praise and prayer. I pray that You would give me godly thoughts, songs, and dreams in the night that will encourage me. I will sing for joy on my bed because of all You have done and are doing within me. I pray that I will get sufficient rest so that this little one within me can have the best environment that he/she can possibly have. Nourish him/her today with rest as well. Make me aware of his/her sleep patterns even before birth. I ask that You would always provide a comfortable place for us to sleep each night and that we would get enough rest to feel refreshed each morning. Thank You, Lord. Amen.

Journal Tip: Describe your times of rest during the day or evening. Has God shown you anything during those times of repose? Are you sleeping well?

Notes:

_____

_____

_____

_____

_____

_____

_____

_____

_____

Week 25

WEIGHT GAIN

"For He satisfies the thirsty and fills the hungry with good things." Psalms 107:9

As you reach your final trimester, it is not uncommon to become very, very hungry. The nutritional demands on your body and the increasing growth of the baby are requiring more fuel. Try to not fill up on things with empty calories. Make plans for successful snacking. Stock your cupboards with healthy snacks that can be accessed quickly instead of junk food. Remember that everything you put in your mouth is also feeding your little one. Be sure to also drink plenty of fluids. Dehydration can lead to contractions. Drinking enough water will also prevent some headaches from occurring. Don't watch the scale too much, either. Remind yourself that you are pregnant and weight gain is normal and expected. You can plan on gaining at least 25-35 pounds or more during pregnancy. The more you put on, however, the more you'll have to take off in the end.

Lord,
Thank You for nourishing me and my little one this day. I pray that You would curb any unhealthy eating cravings. Show me what to eat and drink that would benefit us. I ask that You would be in control of my weight and my thoughts about the weight that I am gaining. Set my mind on delivering a healthy baby and not only my weight or my changing physique. I pray that I would gain a healthy amount of weight and that my baby would be a normal weight at birth, not underweight or malnourished. Thank You for satisfying me today with good things. In Your name, amen.

Journal Tip: How much weight have you gained so far? Do you have any concerns about nutrition or healthy eating? What kinds of things do you like to eat right now or crave? How much longer until baby arrives?

Notes:

_____

_____

_____

_____

_____

_____

_____

_____

_____

Week 25

THE VIRTUE OF RIGHTEOUSNESS

"For the grace of God that brings salvation has appeared to all men. It teaches us to say 'No' to ungodliness and worldly passions, and to live self-controlled, upright, and godly lives in this present age." Titus 2:11-12

We are living in a time where there is a great pull toward things that are unrighteous and evil. It is only by the grace of God that when we are saved, He dwells within our hearts and teaches us to turn from the things of this world. One day your child will be out on his/her own. That can be a sobering thought. We have hope through Christ that He will help us to live godly lives despite the increasing evil around us. Galatians 5:24-25 says, "Those who belong to Christ Jesus have crucified the sinful nature with its passions and desires. Since we live by the Spirit, let us keep in step with the Spirit. Read Galatians 5:22 for further instruction on what fruit we should bear when we are living by the Spirit of God.

Dear God,
Thank You for Your grace that comes through knowing You and putting our trust in You. Even though I cannot see the future, I am comforted by the fact that You can. You know what tomorrow holds and You know what lies ahead for my child. I pray that he/she would come to know You at an early age and that You would be teaching him/her valuable life lessons in the spirit. Teach him/her to say "no" to ungodliness and worldly passions. Help him/her life a self-controlled life, an upright life, and godly life. Give him/her vision for their future and keep them on your path.

Journal Tip: What are some things we face in the world today? What do you think will be the greatest things your child will face? Write them down and ask the Lord to help your child in these areas.

Notes:

_____

_____

_____

_____

_____

_____

_____

_____

_____

SPIRITUALLY SOW INTO YOUR CHILD

"A man reaps what he sows. The one who sows to please his sinful nature, from that nature will he reap destruction; the one who sows to please the Spirit, from the Spirit will reap eternal life. Let us not become weary in doing good, for at the proper time we will reap a harvest if we do not give up." Galatians 6: 7b-9

What you sow into your child will be reaped as a harvest of blessing. Learning to pray DAILY, diligently, and consistently is not an easy task to accomplish. With the help of the Lord, you can continue to sow things of the Spirit into your child. Your child must learn this harvest principle from the Lord. Earlier in the Galatians it said, "…those who only live to satisfy their own sinful desires will harvest the consequences of decay and death!" We want to sow things of the spirit to reap things of the Spirit so that he/she might have abundant life!

Lord,
I know that You will not be mocked. A man will reap that which he has sown. I understand that when a farmer plants corn, he reaps corn. If his crop is wheat, he will reap wheat. If we sow to sin, we will reap sin. If we sow righteousness and the things of the Spirit, that's what we'll receive in return. Help this principle to be ingrained in my thoughts, actions, words, and deeds. Help me to instill it into my child. I pray for the discipline and desire to continually sow things of the Spirit into my son/daughter. May I never grow tired of doing well. I pray for Your blessings that result from this sowing to pour forth at the appropriate time. In Your name, amen.

Journal Tip: Write in your own words what it means to reap what you sow. What kinds of spiritual things do you plan on sowing in your children?

Notes:

_____

_____

_____

_____

_____

_____

_____

_____

_____

_____

_____

Week 25

GOD IS THE ONE TO PLEASE

"It is better to take refuge in the LORD than to trust in man." Psalm 118:8

Parenting can be quite a challenge in a world that seems to reflect the importance of exalting self and pleasing others. What about glorifying God and pleasing Him? One of the most valuable spiritual nuggets to instill in your child is that God is their only critic. He is the one they should strive to please. When this truth is ingrained in your mind set, it will not matter what anyone else thinks about you or how the world views you. Our goal is to please God no matter if it is against the current of secular society or not.

Dear Lord,
I pray that my baby will learn the truth that Your opinion is the only one that really matters throughout life. It is much better to please You than to please men. When we live life with You in mind, it becomes much easier to walk in righteousness. I pray that You will help me as this baby's parent to live this truth as an example and to speak it openly so that it might take root in his/her heart. Your opinion of my child is so important. Please help me teach this precept effectively. Amen.

Journal Tip: Write down your thoughts concerning why this truth is so vital in the day we are living in. In what areas of life do you feel this could apply to your child?

Notes:

_____

_____

_____

_____

_____

_____

_____

_____

_____

_____

_____

_____

190

*Week 25*Week 25

CHILD'S HEART OPEN TO INSTRUCTION

"Apply your heart to instruction and your ears to words of knowledge."
Proverbs 23:12

Having a heart that is open to instruction and knowledge is a desire of most parents for their children. This doesn't only apply to higher education or learning, but also life in general. Being able to heed the instruction of a parent or from the Lord is a necessity for a healthy emotional and spiritual growing process.

Lord,
I pray that my son/daughter will be open to instruction, wisdom, and knowledge. I pray that You would prepare his/her heart for instruction and that You instruction, wisdom, and knowledge would guide me as a parent. We all must learn in life. I pray that when he/she makes mistakes that he/she would learn from them and not have to repeat them over and over. I acknowledge that the life lessons my child will learn from You will be essential for development and growth. Let understanding be bound to the heart and mind of this child. I will have a vital role in my baby's learning, even from an early age. I pray that You would be guiding me in how to schedule our day and pattern our routine in a way that would please You, Lord. Let this be a home in where education, wisdom, and knowledge flourish. May it be an environment that's conducive for learning. Amen.

Journal Tip: Have you thought about when your son or daughter would start learning skills like saying their A, B, C's or 1, 2, 3's? Can you imagine their first Sunday School class? You have plans for their education? Have you considered what it will be like to actually parent (teach life skills, etc.) your little one?

Notes:

_____

_____

_____

_____

_____

_____

_____

_____

_____

_____

Week 25

GOLIATH'S CONQUERED

"As the Philistine moved closer to attack him, David ran quickly toward the battle line to meet him. Reaching into his bag and taking out a stone, he slung it and struck the Philistine on the forehead. The stone went into his forehead, and he fell face down on the ground." 1 Samuel 17:48-49

Teaching our children to take a stand for himself/herself and for the Lord is a very important lesson to teach them. We need to learn the lesson, too. We live in a time of Spiritual warfare. It is not the people we are fighting, but the spirit that they are operating with. We need to learn to recognize the enemy. There are many "Goliaths" out there taunting us in this day and time. They make us feel like we are powerless to do anything about them. But, God has equipped us for the very thing that we face today. David didn't run away from his problems, but ran quickly toward the battle line to face them. People or situations that would like to bully us into a life of fear or into slavery (as Goliath would have enslaved the Israelites had he won), can be conquered by going forth with the Lord. God will multiply what we have in order to conquer the onslaught of the enemy. In 1 Samuel 18:14 it is said about David, "In everything he did, he had great success, because the Lord was with him."

Dear Lord,
I thank You for helping us recognize the enemy so that we may fight him. I pray that You would give me and all in my family boldness to face the giants in our lives. There is nothing that we cannot conquer when You have given us the authority and power to do so. Help my child to rise up as a defeater of the enemy and his tricks. Give him/her spiritual eyes to see the enemy coming! Equip him/her for the battles that are ahead. Bring a boldness to quickly meet the opposition and not timidity. I pray for courage and strength in the face of fear. Let him/her realize that the success in battle comes from You and not of his/her own power. You ask for our accessibility and not our ability. David became a conqueror because he was willing to be used of You and You used him! It didn't matter if he was young or old. I pray for such a character to arise in my child. In Your name, amen.

Journal Tip: What kinds of Goliaths come against people? How do you fight the enemy? Think about these things and let your child know what kind of tricks the enemy uses. It will equip him/her to fight!

Notes:

_____

_____

_____

_____

_____

_____

PROMISES

"When he saw her, he tore his clothes and cried, "Oh! My daughter! You have made me miserable and wretched, because I have made a vow to the LORD that I cannot break."
Judges 11:35

Making promises is something that we should not take lightly, especially to the Lord. In this troubling passage, Jepthath (a leader of Israel) had made a vow to the Lord that if He would give him victory in the battle against the Ammonites, he would sacrifice the first thing he saw coming out of his house when he returned. We can't bargain for God's blessings. What he received instead was grief. This "deal" with the Lord backfired when his daughter, an only child, came to meet Jepthath when he returned. Sometimes our oaths, promises, and vows have awful consequences. Jepthath should have trusted God instead of relying on his own efforts to make something happen. We should be very careful what we promise to do. What we decide could have positive or negative consequences toward our children. Teach your child that oaths and vows are important and that such promises should never put one's self or their family at risk. That is NOT pleasing to God. We should consider God's ways and will first before vowing anything to anyone, especially God.

Dear God,
I know You are the God who leads. I thank You for leading me in ways of righteousness and peace. I pray that my words and actions would line up with Your will and desires. Show me the importance of making promises and to weigh them carefully before I decide to do something, especially when it involves my children. At no time would I want an oath or vow that I have made affect my child in a negative way. Also, help me to explain promises to my child in a way he/she would understand. Little children have a tendency to take promises lightly. Help me convey that a promise is something important. May these important instructions from Your Word never leave him/her. In Your name, amen.

Journal Entry: Have you ever made promises that you couldn't keep? What do you want your child to know about promises, oaths, or vows?

Notes:

_____

_____

_____

_____

_____

_____

_____

_____

Week 26

TRUSTING GOD DURING PREGNANCY

"Trust in the Lord will all your heart, lean not upon your own understanding. In all your ways acknowledge Him and He shall direct your path." Proverbs 3:5-6

The idea of putting our faith or trust in God while we are expecting is not a hard concept. When expecting, we look to God daily for sustaining grace and power. We look to His miraculous hand to fashion our child together and to make the functions of our bodies work properly to be a "home" for our child. This idea of trusting God and who He is spreads throughout all areas of our lives. We can trust Him will all of our heart. We don't need to understand everything all the time. Parenting is a daily walk with our children that will require God's daily guidance. His word tells us that when we acknowledge Him in our daily walk, He will direct our path. Just think! There's no guess work with God. Do you have a need today or something that you simply need to put total trust in God for? Let's acknowledge Him in the situation and see what He'll do!

God,
I come to You today not knowing all about _____. Your Word tells me that I don't have to trust in my own understanding about what is happening, but I can acknowledge You and You will direct my path. Bring clarity to me and a sure understanding of what Your will is for the situation. I ask that You help me to bring everything to You on a daily basis, whether it seems big or small to me, possible or impossible. I need Your help in parenting this child and making decisions for him/her. Father, I pray that I would lead by example in this precept of trusting in You and that my son/daughter would do the same. I pray he/she will acknowledge You in all situations and walk in the path You have set forth for him/her. Direct my path today, Lord. Thank You for the hope that You have given to me, even in this very hour. Blessed is Your name. Amen.

Journal Tip: If you are facing something today, write it down and trust God to set you on the right path. Perhaps you aren't facing something today, but there has been a time in your life where God has been faithful to you. Give an account of what happened and how that has strengthened your walk in Him.

Notes:

_____

_____

_____

_____

_____

_____

_____

EDUCATION AND EXCELLENCE

"To these four young men God gave knowledge and understanding of all kinds of literature and learning. And Daniel could understand visions and dreams of all kinds."
Daniel 1:17

Christians should be counted among the smartest, most innovative, creative, and highly regarded people in the world! I love this passage in Daniel that gives insight into four Hebrew young men (himself included) who were called upon to be servants of the king. God describes them in verse 4 as noble, without any physical defect, handsome, showing aptitude for every kind of learning, well informed, quick to understand, and qualified. God gave all of these characteristics to the young men.

When it comes to educating our Christian children, we have a lot of options out there. Home Schools, Christian Schools, Magnet Schools, Private Schools, Public Schools, etc. Let's ask God to not only give you wisdom when it comes to educating your child, but also that He would bless them like He did the four Hebrew young men.

Dear God,
Thank You for being a Father that knows how to give good gifts to His children. I stand here today and feel like your thoughts toward me are immense. You see me and my baby as the "cream of the crop". Grant me the knowledge I need when it comes to educating my son/daughter. Lead me in the direction that I am to go and open and close doors as needed. Prompt me to action (concerning education) when I need to be prompted. Show me when and if I should begin pre-school and where to go. Direct me when/if I need daycare or other childcare provisions. Meet the needs I have in those areas. I ask that You would show favor to my son/daughter today and raise him/her up to be a person of great knowledge, honor, integrity, and skill, just as you created the four Hebrew young men to be. Design him/her as You have promised with every attribute he/she will need in order to accomplish the work You would have called him/her to do. Raise him/her up to break the molds of society and to bring glory to Your name. Help others to see Your favor resting on my child because he/she has decided to be Your child. In Your name, amen.

Journal Tip: Do you think of your child as "the cream of the crop"? What kinds of characteristics, skills, etc, do you feel are important to make an impact on the world for Christ?

Notes:

_____

_____

_____

_____

_____

_____

GOD NEVER FORGETS

"Can a mother forget the baby at her breast and have no compassion on the child she has borne? Though she may forget, I will not forget you! See, I have engraved you on the palms of my hands; your walls are ever before Me." Isaiah 49:15

God has constant concern for us. It doesn't matter where we are in life, He is always watching over us. It seems unimaginable that a mother could forget about her child or not express compassion toward her son or daughter. Even if that were the case, we find comfort that God has us engraved in the palm of His hand. Make every attempt possible to show concern and care over your child, but more importantly, teach him/her that God has him/her engraved on the palm of His hand. Where we fail as parents, God never disappoints!

Dear God,
You are a present help to me, Lord and a comfort at all times. I am so grateful that I can look to You when all others around me have failed. You never forget us. Help me during those times when I feel abandoned. When I go through a desert experience, You may also be speaking to me in a way that I may not have heard clearly if I wasn't going through my current situation. How great is Your compassion toward Your children! I pray for compassion to be released in me toward my son/daughter. I pray that I would not become emotionally blocked toward him/her at any time. Keep my concern in balance and don't let me sway over toward fear or worry. Help my little one to know that he/she can count on me for support, but especially that You are the one that never fails. If there are times where I come up short with my child, fill in that gap, Lord. I ask that You build a bond between this baby and me. He/she is written upon my heart. Help me to never forget, even in the hard times as a parent, the love and nurturing that I feel right now towards my baby. In Your name, amen.

Journal Tip: How would you tell your child that they are written on the palm of God's hand? Explain what that means and why it is important.

Notes:

_____

_____

_____

_____

_____

_____

_____

_____

_____

YOUNG USES

"Josiah was eight years old when he became king, and he reigned in Jerusalem thirty-one years." 2 Kings 22:1

When we think about what success may favor our children in life, many seem shocked when God chooses to use them at a young age! Josiah was known for walking in the ways of the Lord and not turning to the right or to the left. He also found the law in the temple and renewed Israel's covenant with the Lord and read the entire law aloud to all of Israel. How in the world would a child of eight know how to walk in the ways of the Lord? He was taught to do so and the Spirit of God was with him! Many parents fail to nurture growth in our children and realize that God may call upon them early in life to be a light for Him. Sometimes He chooses the young to confound the wise. Perhaps God has that kind of calling on your child! At the very least, He is urging us all to raise our children in such a way that they are actively growing in Him from a very early age.

Heavenly Father,
Thank You for keeping me safe today and for watching over my little one as he/she grows in my womb. Only You know what he/she will be called to do in life. I ask that as a parent, You would help me in teaching him/her Your Word and Your ways. Use him/her as You will and help me to encourage growth in those areas. I ask that Your plans for him/her would go forth and that Your Word would not return void. Bless all the time I will spend with him/her in the Word and make those times productive. I ask that he/she would be a light at an early age to those around him/her. I know You could use him/her to witness to family and friends even as a toddler. Let Your Spirit dwell with him/her and grant him/her boldness. Thank You, Lord, for the calling You have given him/her and the special skills that You are weaving together in his/her frame. In Your name, Amen.

Journal Tip: Can you think of any examples how you were used by the Lord at a young age? If so, then how? What is your heartfelt prayer for your little one today concerning being used at a young age?

Notes:

_____

_____

_____

_____

_____

_____

_____

Week 26

ROOTS

"He is like a tree planted by streams of water, which yields its fruit in season and whose leaf does not wither. Whatever he does prospers." Psalm 1:3

What kinds of roots have you grown in your spiritual life? Could you be described as a person who is deep rooted in Christ and His Word? Will you be swayed when the storms of life blow by? Do you have shallow roots that can't nourish the tree because there hasn't been any depth to tap into the source of water? Our goal in our personal lives and our spiritual lives should be to grow strong roots. We must tap into the source of life giving water and hold on tight. Even when we go through dry spells, it will take effort on our part to reach toward God, just as the roots must grow deeper in order to live.

On another note, we are growing roots in the communities that we live in and with people around us – our network of relationships. I would ask the same questions of you as before... are you shallow or well rooted? What kinds of family roots are you from? Roots are important for children. We must help cultivate those roots in his/her life. Sometimes it's necessary to uproot and replant to get closer to the stream. Regardless, firm roots must be formed eventually. This is a sign of maturity in our own lives and perpetuates healthy living in our children.

Dear God,
I stand here today wanting to grow deep roots in You. You are the living streams of water that I want to be planted by. I ask that You would help my roots to grow, not only in my life, but in relation to the community and relationships around me. I pray for strong roots and well nourished roots that will hold on tight when the storms of life come. Teach me what that means and why that is important in my life. I want to give my baby a strong foundation to build upon. Make his/her life fruitful in all areas. Don't ever let him/her wither because he/she has a shallow root system. Deep roots can be forged in times of great distress and trial. I pray just enough trial in his/her life so that he/she can tap deep into the source of living waters. Help this family to have strong roots into the community we live in. I ask that we would be a household of light that would bring Your name glory. Thank You, Lord. Amen.

Journal Tip: Describe what kind of root system you have in life. Why do you feel a strong root system is important to your baby? Have you ever been uprooted and replanted? If so, describe that process.

Notes:

_____

_____

_____

_____

_____

_____

GOD'S WORD EMPHASIZED

"I have hidden Your Word in my heart that I might not sin against You."
Psalm 119:11

God's Word is the blueprint for us to live by. From it, we learn about who God is, what He has done, and what He is going to do. Many answers for life's most difficult problems are found within the pages of the Bible. It introduces us to the Lord of the Universe and how we can have a personal relationship with Him. You should plan on reading your Bible to your child regularly as he/she grows up. His Word is the bread of life!

Lord,
Please plant in me the desire to read to my child from the Word of God every day. I want this discipline in my life as well as my child's life. I pray that the words will come alive and that You would speak to me through Your Word. I want the Holy Scriptures to become a vital part of his/her walk with You. Help me begin today to read the Scriptures aloud to my baby. I pray that when Your Word goes forth that it will set off a spiritual blessing and victory in my home and life. Thank You Lord for Your living Word! Amen.

Journal Tip: What are some of your favorite scriptures in the Bible and why? Do you have a "life verse" or maybe "life book" (a verse or book of the Bible that seems to summarize your walk with the Lord?)

Notes:

_____

_____

_____

_____

_____

_____

_____

_____

_____

_____

_____

_____

_____

Week 26

ACKNOWLEDGE GOD & PRESS IN

"Let us acknowledge the LORD; let us press on to acknowledge Him." As surely as the sun rises, He will appear; He will come to us like the winter rains, like the spring rains that water the earth." Hosea 6:3

I believe in acknowledging God in all the important events that change a person's life. Marriage, during family tragedies, job changes, college choices, financial decisions, and having children are just a few! I am amazed how many Christian people don't recognize God during pregnancy, let alone pray for their baby. This is not a criticism, just an observation! So many of us believe and acknowledge (to some degree) that the Lord allowed our pregnancy, but then don't press in. Today I would like to challenge you not to simply let pregnancy progress without pressing in and seeking God. This is a challenge to pray and meditate on the Lord during these next few months and expect God to do great things. You're not only laying a solid foundation for your child, but you'll also grow yourself. Press in and He will surely appear. I expect you to be refreshed, renewed, restored, and rejuvenated. As the verse says, "He will appear like the sun! He will come like winter and spring rains and water the earth!" Let him reign in your life and family. Let Him rain his blessings and anointing upon you today.

Dear Heavenly Father,
I want to acknowledge You today as the source of my life and life of my baby. I want to press in and see You do marvelous things during the next few months. I want to feel Your presence and rest in Your assurance during my pregnancy. I want You to reign in my home and my life. I want You to rain down in the Spirit upon me and my baby today. I don't want to be satisfied with the status quo. I am asking for a supernatural experience during my pregnancy and childbirth. I want to grow closer to You and depend on You during this pregnancy. I want my baby to be raised in the best Christian home as possible. I ask that You be with me right now. Give me the discipline to seek You each day uninterrupted. Help me start my day with Your praise on my lips. In Your name, amen.

Journal Tip: Acknowledge God today in your own words. Are you committed into pressing in toward Him during the remainder of your pregnancy? Why is it important to you?

Notes:

_____

_____

_____

_____

_____

_____

PART 4
The Third Trimester

"LIFE WORDS" INTO OUR LIVES

"The Spirit gives life; the flesh counts for nothing. The words I have spoken to you are spirit and they are life." John 6:63

Our words coupled with faith are a powerful tool. Over and over in scripture we are told that the power of life and death are in the tongue. As Christians, we should not have negativity and doubt coming forth from our mouths. We are not defeated when we are in Christ, so why do we confess that we are? We need to start declaring "life" into those areas where we struggle. This is not "name it and claim it faith". This is asking God to renew, restore, regenerate, and revitalize things in our life that seem to have no hope. No matter what the struggle; relationships, finances, your pregnancy, your job, your home, your future, God comes to give life and life more abundantly. He is a God of resurrection. What does God tell you about the area you are struggling with today? Begin speaking and professing life into those areas through faith and the power of Christ who is in You.

Dear Lord,
You have come to give me life... abundant life! I praise You for the power to bring goodness out of any situation. Today I ask You to raise up a new mind set in me that would declare life back into me and situations that I am facing. I ask that Your will be done on earth as it is in heaven. Bring life into my physical body today. Bring life into my finances today. Bring life into my relationships today. Bring life into my future today. The enemy comes to steal, kill, and destroy, but You come to set the captive free and to restore life. I ask for the newness, regeneration, restoration, and redemption that only come from declaring You into my life today. In Your name I pray, amen.

Journal Tip: What areas are you needing "life" in today? What are some areas that the enemy is attacking you in…where he would like to steal, kill, and destroy? Recognize the enemy's attacks and then begin to declare life over those areas.

Notes:

_____

_____

_____

_____

_____

_____

_____

_____

Week 27

WISDOM AND INSTRUCTION

"The wise in heart are called discerning, and pleasant words promote instruction."
Proverbs 16:21

The first part of today's focus verse deals with wisdom. Wisdom is one of the most sought after characteristics of all parents. It is a valuable tool. Godly wisdom is a result of a parent who spends time with the Lord and is a fruit of that labor. Being a parent of wisdom will save your child and yourself from much heartache. You must be able to discern many things in regard to spiritual matters, family, and life. The second part of this verse is dealing with our speech in instruction. It tells us that pleasant words promote instruction. We should strive for our instruction and correction to be in kindness and never delivered in a harsh, bitter, or damaging tone. When we take on a bad tone, it nulls and voids any good we may have been trying to accomplish. Let's ask the Lord to help us in these areas today.

Dear God,
Thank You for Your wisdom and instruction that You give freely to all. I want to be a parent who is discerning and wise. Show me how to cultivate these characteristics in my life. I want the fruit of those characteristics to bless not only my personal life, but the lives of others around me. In times where I may not have acted accordingly, I pray that there would be healing and restoration quickly. Help me be a person who flows in forgiveness, too. Remind me when situations arise to learn from my mistakes and to grow continually. Raise me up to be parent who expresses the love of Christ to my child through word and deed. My desire is for my little one to grow up in godly wisdom and instruction. In Your name, amen.

Journal Tip: Are you a person of wisdom? If not, what can you do to grow in wisdom? How do you speak to others where there is conflict? Do you need work on this area?

Notes:

_____

_____

_____

_____

_____

_____

_____

_____

_____

_____

BABY'S FIRST TEACHER

"A student is not above his teacher..." Matthew 10:24a

Did you know that you are your child's first teacher? Many of the things that he/she will learn will happen at home. What kinds of things do we teach our children? We teach our children about God, relationships, the world, responsibility, habits, speech, character, knowledge... the list goes on and on. We prime our children for how they will learn the rest of their lives. Perhaps you are struggling today because you know that you will need to return to work at some point after your child is born. God still has a plan. Whether you stay at home or enter back into the workplace, God has commissioned you as your child's first educator. Also, parents sometimes fall into the trap of thinking that they have to be a friend to their child above parenting. Parent, God has called you to lead and not to be led! A child is not above his parent, even if your child is extremely gifted or intelligent. Be a parent! Lead your child in the way he/she should go. Think about what being a successful person means to you and then strive to meet those goals. Communication is important, but your child will also learn by your example.

Lord,
I realize that You have set an order in raising this child I am carrying. I pray that You would help me to grasp and bring forth all the training that he/she is to learn, especially during the first few years of his/her life. I pray that You will encourage my heart to be a godly example of a believer at all times and in all types of situations. I pray that I will learn how to parent this child and to nurture him/her in You and increase his/her knowledge. In a world where so many leave the raising of their children to others, I pray that it would not be so in this house. Whatever additional work You have called me to do, help me to always realize that parenting my child is a top priority. Give me the knowledge, patience, diligence, dependability, and love that it takes to teach my child. Give me creative ways to instruct him/her. I pray that my child would have a heart that would receive instruction easily. Thank You, Lord, for this task of teaching. Help me to seek You for instruction concerning him/her daily. In Your name, amen.

Journal Tip: What kinds of things came to mind as you read about being your child's first teacher? What will your life include once baby is born? Will you return to work? Will you be at home? Will there be others in your child's life that would help with educating your child or teaching him/her about life? Who would those be?

Notes:

_____

_____

_____

_____

_____

_____

Week 27

ORNAMENTAL CHILDREN

"Lift up your eyes and look around; all your sons gather and come to you. 'As surely as I Live', declares the LORD, 'you will wear them all as ornaments, you will put them on, like a bride.'" Isaiah 49:18

Children can be such a blessing to a mother! As your child grows and begins to mature, you will notice lost of changes. I appreciate when they are old enough to make individual thoughts and choices. Those are the cherished times when my children have come up and said, "Mom, I love you!" unprovoked and unprompted. When children begin living for the Lord and displaying the fruits of all the teaching you have given them, it is quite rewarding. In times when you feel like giving up... don't! All your daily training will pay off in a lifetime of rewards. This verse tells us that your children will be drawn to you and that they will as priceless as jewels to you. It even says that you will wear them as ornaments. They will be displayed proudly.

Dear Lord,
Thank You for this blessing of motherhood today. I thank You for this promise in Isaiah 49:18 that I will be honored, adorned, and blessed by godly children. My son or daughter is so special to me and I know he/she is special to You. I ask that You would go before me in all the training and teaching that this child will receive. I pray that You will be Lord over our good times and our bad times. Come into this home and be Lord over every aspect of it. I want to be a family that reflects You, Lord. Display these children for the Lord to see. Let them be as ornaments to me. I thank You, Lord for all Your involvement in this pregnancy. I am totally depending on You to give me the strength, ability, and endurance I need to become a mother and parent this child in Your ways. Be with me now and in the days and months ahead. Amen.

Journal Tip: How are children like ornaments? Are you already proud of your child even though he/she hasn't been born yet? What are your thoughts today?

Notes:

_____

_____

_____

_____

_____

_____

_____

_____

_____

Week 27

PLANS FOR YOU AND YOUR BABY

"'For I know the plans I have for you,' declares the LORD, 'plans to prosper you and not to harm you, plans to give you hope and a future.'" Jeremiah 29:11

God has plans for you and your baby. He has a specific direction He is leading you in. He also has perfect plans for your baby. God sees our days from first to last. He knows what every one will hold. He knows what He fashioned your child to become in life. The enemy has plans for your little one, too. You must uphold your child through prayer. Let's pray that God will make known the plans for your child and that he/she will walk in the path of the righteous.

Lord,
Thank You for the perfect plans you have for my baby. I know that those plans are to prosper and not to harm. They are for a future and a hope. Your ways are perfect. Even when we stray from Your plans, You are able to bring us back onto the path of righteousness. I bind the enemy's plans for me and my baby. The enemy's plans are stopped by the blood of Jesus. Bring forth Your plans for my child, Lord. May he/she come to know Your plans at a young age and have a desire to follow the path You have set for him/her. Thank You, Lord. Amen.

Journal Tip: Include some specific things you would like to see your child become when he/she is older (e.g. character traits or personality traits). What type of person do you think God would desire for them to become?

Notes:

_____

_____

_____

_____

_____

_____

_____

_____

_____

_____

_____

_____

_____

SOUND DOCTRINE & DECEPTION

"For the time will come when men will not put up with sound doctrine. Instead, to suit their own desires, they will gather around them a great number of teachers to say what their itching ears want to hear. They will turn their ears away from the truth and turn aside to myths." 2 Timothy 4:3

There is no doubt that we are living in the gap of time directly preceding the return of Christ. These are known as the last days. Our children will be growing up in such days and we must warn them, as the scriptures do, of what the day they are living in will bring. We need only look to such chapters as Matthew 24 or 2 Timothy 4 to learn some of these signs. One of the most disturbing is the deception of the church. Some of it will come in the form of sound doctrine being replaced with whatever it is that people want to hear. You need to ask yourself as a parent, "What is it that I believe and why do I believe it?" Do you have a church home? What doctrines do they follow and what do they believe? Are there ordinances of the church that you follow? Why or why not? If you do not know why you believe what you do, how will you be able to share your faith effectively with your children? Let me challenge you to read your Bible <u>daily</u>. Know His Word so that your feet will not stumble. Know His ways and test everything you hear (in preaching, in books, etc.) to see if it stands up to the Word and God's character. Another helpful suggestion with your children would be to get into the habit of referring your child to the Word of God when they have life questions. Ask, "What does the Word of God say about that?" Be as Paul and guard your life and doctrine closely. Contend for your faith. It will only benefit you and your family.

Dear Lord,
Thank You for Your Word that never leads us astray. I ask that Your Word would be bound to me and that I would not depart from it. Help me to understand what I believe and why I believe those things. If I have been in error in any part, reveal it to me and lead me back to the path of righteousness. I ask that I would be a parent who can effectively relay Christian beliefs to my children. Help me to point them to the Word for the answers to their questions. Help me to recognize the truth and speak it. Give me a discerning heart that can spot deception and keep it from harming my child. Remind me that Your Word is the standard that man should live by, not the teachings of men or the fancies of the heart. You alone hold the complete truth and I ask that You lead me in it, as well as my child. Keep him/her safe in these last days. May he/she live in such a way as to lead others in the truth. In Your name, amen.

Journal Topic: Why is sound doctrine important? Do you know what your beliefs are and why you believe them? What beliefs will you share with your child?

Notes:

_____

_____

_____

_____

Week 27

THE SPIRIT INTERCEDES

"In the same way, the Spirit helps us in our weakness. We do not know what to pray for, but the Spirit Himself intercedes for us with groans that words cannot express."
Romans 8:26

Isn't it good to know that the Spirit is in operation in us today? If we are in Christ, His Spirit abides in us. He is there to help us in our weakness. There may be times during your pregnancy that you'll have to cling to Him for help. The Spirit is also there, interceding for us to the Father. He prays for us! Isn't that something that in our weakness, He prays for us?

Dear God,
I thank You for Your Spirit today. I am amazed that in my weakness, You are there interceding for me. I pray that whatever You are praying about today, that it would be done in my life and in the life of my little one. Give me a heart that is sensitive to Your Spirit and a desire to do Your will. Bless this baby today with health and vitality. Even though he/she isn't old enough to understand Your Spirit, I am convinced that He is in operation on the behalf of my baby already. Thank You, Lord. Amen.

Journal Tip: Have you ever been at a loss of what to pray for? Isn't it exciting to know that the Holy Spirit intercedes for you? Write down your thoughts.

Notes:

_____

_____

_____

_____

_____

_____

_____

_____

_____

_____

_____

_____

Week 27

DAILY TASKS AND CHORES

"Make it your ambition to lead a quiet life, to mind your own business and to work with your hands, just as we told you, so that your daily life may will the respect of outsiders and so that you will not be dependent on anybody." 1 Thessalonians 4:11-12

Wouldn't it be nice if the world around us would just stop when we find out we're pregnant? There would be nothing to do except care for ourselves, kick back, and relax! Unfortunately, that's not reality. Even though you are pregnant, there are still daily chores and activities that you will need to accomplish. Sometimes you will feel like you don't even have the energy to get out of bed. Set priorities during the day and consider what is important and what is superficial. Tackle those tasks that <u>must</u> be done and pace yourself. Remember to rest and not to overdo. There must be a balance. The further along you get, the more sapped for energy you may feel. Also, if there are any medical reasons that would limit your activities, perhaps you could call in some family and friends to help with your workload on the things that <u>must</u> be taken care of. Don't sweat the things that aren't important. It's alright to let a few things go!

Dear Heavenly Father,
I thank You Lord, for giving me the wisdom and strength that I need to accomplish my daily tasks and chores. I pray that as my pregnancy progresses that I would continue to feel as good as possible and to be able to accomplish the tasks that I need to do. Help me to let go of those things that are not important. I ask that You give me knowledge in how to orchestrate my days to be productive. Remind me to rest when I grow weary. Keep me from workplace environmental hazards, such as chemicals, toxins, or any other biohazards that may affect me or my baby. Remind me to pamper my body more than normal during this special time. In Your name, amen.

Journal Tip: What kinds of things fill your day? Are you working or not? What are you doing to keep yourself and baby safe and healthy when working at tasks or jobs?

Notes:

_____

_____

_____

_____

_____

_____

_____

_____

Week 28

STRENGTH FOR YOU TODAY

"We are glad whenever we are weak but you are strong; and our prayer is for your perfection." 2 Corinthians 13:9

Need a little strength today? There are points in your pregnancy, particularly in the last trimester, in which you will begin to feel weak and sluggish. God says that His grace is sufficient for you and that His power is made perfect in weakness. Isn't that a comforting thought? When we are weak, He will display His power in us! Whatever area of your life needs a boost today, rest in the fact that God himself is working on your behalf. His power will work in your weakness.

God,
Thank You for Your limitless grace. When I am feeling down and tired, You raise me up and give me strength. Your Word says that in my weakness, Your power is made perfect. Perfect it in me today. I ask that You would strengthen my body, soul, emotions, and mind. Let me not rely on my own strength or power when Yours is readily available. I rejoice that You are working to help me in my weakness. I praise You for Your marvelous works! Amen.

Journal Tip: Has there been a time during your pregnancy yet where you have felt weak (in mind, spirit, or body)? If so, write a simple statement that says you are going to allow God's power to be made perfect in that specific situation.

Notes:

_____

_____

_____

_____

_____

_____

_____

_____

_____

_____

_____

_____

_____

212

Week 28

THE GRACE OF GOD

"And God is able to make all grace abound to you, so that in all things at all times, having all that you need, you will abound in every good work." 2 Corinthians 9:8

Grace from God is something that we receive freely. It is the divine assistance given from God to us that helps us to live a godly life. It also recharges our spirits. With grace imparted, we can endure more than we ever thought we could in our own strength. If it weren't for God's grace we wouldn't get very far in life. During pregnancy, you may have times where you feel like you can't go on. Let God's grace adorn you today. He gives freely to those who ask. He is more than able when we are not.

Dear God,
Your grace is sufficient for me today. When I feel like I cannot go on or that this pregnancy is more than I can bear, You give me grace. I ask for Your grace in this hour. Touch me, Lord and lift me up. Your word says that You are able to make grace abound to me, that in all things, at all times, I will have what I need. Help me to abound in every good work. Pour Your grace and mercy upon me. May my child live a life full of grace. Impart Your grace in his/her life at the very moments that he/she may need it. Thank You, Lord. Amen.

Journal Tip: How are you feeling about your pregnancy today? Do you need God's grace?

Notes:

_____

_____

_____

_____

_____

_____

_____

_____

_____

_____

_____

_____

_____

Week 28

IMAGINING WHAT BABY LOOKS LIKE

"And the very hairs on your head are numbered." Matthew 10:30

It's fascinating (on delivery day) to admire the features of your baby. Those little fingers and little toes! Whose nose does he/she have? Are there any birthmarks? What color is the baby's hair and how much or how little does he/she have. God's creating abilities makes us sit back in awe. How can He make all of us different? How did He make our cells so precisely that they can carry DNA and certain genes that determine the features we are created with? What a wonder. God knows all about us even before we are born. His Word tells us that even the hairs on our heads are numbered. He's personally involved with you and your baby. He has an interest in you. That just makes my day! It's heartwarming to know that You have value to the God of the Universe. He loves and cares for you deeply.

Heavenly Father,
I am so excited to hold my baby in my arms for the very first time and see what he/she looks like. I am so thankful to You that he/she has been designed of You. You know so much about him/her that even the hairs on his/her head are counted by You. Oh, Lord, if You care so much about even the little details of my baby's features, You must care about the larger details of his/her life. I know Your eyes are continually on my little one. That assurance brings me great comfort and peace. I understand how much You care for Your people. Thank You, Lord, for loving us with a great, unfathomable love. Amen.

Journal Tip: What features do you think your baby will have? Why? How does it make you feel to know that God has even the hairs on our heads numbered?

Notes:

_____

_____

_____

_____

_____

_____

_____

_____

_____

_____

Week 28

COMMUNICATION & BABY SIGNS

"Come, let us go down and confuse their language so they will not understand each other."
Genesis 11:7

The Towel of Babel is one of the most interesting stories in the Bible. It's fascinating that up until this point, there was only one language in the world! But men's hearts declared to do evil and God couldn't allow that to happen. How frustrated they must have become when they turned to each other and had no idea what the other one way saying. It reminds me of when our children are beginning to learn language. Over ten years ago, when my first son was born, the Lord showed me that there are many ways to communicate. I began thinking about the deaf and that they can talk without speech. I suddenly realized that if I did some simple hand gestures that my son and I could communicate much easier. A few years later a doctor came out with an entire book called "Baby Signs". Now it is pretty common to hear of communicating with infants in this way. For the first time mom, it can be a real help in knowing what your child is wanting before the verbal skills have matched their physical aptitudes. Opening those doors of communication will be vital in the early months of your child's life. Their first words will be music to your ears. Cherish these moments and continue to work as hard as you did in the first months to communicate frequently with your child. Remember that communication takes both listening and talking. Communication is also a process. It will produce results over time. Let's ask God to help us in this area.

Dear God,
I pray that as I grow closer to delivery that You would begin speaking to me about communicating with my baby. Our first communication won't be simply with words, but also with touch. Later there will be communication with expressions and eye contact, gestures, and speech. I pray that You would orchestrate each phase of communication with my baby and show me new, creative ways to communicate. I pray that our communication would produce contentment instead of frustration. Let there be great understanding between my baby and me. Even while baby is in the womb, I know he/she is coming to recognize the sound of my voice. His/her little kicks seem like attempts at communication. Thank You, Lord, for giving me clarity in this area and for already forming bonds of communication between my baby and me. In Your name, amen.

Journal Tip: Describe some ways that you could communicate with your baby. Do you talk to your baby? Have you imagined your baby's movements as ways to get your attention or as responses to your voice or sounds?

Notes:

_____

_____

_____

_____

Week 28

GOD OF THE INCREASE

"May the Lord make you increase, both you and your children. May you be blessed by the Lord, the maker of heaven and earth." Psalm 115:14-15

To increase means to grow or become greater. May the Lord make you increase today! I'm not talking about your enlarging size or other growing parts of your anatomy! May your spirit increase! May your borders increase! May your territory increase! May your expectations increase! May your testimony increase! May your praise increase! May your skills increase! May your harvest increase! May your finances increase! May your ministry increase! May your faith increase today! He IS the God of increase!

Lord,
Thank You for increasing me in parts of my life that may have seemed boxed in. Break me out of my comfort zone and let me see life in a different way today. Your Word declares increase for both me and my child. Reveal to me the areas that I am expanding in. Show me how to pray specifically and affirmatively concerning what You are doing in me and my family. I thank You for it, Lord! Amen.

Journal Tip: What is God increasing in you today? Ask Him to show you.

Notes:

_____

_____

_____

_____

_____

_____

_____

_____

_____

_____

_____

_____

LISTENING AND LEARNING

"Does not the ear test words as the tongue tastes food?" Job 12:11

Listening to what our children have to say is a valuable part of parenting. It's as important as talking when communicating. Like the old saying goes, God gave us two ears and just one mouth because we need to do twice as much listening as talking. Just as the tongue in our mouth have special sensors on them called taste buds, our ears are the discerner of words. If the Spirit of God is in us, we should be able to identify the truth when it comes to our children. We will also be able to detect that "tone" of voice in our child that warns us something is bothering him/her. Our children also need to know that their thoughts and feelings are valued by us. We need to let our sons and daughters know that we care and are willing to listen to them. Let's make sure that how we talk and listen to one another is done in a godly manner.

Dear Lord,
Thank You for giving me Your Spirit and conforming me to Your likeness. Though I am not perfect, I am continually being perfected in You. I ask right now that my speech and testing of words would be filtered through the Spirit and that when I speak or listen, it would be done through Christ who strengthens me. I want You to be glorified in my body, as well as in my home. Help me in the days to come to keep my ears and mouth in check when it comes to my little one. Make our efforts at communication successful in this home. Open our understanding and receptivity. Protect us from the enemy who would like to come in and cause havoc through broken communication. If there is ever a time where damage has been done, help us to be quick to remedy the problem and remove any harmful seeds that the enemy may have tried to sow. I don't want anything I have done to cause permanent harm to my baby at any time. Thank You, Lord for my little one today. Touch his/her ears with discernment, his/her physical features with wholeness, and his/her spirit with love today. Amen.

Journal Tip: How is discernment important when your child is communicating with you? Do you have examples from when you were younger of both helpful and harmful communication?

Notes:

_____

_____

_____

_____

_____

_____

_____

Week 28

HE'LL FINISH WHAT HE'S STARTED

"From the first day until now, being confident of this, that He who began a good work in you will carry it on to completion until the day of Christ Jesus." Philippians 1:5b-6

Sometimes during pregnancy, we have times when we doubt we will ever get through. Time seems slow as our perception of time seems to change. You learn a lesson in how long seconds or even minutes can feel, especially during delivery. Unexpected complications or unrelenting fatigue can leave us in despair. You need to stand on Philippians 1:5b-6 today. God sees every second, every minute of your pregnancy and knows what will come in the next minute. He has ordained an exact minute for your baby to be delivered. He'll give you strength for the minute ahead.

Dear God,
I am standing on Philippians 1:5b-6 today. I know that You began a good work in me and that You will carry in on to completion until the day I am to deliver. I put every minute I face, even every second, into Your hands. I put my trust in You, father, from the first day of my pregnancy until now. I ask that You give me strength and endurance today. Grant me confidence in You. I believe Your Word. Thank You, Lord. Amen.

Journal Tip: How are you feeling today? How far away are you from your due date?

Notes:

_____

_____

_____

_____

_____

_____

_____

_____

_____

_____

_____

_____

INTRODUCING JESUS

"Since the children have flesh and blood, he too shared in their humanity so that by his death he might destroy him who holds the power of death- that is the devil- and free those who all their lives were held in slavery by their fear of death." Hebrews 2:14

Today, I ask you to consider Jesus. It's hard for our minds to wrap around the thought that the Savior of the World came as a baby. He grew within Mary's womb just as your baby grows inside of you. His supernatural conception was from the Holy Spirit. He is one hundred percent God and one hundred percent man. Jesus shared in our humanity by becoming flesh and blood. He was offered up as the perfect sacrifice for our sins. The shedding of His blood brought the remission of those sins and also conquered the power of death, hell, and the grave. Believing who Jesus is and what He came to do is the core of our Christian belief system. Change who Jesus is or what He was called to do and You no longer have Christian beliefs. Satan is trying to erode Christian beliefs in this day and time. Call it last days prophecy being fulfilled. Many are coming claiming to be the way to Christ. Others tell us that there are many ways to God. Still others are twisting and distorting the major foundations of the church. If you are a Christian, you must believe (as the Word declares) that the only way to the Father is through Jesus. Who is Jesus to you? Perhaps you have never thought of it in depth before, but consider Him today. How will you present Christ to your child?

Dear Lord,
I thank You that You are the risen Savior who died for my sins. Without that sacrifice, I would still be bound to sin and doomed to death. You mean so much to me, Lord, and I ask that You would show me exactly who You are and how I can share that with my baby, even at a young age. Show me tools I could use, daily scripture reading, picture books, etc. that would even further shed light into the mind of my child concerning You. Help me to present You in such a way that would be easily understood and accepted by my child. Let living with You in our lives be a daily process. Let your name be talked about and expressed openly and freely thought out this home. I pray that leading my child to know You will become a priority of my day. Protect my child from the voices of doubt or deception that would lead him/her away from you. May they know You so well that he/she would be able to quickly realize what truth is and what is not. In Your name I ask it. Amen.

Journal Tip: Who is Christ to you? What do you know about His character? Name a few ways you could help your child learn about Christ.

Notes:

_____

_____

_____

_____

_____

Week 29

TREASURES

"For where your treasure is, there your heart will be also." Matthew 6:21

Is there anything that you would consider as a "treasure" in your life? A treasure is something that is held in high regard or value. Perhaps you treasure certain possessions (a family heirloom, a vintage car, an antique, etc.). Maybe your career or relationships are what you regard in high value. God speak to us in His Word that we are His jewels. We are His treasure. Consider what Jesus spoke in this verse... where your treasure is, that's where your heart will be. What are your priorities? Honestly ask yourself what is important in your life. What is your heart set on? As parents, our treasures seem to rub off on our kids. If we like something, chances are, your offspring will too. What do you value today? Is it worth valuing or is it something that we need to give over to the Lord?

Dear God,
I thank You that You see me as a precious jewel. I treasure my relationship with You and the family that You have blessed me with. I treasure this precious little baby and I hope that he/she will grow up to feel treasured by both of his/her parents and by You. Help my priorities to line up with Your will at all times. If there needs to be adjustments to what I have set as a priority, illuminate it to me and help me to reorganize my treasures where I need to. I want my heart to be fixed on You and what Your will is for my life and for the life of my baby. Thank You for thinking of me as special. Amen.

Journal Tip: Write down what "treasures" you have in life and what God might be speaking to you about them.

Notes:

_____

_____

_____

_____

_____

_____

_____

_____

_____

_____

220

PLAY AND DISCOVERY TIME

"Play skillfully... and shout for joy." Psalm 33:3

As your child grows and you strive to teach him/her all kinds of things, don't neglect the play time. Kids need time to learn and develop through structured play time. It's also a way for little ones to work off stress, anger, anxiety, or excess energy. Creativity blossoms during play. Little minds work all the time, but the body needs attention, too. Let's ask the Lord to make our homes and lives open to the wonder and discovery of play.

Dear God,
Thank You for the wonder and discovery that happens during play. I pray that my little one will find great joy and skill in the play time that he/she will engage in each day. Help him/her to grow and develop at a normal, healthy rate and to learn at a consistent pace. Give me ways and ideas that could help stimulate his/her mind and to always be willing to share in his/her playtime experiences. Let me expressively participate during times of interaction with him/her. I pray that his/her body, mind, and emotions would benefit greatly from the experiences he/she will have during play. Help me to introduce my child to Your wonderful creation through our times outside. Thank You, Lord, for this wonderful way to teach us about life.
Help me, Lord, to not always be consumed with work or chores that I can't take time to stop and enjoy life. In Your name I ask it. Amen.

Journal Tip: What are some fun things that you did as a kid? Do you have any toys yet for your baby? What are some things you can imagine your child doing during play?

Notes:

_____

_____

_____

_____

_____

_____

_____

_____

_____

_____

Week 29

A CHILD'S LAUGHTER; HAPPINESS

"A cheerful heart is good medicine, but a crushed spirit dries up the bones."
Proverbs 17:22

What wonder there is in a child's laughter! It seems so unprovoked. It seems to radiate from every inch of their being! Your child will begin laughing sooner than you may think. That's something to look forward to around the four month milestone or even sooner! A home where laughter is a regular event is a sure indication of a happy home! Even when you feel low, a good laugh can trigger something in you that seems almost healing. Perhaps you are feeling a little down today. Can you think of something that brings you joy or something that at one time caused a lot of laughter?

God,
I pray that my home would be one where laughter would genuinely abound. Let there be merriment and joy flowing freely! Let Your laughter work as a medicine to the ailments that life can sometimes bring. I know that pure joy comes from You and You delight in Your creation. I pray that my son/daughter will experience a life of great delight, full of fun and laughter. Give him/her a good sense of humor and be able to laugh at himself/herself as well. Give me a special touch today, Lord, which would trigger joy overflowing in me. Let it bubble up and spill out. I give You all the praise and glory today for this expression You have created in us... laughter. Amen.

Journal Tip: What are some things that make you laugh? Can you think of a time when you were so happy that it just overflowed?

Notes:

_____

_____

_____

_____

_____

_____

_____

_____

_____

_____

_____

222

CLAY IN THE POTTER'S HANDS

"Yet, O Lord, You are our Father. We are the clay, You are the potter; we are the work of Your hand." Isaiah 64:8

I love the picture of the potter and the clay. What creative, masterful, powerful hands that form the clay! When I think about the Lord and how He can take something as unformed as us (the clay) and turn it into something useful... I am in awe. What a revelation!   I see your little one in the hands of God today. We are a work of His hands. Sometimes we are as broken pottery. The cares and trials of this life have left us in nothing but pieces. Praise God that the potter can put us back together again. We are constantly being formed by the Potter. Let's yield ourselves to Him today and let Him create something new in us.

Father,
Your masterful hands are forming my little one today. I can't express my wonder and praise for the mighty act You are doing within me! I am also continually being molded by Your hands as I get older. The potter is always working on His creation! If there are areas in me that are broken and of need of repair today, I ask You to mend them, Lord. Create in me something new today. Make me into the vessel that You desire. Fashion my little one just as You would have him/her to be. Thank You, Lord, that Your hand is continually upon me and my little one. Amen.

Journal Tip: Does the thought of the potter and the clay speak to you? What come to mind when you think about it?

Notes:

_____

_____

_____

_____

_____

_____

_____

_____

_____

_____

Week 29

JESUS LOVES CHILDREN

"Then little children were brought to Jesus for Him to place His hands on them and pray for them. But the disciples rebuked those who brought them. Jesus said, "Let the little children come to me, and do not hinder them, for the kingdom of heaven belongs to such as these." When He had placed His hands on them, he went on from there."
Matthew 19:13-14

Jesus loves little children! He acknowledged their importance in front of others. We should never look down on little ones or act like they are not there. Jesus took the time to pray for them and so should we. I get somewhat annoyed at people who ignore children in their midst. God can and does use children. They are important because 1.) Each individual is important to God 2.) Everyone has gifts and fruits that would benefit the body 3.) They are the church of tomorrow. We should want our children to be surrounded by others who will encourage them in the things of the Lord, look upon them with love, acknowledge their importance, and value their place in the Kingdom of God!

Dear Lord,
I thank You for taking the time to pray for the children. I ask that You would bless them today from Your heavenly throne. I ask that You extend Your hand to my child today and pray for him/her. Your Word says that You are there at the right hand of the Father praying for us. Thank You. I ask that my child would be surrounded by adults who would pray for them, cultivate Your Word in them, encourage them to use their gifts, encourage them in their walk with You, and to praise them for jobs well done. Oversee the teachers, mentors, Sunday School leaders, pastors, and all others who will come into his/her sphere of influence in the future. Thank You, Lord. Amen.

Journal Tip: Who prayed for you as a child? Who encouraged you? Do you remember a favorite teacher? Why is it important for your child to be encouraged by others?

Notes:

_____

_____

_____

_____

_____

_____

_____

_____

_____

OVERCOMING THROUGH CHRIST

You dear children, are from God and have overcome them, because the one who is in you is greater than the one who is in the world." 1 John 4:4

There have been some great deceptions by the enemy in our world. One of the greatest of these is to make the Christian feel and believe that God is not really God (all powerful, all knowing, and all present). Even some current children's books depict the powers of darkness as being equal to or even sometimes greater than the power of good (God). Our children need to know that the devil never has nor will he even be on the same level as God. He was a created angelic being that God cast out of heaven. At no time has he been or will he be greater than God. God HAS always been greater. When we are in Christ, Christ is in us. This verse reminds us that through the power that Christ has... and because He is in us... we can be over comers of the enemy. Empower your child by teaching him/her this valuable truth.

Dear God,
You are the Almighty One! The Risen Savior! The Lord of Hosts! The First and Last! The Good Shepherd! The Creator of the Universe! The Beginning and the End! The I Am! The Lion of Judah! The Prince of Peace! The Light of the World! I acknowledge Your power and authority over me today and over the members of this household. God, remind me often to express to my child that You are all powerful and that because You are in us, we can overcome anything that comes against us in this world. I want my child to know that there is none greater than You and that the enemy has no authority over me because of the work You did on the cross! He has been overcome by the blood of the Lamb! You have given us the keys to Your power and authority if we will only use them. I pray against the world view that says that the enemy is as great as You. You are the I AM! Let it rise up in might within this household and to my child. What weapon of the enemy can stand against You? Sickness? No, You are greater! Attacks against our minds? No, You are greater! Sin? No, You are greater! Praise God! Amen.

Journal Tip: Express why you think this is an important tool in teaching your child who he/she is in Christ!

Notes:

_____

_____

_____

_____

_____

_____

_____

Week 30

FEEDING YOUR BABY

"As newborn babes, desire the pure milk of the Word, that you may grow thereby."
1 Peter 2:2

What a wonderful design God made in milk. It's a pure complete food. Babies don't come out of the womb and start asking for steak and potatoes (although you may feel like they might after the cravings you may have had during pregnancy). Infants require milk as their sole food source during the beginning of their lives. Likewise, baby Christians require the pure milk of the Word as their soul food source. As an infant grows and matures, then the more solid forms of food will be acceptable to them.

God,
I thank You for perfectly designing a food source for children when they are born. Whether I choose to breast feed or formula feed, I pray that You would guide my decision. Only You know what circumstances I will face after delivery. Only You know the journey I am on. I pray that my steps would be ordered of You so that my child will receive the nutrients that he/she needs for healthy growth and development. I pray that You would keep me protected from comments that might be harmful to me in any way and that You would be my confidence in this area. I pray that I would not give way to any outside ideals or pressures, but seek Your will for my life.
As my baby grows, help him/her to be fed the pure milk of the Word day by day. I would never dream of neglecting the physical feeding of my baby. Let me have the same unction toward sharing the Word of God with my child so that he/she may grow thereby.
I pray that You would also give me wisdom and knowledge as the "solids"(in food or spiritual teachings) are introduced to my child. I pray that I would be attentive to his/ her growth and needs. I come against any possible allergies or adverse reactions. Let this baby grow strong in his/her physical body and in his/her spirit. Thank You, Lord, for Your help in this area. Amen.

Journal Tip: Can you imagine what it will be like to feed your baby for the first time? Have you been learning about the stages of development in infants? Have you thought of ways you would feed his/her spirit during the first year (Christian Music, simple Bible readings, praying, etc.)?

Notes:

_____

_____

_____

_____

_____

_____

Week 30

INHERITANCE OF GOD

"Houses and wealth are inherited from parents..." Proverbs 19:14a

What are you going to leave your child when you are gone? Do you have anything of value that is worth giving? As we have children, there are many things that we would like to give them. Some of these things would include material things such as a nice house to live in located in a safe neighborhood, decent clothes to wear, food, toys to play with, and a sound education. Have you also considered what you are giving to your child that isn't seen? What about faith, love, respect, courtesy, kindness, gentleness, or diligence to name a few. Clothing wears out and goes out of style, houses fade and crumble. What can you give your child that won't pass away with time? Yes, we should be planning and saving for our children, but there is more to their upbringing than materialism.

I love the verse in Numbers 18:20 when God tells Aaron 'I am share and your inheritance'. God wants to be our portion in all things. He wants us to walk in close relationship to Him and depend on Him. If all else fails us in life, God never will. He is more than enough when we are redeemed in Him. No matter if you are the poorest person in material possessions that you know or the richest, the most important inheritance you will leave your child is their faith in God. That is something that will never lose value throughout eternity!

Dear God,
I thank You that You are my inheritance. Thank You for being a lasting legacy to me and to the children that I will raise. Show me in Your loving ways how to raise my little one in Your ways so that You will be an inheritance for him/her. You are my inheritance and I ask that Your presence will pass forth in this family from generation to generation. Meet the material needs that we have, but help us to never put our hope or trust in them. Remove the scales from our eyes that blind us to righteousness and replace our heavenly vision with things that are only temporary. Help us to see You in all things at all times. Bless this baby as he/she comes into this family. Bless this house for having our new baby in it. May we leave great inheritance to our child. Amen.

Journal Tip: Describe your household and what kind of life your child will be brought up in. What are your thoughts about God being our inheritance? What does that mean to you personally and what does that mean for your child?

Notes:

_____

_____

_____

_____

_____

_____

DISCOURAGEMENT

**"But my mouth would encourage you; comfort from my lips would bring you relief".
Job 16:5**

Discouragement comes to us many times in life. Perhaps you're discouraged because of your growing waistline, your lack of energy, your finances, family situation, friendships or lack of time to grow in the things of the Lord. Take heart. God has not abandoned you. He knows just what you are going through, how you feel, and what you are facing. His shoulders are big enough and strong enough to bear your burden today. Sometimes the best thing is to roll that discouragement onto the Lord and allow Him to work in your life. No matter what you're facing, there is hope in Him. He can not only make a way in the desert, but He can give you the encouragement and relief you need!

Dear God,
Your shoulders are big enough and strong enough to bare the discouragement or disappointment in my life. I cast it off onto You and ask that You sustain me today. Encourage my spirit and bring relief to my mind and heart. You are concerned about every area of life (body, soul, and spirit) and You desire health and wholeness in all three areas. Work in me even in this moment. Bind up my emotional wounds and apply Your healing balm of Gilead. I ask that You would remove any and all discouragement from me today and bring life into that area. Even though I may not see the solution, I trust in You and know that there is a divine answer on the way. In Your name, amen.

Journal Tip: What came to mind when you read the word "discouragement"? Roll that burden over to the Lord today and then be sure to come back tomorrow and record how you are feeling!

Notes:

_____

_____

_____

_____

_____

_____

_____

_____

_____

228

Week 30

THE SPIRIT TESTIFIES THAT WE ARE GOD'S CHILD

"The Spirit Himself testifies with our spirit that we are God's children. Now if we are children, then we are His heirs- heirs of God and co-heirs with Christ, if needed we share in His sufferings in order that we may share in His glory." Romans 8:16

Do you feel like you are suffering today? Sometimes the demands of pregnancy touch every facet of our lives. The suffering is all worth it when you see the glory of the Lord revealed through the child He is blessing you with. Yes, remember that pregnancy is a blessing! Let the Spirit speak to you today and bring you comfort.

Dear Lord,
Thank You for Your Spirit that is continually with me through my pregnancy. When I am down, when I am uplifted... You are continually there. I ask that You would ease my load today and keep me healthy in body, spirit, and soul. I thank You that I am Your child and you care for me so deeply. You know my every thought, every weakness, and every load I have to bear. Reveal to me the joy of my salvation today. I ask that ministering angels would surround me and my household. Bless this little one within me who relies on me for life. I ask that he/she would be nourished today in his/her body. Keep my placenta healthy and right where it is supposed to be located. I come against Placenta Previa or any other condition that may cause my child to be in danger. Continue to strengthen the bond that I have with my child. Meet every need that I or my baby may have today. Let Your plans go forth. I ask all of these things in Your name. Amen.

Journal Tip: Have you had a physical exam at your doctor lately? Are there any problems to report? Are you in great condition? Do you feel like God's Spirit is with you during your pregnancy? Why or why not?

Notes:

_____

_____

_____

_____

_____

_____

_____

_____

_____

_____

Week 30

SALT AND LIGHT

"You are the salt of the earth... You are the light of the world.... In the same way, let your light so shine before men that they may see your good deeds and praise Your Father in heaven." Matthew 5:13,14,16

How is a Christian like salt and light? Salt was used as a preservative in Biblical times, as well as a flavoring for food. In this way, we can see a perfect picture of how God intends for us to be "salt" in the world. He has also called us to be light. If you have ever been in a dark room and lit a small candle, you understand that one little light dispels the darkness! We are to be His light in this dark world; representatives of God and His love to those around us. Let's ask the Lord to make us and our children salt and light.

Dear God,
Praises flow from me today when I think about Your light shining in my little one. I pray that You would send me and my child forth as salt and light. Give me understanding in this area and a desire to see it accomplished in the world around me. You make us salt and light for Your glory among men. You do not desire for Your salt and light to be hidden. Bring us forth so that You may be glorified. I pray that You would give me creative ways to teach this "salt and light" concept to my child, such as songs I have heard in the past (e.g. "This Little Light of Mine"). Show me how to be a light to those around me, especially my family and children. In Your name, amen.

Journal Tip: What do you think about when you consider being salt and light? Do you think your child can be salt and light to others, even at a young age?

Notes:

_____

_____

_____

_____

_____

_____

_____

_____

_____

_____

BALANCING YOUR TIME

"Then He said to them, 'Suppose one of you has a friend and he goes to him at midnight and says, 'Friend, lend me three loaves of bread...' The one inside answers, 'Don't bother me. The door is already locked, and my children are with me in bed. I can't get up and get you anything.'" Luke 11:5, 7

One of the dangers in parenting is getting so absorbed with our own personal and family needs and comforts that we do not have time to give to others. Many times, we commit to a task with family or at church which we soon find abandoned because we have failed to create a balance. Some may be faced with the opposite end of the spectrum, which would need to be scaled back. It's alright to have to say no to people or activities while you are pregnant. I challenge you today to not allow either extreme to overtake you. Don't let that to happen to your family! Create a balance.

Dear Lord,
I thank You that You have designed our lives and created them with purpose. I pray that You would help me find a task that I can do while I am expecting. As my life is changing, so are my personal ministry opportunities. I know there is something for me to do and a specific area where You would have me give to others. Where would You send me, Lord? What would You have me to do? I pray that You would open and close doors in my life that I would clearly see the path I am to be on. Lay someone on my heart that I can uphold in prayer today- perhaps another new mother or expectant mother that may need prayer. Help me to find the balance in life between family life and reaching out to others. I pray that my child would be a person who would reach out to others, even at a young age. Help everyone in this family to grow together and individually in ministering to others. In Your name, amen.

Journal Tip: Do you think it's important to give of yourself to others? How would you express your thoughts to your child? What kinds of things do you do to reach out to others? Has God given you direction in ministry during pregnancy?

Notes:

_____

_____

_____

_____

_____

_____

_____

_____

Week 30

LEARNING TO TALK

"When I was a child, I talked like a child, I thought like a child, I reasoned like a child"
1 Corinthians 13:11

Children are so enjoyable when they are learning to talk. It's exciting to hear them utter their first words and babble in their own language. Children think and reason like children... because they <u>are</u> children. Don't strive to make your little one grow up too fast or place unrealistic developmental or educational expectations on them. Children need to be children. Cherish every minute that you have with them because you won't believe how fast the first year moves along. It's a fantastic journey.

Lord,
I pray that You would help me savor every minute of my child's first year. Help me be attentive to his/her first words, steps, and accomplishments. There will never be another year like the first one. There's so much growth and new skills developing. Give me creative ways to preserve all the "first" memories that we will make. I pray that my baby would progress in Your time frame. Help him/her to develop in a healthy way. Help me to grow and develop as the parent of this little one. I pray that I would play an active role in his/her growth and development. I pray that You would keep him/her from any speech disorders or communication deficiencies/problems of any kind. May he/she be fluent in verbalizing thoughts, feelings, prayers, praise, and love. Give understanding to speech patterns and language, especially if he/she is to be bilingual. Show me if there ever comes a time when he/she needs assistance or help. I ask it in Your name, Amen.

Journal Tip: What are some things that you can imagine will happen during your baby's first year? What are some ideas of how you could record your memories of the baby's first year?

Notes:

_____

_____

_____

_____

_____

_____

_____

_____

_____

_____

Week 31

PROVERBS 31 WOMAN (1)

"She is clothed with strength and dignity; she can laugh at the days to come."
Proverbs 31:25

Proverbs 31:10-31 gives us an insight into a "wife of noble character". You only need to read it to find inspiration for your life. Does the focus verse describe you today? Are you clothed, literally wrapped in strength and dignity? Do you feel worthy? Sometimes when you are expecting, it seems like everyone is looking. At times that may be true. So do you reflect a nobility and worthiness of a King's Kid? And what about the end of this verse that says 'she can laugh at the days to come'? Can you resemble that or is there fear, trepidation, and thoughts of inadequacy lingering in your mind? Let's pray and ask God to make verse 25 a reality in your life!

Heavenly Father,
I thank You for giving wisdom, insight, and inspiration throughout the book of Proverbs. I pray that I would resemble the "wife of noble character" in Proverbs 31. Wrap me literally in strength and dignity. As others view me during pregnancy, I want Your reflection to shine through me. I know that a close walk with You is what brings nobility to the Proverbs 31 woman and I ask that You draw me closer and closer to You in the coming days. I want to be able to trust in You and not fear the days ahead. I pray that joy, laughter, and peace would flood my soul in this hour. My baby deserves a mother that is confident in You. Thank You, Lord, for creating life in me this day. Amen.

Journal Tip: Does this verse describe you or are there things in it that set off bells? Write down your thoughts and then take them to the Lord in prayer.

Notes:

_____

_____

_____

_____

_____

_____

_____

_____

_____

_____

PROVERBS 31 WOMAN (2)

"She speaks with wisdom and faithful instruction is on her tongue."
Proverbs 31:26

What mother wouldn't love to be thought of as wise and a giver of faithful instruction? As our children age, we should desire to have a good reputation in their eyes. Can he/she trust us with advice? Are we faithful to keep what they have told us in confidence without sharing with others? Are we faithful to be there for our children when we need them? Even when we fail in this area as parents, God will never fail our children. That doesn't give us reason to slack off when it comes to giving advice, wisdom, or instruction, but it does take the pressure off to be perfect! Commit this area to God.

God,
I acknowledge that all wisdom comes from You and your Word. I thank You that You freely give to us faithfully when we ask. I pray that as I raise my child that You would be there ever present, guiding me with faithful wisdom and instruction. May I in turn give those same nuggets to my children. Help me to watch my tongue in all instances. May I speak with words that will bring life and encouragement and not works that would bring destruction. When I am in need of wisdom, let me ask. Help me to guide my child in wisdom and integrity. I want to be a mom that my child would want to come to for advice instead of avoid. I pray that we would find each other faithful in giving and receiving instruction, correction, wisdom, encouragement, and love. In Your name I ask it. Amen.

Journal Tip: How did you feel when you went to your parents for advice? How do you want things to be between your children and you when it comes to asking for advice, wisdom, or instruction?

Notes:

_____

_____

_____

_____

_____

_____

_____

_____

_____

PROVERBS 31 WOMAN (3)

"She watches over the affairs of her household and does not eat the bread of idleness."
Proverbs 31:27

I haven't met a mother yet that would be described as "idle"! Maybe it's all the running after kids, picking up toys, cleaning dishes, or carting them off to wherever. Even during pregnancy, before baby has arrived, there are so many things to take care of inside and outside of the home. No matter if you are working or not, it is usually mom that keeps the house affairs in order. That can be a tall order if you are stretched too thin. I believe that God can give grace in any situation and organize your time when you are feeling overwhelmed by the many tasks that must be done during your day. God can prompt others to help you as well. You don't need to feel like Super Woman! Shared responsibility can be very rewarding. Whatever your situation is today, God would like to create peace in your life and make sense of all your loose ends.

Heavenly Father,
You see my coming and my going. You see each time I rise and when I lie my head down for a night's sleep. Your eyes are always on me watching the affairs of my day. Your arms are there to hold me during the difficult times when it seems like I can't get anything done. When I rise, help me to commit my day to You. Order it in the way You would have it go and help me to achieve the goals that I must accomplish in my day. Put my house in order and give me the wisdom, endurance, strength, and diligence needed to manage my household. I ask that where there seem to be mountains, that You would make them like tiny mole hills. Bring others in to help carry the load when I need it. Help me to accept assistance when I need it. Sometimes I feel too busy, running to and fro. Quiet my spirit this day. Renew me. Revitalize me. Show me when I need to rest to recharge myself. I thank You, Lord, for caring for my entire household this day. Bless my household I pray, Amen.

Journal Tip: What kinds of things are you in charge of concerning your household? Do you feel like you have too much to do sometimes? Let God show you where you can cut back and what things are important. Perhaps it's time to call someone to help share the load?

Notes:

_____

_____

_____

_____

_____

_____

_____

_____

PROVERBS 31 WOMAN (4)

"Her children arise and call her blessed; her husband also, and he praises her:"
Proverbs 31:28

There have been many people in my life that I have had the honor of standing up and saying wonderful things about. Sometimes it's been at birthdays, others at graduations or anniversaries. Perhaps you have had similar experiences. My most cherished are when I have had the chance to honor those women in my life that have mothered me; my own mom, my mother-in-law, my spiritual mothers... all have a special and blessed place in my heart. When children arise and bless their mothers they are saying that all their hard work has paid off. When they taught you, instructed you, corrected you, praised you, encouraged you, it meant something life changing. They are truly blessed by the life they have chosen to live in Christ and in turn have passed a legacy of righteousness and godliness onto others. My younger children are just getting to the age when they are saying truly touching things to me. It builds up my faith and determination to persistence to keep on in the things of the Lord. When you hear these words of blessing from your little one, you will know that God has answered your faithfulness.

Dear God,
The mere thought of my child blessing me thrills my heart. I hope that one day I will be able to see the fruits of the prayers and laboring of love that I have already sown into my little one. I want to stand as a mother that is praised by her children for teaching them, instructing them, correcting them, and persuading them in the things of the Lord. Show me how I can accomplish this each and every day. I know that it takes consistency to see such fruit. Help me to be diligent and steadily paced in the race set before me. I ask that You watch over my baby today. Continue to help him/her grown healthful and strong. Thank You for his/her life. Amen.

Journal Tip: Who are those that you would bless today if given the chance. What would you say? Imagine your baby saying the same things about you when he/she is grown. Be blessed today!

Notes:

_____

_____

_____

_____

_____

_____

_____

_____

PROVERBS 31 WOMAN (5)

"Give her the reward she has earned, and let her works bring her praise at the city gate."
Proverbs 31:31

The reward of motherhood would have to be raising children who fear and serve the Lord! When they are grown, having been raised in the faith, they will begin passing that godly heritage throughout generation after generation. Perhaps you come from a family that hasn't served the Lord. You have a chance to totally change the spiritual history of your family forever! Godly persistence doesn't go unnoticed. Those who are watching you are learning from you and will spread the word loud and clear. The verse says 'let her works bring her praise at the city gate'. God will honor you when you honor Him and you will be a blessing to more than those in your household!

Heavenly Father,
I ask that You would make me a blessing to all those who know me and are around me. I want to be counted as a worthy servant and a great godly mother. I know that a life of righteousness is rewarded. Perhaps not from the lips of men, but nonetheless YOU honor me. Verse 30 of Proverbs says "A woman that fears the Lord is to be praised." If I am to be found praiseworthy for anything, Lord, it is all because of You! I ask that You would begin a new era in the spiritual lineage of my family. I pray for more to rise up that would be counted as righteous. Continue to bless generation after generation with God fearing men and women who would devote themselves to Your will and Your way. Help my family to be a voice for righteousness in a dark world. Place Your hand upon this child and the children that may come in my family. Mark him/her as Yours and bless him/her. I want this baby to bless the nations through the ministries and gifts that You have given to him/her. I ask it in Your name that Your kingdom might be advanced. Amen.

Journal Tip: What kind of legacy do you want to leave to your children? What kind of spiritual heritage did you come from? In your own words, speak about what you would view as your "reward" for being a godly mother.

Notes:

_____

_____

_____

_____

_____

_____

_____

PRUDENCE

"But a prudent wife is from the Lord." Proverbs 19:14b

Are you a blessing from the Lord to those around you because you are prudent? What is prudence? Prudence is defined as the ability to govern and discipline oneself by the use of reason, shrewdness in the management of affairs, or skill and good judgment in the use of resources. As a mother, you will want to show great prudence in the affairs of your children. You will set the tone of discipline, learning, morals, and spirituality in your home. Let's ask God to bless you with prudence during your season of motherhood.

Dear Lord,
Thank You for placing me right where You want me to be in life. I know I am here, experiencing exactly what You have ordained for me from the beginning. I thank You for the power of choice. Sometimes this ability to choose is used in a good way and other times it is used in a harmful way. I ask that You would help me to develop a life that is pleasing to You. Help me to make good choices, such as choosing to be prudent in life. I want to be disciplined, shrewd, and full of sound judgment. I want to be creative and frugal in the use of the resources You have given me. Help me use my talents to the best of my ability. Bless me in this area of prudence today that I may be a breath of fresh air to my husband, my children, and my extended family. Amen.

Journal Tip: Look at the definition of prudence again. Which terms describe you? Which ones do you need to prayerfully work on? How does being prudent help you in motherhood?

Notes:

_____

_____

_____

_____

_____

_____

_____

_____

_____

_____

CHOSEN LADY

"To the chosen lady and her children, whom I love in the truth- and not I only, but also all who know the truth- because of the truth, which lives in us and will be with us forever."
2 John 1

Read this entire short book of 2 John today if you get the chance. The focus of it is to keep on target spiritually. It encourages you to watch out and to be certain about what you believe and how you live. You are such a woman as the addressee in this letter- a chosen one. Sometimes you may feel like you don't get very much credit for being a mother or very much appreciation. Let me encourage you today that if you are reading this, you have already been prayed for! I appreciate your dedication to motherhood and your child! God is keeping a record of all your diligence and faithfulness. So, I say to you as John said to this woman, "Grace, mercy, and peace from God the Father and from Jesus Christ, the Father's Son, will be with us in truth and love."

Dear God,
I pray for grace, mercy, and peace to surround me today. I pray that I would be encouraged in spirit and in truth. I feel blessed that You have chosen me to be a mother. Help me to do my best at all times, even when I don't feel noticed or appreciated by others. I want to please You in all I do. Remind me that there are people praying for me. I thank You that You are making me sure of what I believe and how I live so that I can pass the best spiritual heritage to my child that I possibly can. Guard my heart and mind today and help me to be diligent to watch out for the tricks of the enemy. In Your Name I ask it. Amen.

Journal Tip: How do you feel knowing that God chose you to bring this little one into the world? How are you feeling today?

Notes:

_____

_____

_____

_____

_____

_____

_____

_____

_____

Week 32

RIGHTEOUSNESS

"The righteous man leads a blameless life; blessed are his children after him."
Proverbs 20:7

Would others look at your life and say that you are a righteous woman? Would they say that you live with integrity, believe in God, and strive to align your life with God's? If you are, your children will be blessed because of the life you have led. Let's ask the Lord to prosper our children even as our souls prosper.

Dear God,
Thank You for the blessing that follows after righteousness. Not only does a life patterned after You affect me, but it will also benefit my child. Prosper my child even as my soul prospers. I ask for spiritual understanding to grace him/her and wisdom to adorn him/her even as a toddler. I pray that I will continue to be a blessing to my little one as long as I am alive. Bless me today with health, joy, and vitality today. Nourish my body as I nourish my soul. In Your name I pray it. Amen.

Journal Tip: Do you see your life of righteousness as a blessing to your child? How so?

Notes:

_____

_____

_____

_____

_____

_____

_____

_____

_____

_____

_____

_____

_____

_____

Week 32

GODLY PARENTAL QUALIFICATIONS

"Here is a trustworthy saying, if anyone sets his heart on being an overseer, he desires a noble task. Now the overseer must be above reproach..." 1 Timothy 3: 1- 2a

In this chapter of 1st Timothy, Paul is giving instruction to Timothy about the qualifications for those who would lead in the church (deacons and overseers). I have often read this chapter and wondered what it would be like if the word "parent" was inserted in the place of "overseer" or "deacon". Would this describe you at least in part? The listed qualifications include: being above reproach, self-controlled, respectable, temperate, hospitable, able to teach, not a drunkard, not violent, gentle, not a lover of money, and of a good reputation, and trustworthy. If you had to describe what kind of parent you would want for your child, what kinds of things would you include? Look to chapter 3 of 1 Timothy for some more inspiration!

God,
I thank You that Your Word brings light and life unto me. I ask that You bring to my mind the description of the type of parent You would desire for my child. I ask that in the areas where I am lacking that You would show me how to improve in those areas. I want to manage my family well. Guide us in the fear and admonition of the Lord. I want to take care of my child in the way You have designed. I ask that You bring me revelation today and that Your Spirit would bring light onto the path that I am about to walk. I want to become a parent with confidence and not doubt the role that You have given to me. My child deserves the best parental figure in his/her life that You can give. Help me to have knowledge and understanding towards the raising of my child and what I will need to supply for him/her. Equip me for the job ahead. Bless the growth of this little one today. In Your name I ask it. Amen.

Journal Tip: Describe the type of parent that you want for your child. Put a mark by the ones you feel you may be falling short in and then take those things to the Lord in prayer.

Notes:

_____

_____

_____

_____

_____

_____

_____

_____

Week 32

TEACHING THE FEAR OF THE LORD

"Come, my children, listen to me; I will teach you the fear of the LORD."
Psalm 34:11

Can you envision yourself gathering your child/children around and teaching them about the Lord? Perhaps you will read to them the great stories of the Old Testament, teach them how to praise God though worship, or even how to pray through simple prayers at meal time or at bed time. You are their first window into how to serve God and who God is… way before they will begin talking, or reading, or even fully understanding. Commit yourself and your ways to the Lord now so that you can effectively teach your children to fear the Lord when they are born.

Dear Lord,
Thank You for Your love that is extended to me and through me. I thank You for showing me how to fear You so that I can pass on that reverence to my child. Begin to work in my heart and mind to cultivate Your Spirit and help me to plant good seeds of righteousness into my son/daughter. Give me creative, simple ways to share your truths, Word, and characteristics with my child. Help me to grow in the areas that I need to work on so that I can be a whole person, ready to minister to my child. Thank You, Lord. Amen.

Journal Tip: Imagine yourself sitting down in a room to teach your child about the Lord. What do you see yourself doing? What are some spiritual things you know will be part of their daily routine?

Notes:

_____

_____

_____

_____

_____

_____

_____

_____

_____

_____

_____

_____

Week 32

USED TO REACH THE WORLD

"He said to them, 'Go into all the world and preach the good news to all creation.'"
Mark 16:15

Everyone can touch the world! It starts in your immediate circle of family, friends, and neighbors. Then it branches out regionally to perhaps co-workers or people at church from all over the city. By starting with these small areas, God then can launch us further to affect our state, our nation, and then the world. It's easy to understand that we can reach the world when you think about giving, prayers, and missions. As God has called you and equipped you to do certain things in life, your child will be gifted and equipped as well. It may be areas similar to yours, or it could be gifts that are drastically different. Encourage him/her to use whatever they have for the good of the Lord and to take Him to the circles that they are involved in. Let's pray for your child that his/her life will be used to reach the world for Him.

Dear God,
Thank You for the gifts You have place in me and in my child. I ask that You would expand my borders and increase them today. I can be used to reach a circle of people that no one else has audience with. I know that You have divinely planted me and positioned me exactly where I am supposed to be, dealing with the people You have me to deal with. You also have a plan for my baby. I pray that he/she will rise up and impact their social circles for You. Extend those circles to the world. May a harvest be reaped because of what my child will sow? I pray that the good seed he/she plants will not be choked out by weeds, fall on rocky soil, or be snatched away by the enemy. I pray for good soil, uncontaminated fields, and protection by You. I pray against tunnel vision that would keep my son/daughters eyes focused just on the immediate circle around them. May he/she have a world vision. You may choose to call him/her to another nation through missions. I pray that my heart would rest in knowing that Your plans are being accomplished in his/her life. Bless the good news going into all the world today. In Your Name, amen.

Journal Tip: How have you been used to reach the circles of people around you? What gifts are you used in? What is your prayer for your child concerning taking Christ to the world?

Notes:

_____

_____

_____

_____

_____

_____

_____

Week 32

<u>WARRIORS</u>

"May the praise of God be in their mouths and a double-edged sword in their hands."
Psalm 149:6

This generation of children coming up is facing a totally different world than when you and I were children. Just think how things have changed since our parents were new parents. In these last days that we are living in, we need to make it a priority to raise children who will openly profess the things of the Lord and to do battle in the spiritual realm. Our freedoms in Christ are being challenged daily. We must teach our children the Word of God. The Word is the sword of the spirit. Let's pray for our children to rise up with a warrior spirit to fight against the enemy and the things of this world.

God,
I thank You that You have chosen such a time as this to bring my baby into the world. I do not face it with fear or trepidation, but with confidence that he/she will have a purpose in Your kingdom. Help me to plant spiritual truths in his/her life at a young age. Let he/she grow strong, deep spiritual roots early in life so that when the storms of life come raging by, they will not be destroyed by them. I pray for a tenacity to rise up within their little spirit, even now. Give him/her a warrior spirit that will not be shy from battling in the spiritual realm. May he/she learn Your Word and use it to fight the works of darkness. I pray that You would keep his/her feet firmly planted in You, even when days seem grim. Every day is in Your hands, no matter what it holds. We will not fear the coming days. Raise others up to stand along side my child; friends, mentors, teachers, pastors, all who will encourage them to fight the good fight of faith. In Your name I ask it, Amen.

Journal Tip: How has the world changed from the time your parents were parents until now? What came to mind as you read the devotional and prayer today? Are you fearful of the coming days and what the world will be like when your child is growing up? Find some verses about trust and write them down.

Notes:

_____

_____

_____

_____

_____

_____

_____

Week 32

COUNTING DOWN THE DAYS

"Do you count the months till they bear? Do you know the time they give birth?"
Job 39:2

Are you counting the months, days, and hours until delivery? The time of delivery is drawing closer and closer. At each doctor visit, you will be reminded (as if you need it) how far along you are. You are fully aware of the number of weeks you are to the exact day! As your last few weeks approach, your doctor visits will get more and more frequent. Your pelvic exams will resume as well, as the doctor tries to determine if you have dilated and by how much, how thinned out your cervix is getting, and whether or not your baby's head has dropped. All of these things are simply hurdles that you must cross before you reach the final prize. So keep counting those days! Don't focus on the "negatives"- remember to count your blessings along the way, too.

Dear Lord,
Thank You for sustaining me during my pregnancy. I look forward to the day when I have delivered my baby and can hold him/her for the first time. Keep me pressing on toward the goal, though I know the final days will be my most difficult. Show me the positives and keep me from dwelling on the negatives of pregnancy and childbirth. Anoint my doctor/ midwife with words of wisdom, encouragement, and with kindness. Help my doctor/midwife remain sensitive to my personal fears, concerns, and questions and at no time treat me as if I am not intellectual. Use them as a tool in my life, Lord. I thank You for the days I have left. Continue to speak to me and teach me truths during this time. Keep this baby safely protected and prepare us both for delivery day. In Your name, amen.

Journal Tip: How many weeks/days do you have left in your pregnancy? What kinds of things are you experiencing at your doctor visits and how often are you going? Has your doctor/midwife given you any added encouragement in the past few weeks?

Notes:

_____

_____

_____

_____

_____

_____

_____

_____

Week 32

WHEN YOUR CHILD IS SICK

"David pleaded with God for the child. He fasted and went into the house and spent the nights lying on the ground." 2 Samuel 12:16

Although this story in 2 Samuel doesn't end well, it gives us a good example of what to do when our children are sick. Pray and sometimes even fast! How often do we run to the doctor or put our trust in over the counter medicine to do the trick? When we are sick, we should pray... especially when it comes to our children. Even if we do need to enlist the services of doctors or hospitals, prayer should be our primary resource for the help we need. We serve the one who fashioned our bodies. Who better than the maker of the body to heal it? God does use doctors and medicines as tools to heal, but ultimately it is up to Him to bring about your healing.

Dear Lord,
Help me to remember in times of trouble in the health of my child, myself, or anyone else in this house that we would seek You first for healing. Give us the wisdom and discernment to know when medical attention is needed, even if presenting symptoms may not indicate a problem. You who fashioned the body are able to heal it. Doctors cannot heal, they can only aid in healing. You are the healer. I thank You for paying the price for my healing with the stripes you bore on your back (Isaiah 53:5). I ask that You protect my child from diseases and illnesses. Give us grace and mercy if we ever have to face a medical situation, accident or otherwise. Help me to keep a clear head about me, calmness in my actions, and peace in my heart when my little one is sick. In Your name, amen.

Journal Entry: Can you remember a time when you were sick growing up and a parent made you feel better? What did they do? Write a short account.

Notes:

_____

_____

_____

_____

_____

_____

_____

_____

_____

_____

Week 33

REMEMBERING OTHERS

"And do not forget to do good and to share with others, for with such sacrifices God is pleased." Hebrews 13:16

Do you have friends or relatives that have blessed your life? It's easy to take from friends or family and not give back during times like pregnancy. Remember you have to BE a friend as well! Don't neglect to pray for them, to encourage them, and share with them from the Word. Just like you, they are going through things and may need a friend to lift them up. You may not feel like you have much of a ministry right now, but everyone can pray and share with others. Perhaps you can be used to meet a need in someone else today. Let's ask the Lord to reveal avenues of ministry for you.

Dear Lord,
I thank You for using me, even when I feel like there might not be too much I have to offer right now. Bring to mind people that I can pray for, encourage, or share with today. Use me in whatever way You can, I pray. I know others have blessed me and I want to be a blessing, too. Help me not to focus only on me during my pregnancy, but others as well. Remind me to do good and do what I can for others. Open up doors of opportunity for me this day. I want my child to be a person who does not forget others. Help me to raise him/her up in a way so that he/she would be thoughtful and compassionate toward others. Instill a desire to pray within his/her heart that he/she may learn to pray for others, share, or do good towards others even at an early age. In Your name I ask it. Amen.

Journal Tip: Write down a few names that come to mind that you could pray for or share with today. Perhaps someone you know is also an expectant mother. Write down what you would pray for the mother and her baby. You may be praying for your child's future friends!

Notes:

_____

_____

_____

_____

_____

_____

_____

_____

_____

_____

Week 33

EACH CHILD IS BORN WITH GIFTS

"But each man has his own gift from God; one has this gift, another has that."
1 Corinthians 7:7

Isn't it fitting that God designed us so perfectly? That design also included "gifts" that we would be given in order to minister to others. Your baby has a gift(s) that God wants to use. It will be your parental job to help your son or daughter recognize that gift. You'll have to nurture it and help it develop as he/she grows. Helping a child find out who they are in the Lord is one of the most important roles a parent can have.

God,
I thank You that You have planted a gift into this little one. I pray that as he or she grows, You will bring forth that gift so that it will be evident to him or her and to me as the parent. I pray that You will supply the necessary experiences, resources, opportunities, and environment in which they can nurture, expand, develop, and use their gifts. Whatever it is Lord, I pray that it will be revealed at a young age so that it can be brought forth in due time. You have created them just how You intended to. I will not force unrealistic expectations on them or try to make them into something that isn't of You or in Your design for them. I pray that he/she will use their gifts all through their life and that they will at no time lay dormant. I pray that they will not seek to use their gifts for their own selfish gain, but will dedicate them back to You to be used for Your purposes. I pray that he/she will delight in the gifts You've given to them and will at no time seek the gifts of others! Thank You for the workings of Your body. I pray that I will continue to seek You for guidance and instruction concerning my child's gifts. In Your name, amen.

Journal Tip: What are the gifts/skills that God has given to you or members in your family? How are you using your gifts for the Lord? How will your gifts help you as a mother?

Notes:

_____

_____

_____

_____

_____

_____

_____

_____

_____

_____

CHILD HEARING FROM GOD

**"The LORD came down and stood there, calling as at the other times, 'Samuel! Samuel!'
Then Samuel said, 'Speak for your servant is listening.'" 1 Samuel 3:10**

Samuel had been sleeping when the Lord came to him calling his name. In those days, the Word of the Lord was rare as there were not many visions (verse 1). It was even said that Samuel didn't know the Lord yet, as the Word of the Lord had not yet been taught to him (verse 7). Samuel assumed that Eli, the priest he was working under in the temple, was calling to him. He arose when hearing his name and ran to Eli. Eli had not called however and sent him back to bed. The second time this happened; Eli realized that the Lord must be calling him and instructed him to answer the Lord. Samuel did. God used Samuel in this instance to deliver a message to Eli. In the same manner, we should expect the Lord to communicate with our children. It will be our job to encourage them in these times. Children can be used in their gifs even at a very young age. Samuel was used as a voice of the Lord. Verse 19 tells us "The Lord was with Samuel as he grew up, and he let none of his words fall to the ground." Our children may even be used to be messengers of the Lord into our families through the gifts He's put in them.

Dear Heavenly Father,
Thank You for the gifts and character traits that You have placed in my child. I ask that You would use me as his/her parent to encourage him/her in times when You are speaking to him/her. No matter if they are young or not, You can use anyone You choose. Let me never look down on him/her because he/she is young. Help me to realize that even though they need to grow in instruction concerning the things of the Lord, You can still illuminate their minds to understand things that I do not. Help me to guide as a parent with the discernment and understanding that Your Spirit can give me. Let my spirit recognize when You are doing a work in my child. As You did in Samuel, never let anything fall to the ground that You have gifted my son or daughter to do. In Your name, amen.

Journal Tip: Do you think it was hard for Eli to recognize and receive in humility that God was speaking to Samuel? What can you do to ensure that You will recognize the Lord's working in your child?

Notes:

_____

_____

_____

_____

_____

_____

_____

Week 33

EQUIPPED BY GOD

"Equip you with everything good for doing His will, and may He work in us what is pleasing to Him..." Hebrews 13:21

Feeling a little unequipped today? Don't lose hope! God has not called you to failure. He has a plan for you and will equip you with everything you need to do the job. Of course, we see this in the physical that in order to have a baby, God has created us anatomically different from men! We needed a uterus and a way to feed our babies. God has taken care of those things already. Primarily our doubts in parenting are a battle in the mind. That's where we feel inadequate. We think we don't measure up or could never be as great as so and so. Well, I have news for you. God is going to equip you with everything good you need in order to care for and nurture your child. Just trust in Him for the provision and He will work in You what is pleasing to Him.

Dear God,
I come to You today with thanksgiving for this baby and all the promises and hope that he/she inspires. At times, I may feel like I am not equipped to handle pregnancy, childbirth, or mothering, but I know You do have a plan for us. I want to do Your will and work in ways that are pleasing to You as a parent. I know that with You all things are possible and I have nothing to fear. So today, I am turning over all my fears, apprehension, and doubt to You. I ask that You replace worry with confidence, fear with stability, and doubt with assurance. I ask for an extra measure of grace and mercy today. Please show me in a real, evident way, how You are caring and watching out for me today. Thank You, Lord. Amen.

Journal Tip: Are you confident in Christ today or are there areas where you feel you are not equipped or prepared to handle a baby? Are there ways to prepare and grow towards being more ready to have your baby? What have you learned so far during your pregnancy that would show you that God is equipping you?

Notes:

_____

_____

_____

_____

_____

_____

_____

_____

_____

MISTAKES AS A PARENT

"If the LORD delights in a man's way, he makes his steps firm; though he stumble, he will not fall, for the LORD upholds him with his hand." Psalm 37:23-24

No parent is perfect. We all make mistakes. You might as well accept it. No matter how hard we try, we will still stumble in areas of parenting. The question is, how will you handle it when you do? Will you give up and quit? Will you focus on the failure? Before you answer, let's look at the verse again and get a godly perspective! Psalms tells us that our steps can and will be firm when we are walking with Him and that even though we stumble, the Lord will hold us up with His hand. What do we learn from this? First of all we learn that our steps are to be walked as to please God. If we make that a goal, our steps will be firm and sure. Secondly, we learn that even if we stumble on the path of parental guidance, we will not fall. There is not a hole or article of debris that can bring us down. God will balance us out and make us steady. Thirdly, let's be sure to hold on to His steady hand as He upholds us. It's easier to keep a grip on things in life when we are holding on tight to Him!

Heavenly Father,
I thank You for being my stability today. You balance out my life and create order where otherwise there would be chaos. I pray that I would walk the path of life firmly planted in You. I ask that You would help me to accept the fact that I am not perfect, but You are ever perfecting me. There is a difference. Help me to achieve that balance in my mind and actions when it comes to parenting. Even at times when I may stumble as a parent; help me to regain my footing quickly. I pray that I would openly communicate my faults with my child so that they know that parents make mistakes too. Bless baby today and his/her growth. In Your name, amen.

Journal Tip: Imagine if you made a mistake as a parent. How do you think you'll handle it? Do you expect to be perfect or will you make mistakes?

Notes:

_____

_____

_____

_____

_____

_____

_____

_____

Week 33

PROTECTING FROM EVIL

"Now a man of the house of Levi married a Levite woman, and she became pregnant and gave birth to a son. When she saw that he was a fine child, she hid him for three months."
Exodus 2:1-2

The Israelites had become a large people and their mere size became a threat to the Egyptians. Following the death of Joseph, another king had come into power who did not know about Joseph. From that point on, the Israelites were in bondage to Egypt. During the time of Moses' birth, Pharaoh gave an order to all his people that every boy born to the Israelites was to be thrown into the Nile. He was trying to wipe out his threat. Isn't that like the devil who is intent on killing and destroying anything good that God is doing? There will be times as a parent when you will have to protect your child from the plans of the enemy and possibly people who have evil intentions toward your child. God showed Moses' mother a way to protect her child and if need be, He will show you, too. It meant that the mother would have to take a risk in order to protect her little one and face possible harm herself. What courage. The enemy wanted to harm Moses because it was God's plan to use him to deliver the Israelites. God has a plan for your little one, too. Threats to our children are not only physical harm, but spiritual and emotional as well. Let's ask the Lord for guidance and wisdom when it comes to protecting our little ones to see that they are able to fulfill God's purposes in their lives.

Dear God,
I know that You have a very special plan for my baby. I ask for wisdom and knowledge to recognize when the enemy is trying to destroy my child and for boldness and bravery to protect him/her from all threats, physical, emotional, and spiritual. Help me to rise up and take authority over the enemy. I want to resolve to be a parent that will go to great lengths to see that my child will be able to grow and prosper in the things of the Lord. When I have need of direction, grant it to me just like you did for Moses' mother. I ask that Your Spirit would rise up within my baby and compel him/her to follow the life's journey that You have set before him/her. May he/she be a person who hears Your voice clearly and follows in obedience just as Moses did. Bless him/her with righteousness and determination to accomplish Your will and purposes in his/her life. In Jesus' name, amen.

Journal Tip: Can you think of an example from your childhood where your parents or a spiritual mentor stepped in and protected you from something? Do you think it will be easy for you to protect your children or will it be difficult? How do you handle adversity? Can God help you in that area?

Notes:

_____

_____

_____

_____

HE'LL FIGHT FOR YOU; CONTENTION

"I will contend with those who contend with you, and your children I will save."
Isaiah 49:25b

Contention comes in life. The word "contend" means to strive against others or difficulties. You will contend with your children from time to time. Also, every parent will have to deal with other parents at some point. When you are expecting, it may come in the form of unsolicited advice. When your child is older and approaching the toddler stage, it may be in the form of parents wanting to tell you how to raise your child or pointing out his/her flaws. I think of incidents where children bite or hit other children and there must be confrontation in those areas. Sometimes as a parent, you feel like you or your child is misunderstood. Keep in mind that God is the only one you are trying to please as a parent and that what works for one family may not work for another family. Let God direct your path in parenting and you can be assured that the path you are on will only lead to God's blessing.

Dear God,
Thank You for allowing me to raise this child in the fear and admonition of You. I pray that You would guide my steps this day and put them in order for me and my child. I know that I may have to face people at some point in life that have no idea who I am or what I am about. In those times, come into the situation and remind me as only You can that You are the only one that I need to please. Many may come and tell me to do things this way or that way, but I ask that You would give me ears to hear what You are saying. Where words from others may have been wounding, bring healing and life back into those areas. Surround me with good, godly examples of parents and mentors that I can learn from. Protect me from people with ill intent or others who are critical out of their own fears or insecurities. Bind my feet as a parent to Your will and ways. As Your Word says, You will contend with those who contend with me. Let it be so. Help me to stand up for what I believe, especially when it involves the spiritual, emotional, or physical welfare of my child. Let my child know that I am an advocate for them and will fight for their best interests. In Your name I ask it, Amen.

Journal Tip: How do you deal with confrontation when it arises? Are you good at confronting problems that arise or do you tend to not deal with things? Write down your thoughts and use them in your prayer time.

Notes:

_____

_____

_____

_____

_____

FAITH FOR FEAR

"He said to his disciples, 'Why are you so afraid? Do you still have no faith?'"
Mark 4:40

It's hard to imagine the days of the disciples when they literally walked with Jesus in the flesh upon the earth. In this passage the disciples were in a boat with Jesus crossing the sea. A furious storm came upon them and the waves began to swamp the boat. Jesus was in the stern sleeping on a cushion and the disciples woke him declaring that they were going to drown. Immediately Jesus spoke and calmed the waves and the wind. Who was this man that the wind and waves obeyed?   He is the same God that you serve today! Though He is not here in the flesh, He promised that the Holy Spirit would abide with us.

As you anticipate your labor, deliveries, and motherhood, do not get distracted by the waves of emotion or circumstance that can easily overwhelm you. God is right there with you! He is still the one who speaks peace to your storms of life and calms them. Trust in Him today. Call upon the Master and those waves will cease!

Dear God,
I give You glory and praise today that You name is high above all names. I exalt You and Your majesty. I am comforted that even in my deepest fears, You can calm them. I ask that You would give me peace. I ask that You give me faith. Settle my mind and heart today just as Jesus stilled the waves of the sea. I ask that doubt would not creep in my mind, but that I would be reminded by the gentle nudging of Your Spirit that the Master is with me and I will not be overcome. I ask that you still me. Grant me rest and patience to see this pregnancy completed. Just as Jesus said that they were going to the other side, help me to trust in Your ways that You will bring this pregnancy to completion. Thank You, Lord. Reassure me today in little ways as only You can. Help me to see evidences of You in my day today, as I know You are always working things together for my good. Help this little one within my womb to rest as well. Delivery is not easy on a baby, either. Calm him/her as the labor progresses. Help things to move along at a good pace and to work according to You will. In Your name, amen.

Journal Tip: What are you most fearful or unsure of when it comes to labor and delivery? Ask God to calm that area. If you have someone praying with you during your pregnancy, don't be hesitant to share how you are feeling with them. Pray together and watch God calm your storm.

Notes:

_____

_____

_____

_____

_____

_____

Week 34

ENTERPRISE OF MOTHERHOOD

"Whatever you do, work at it with all your heart, as working for the Lord, not for men."
Colossians 3:23

With any task that we set out to accomplish, we should do all as unto Christ Himself. God has granted you this day the task of housing a new little life, eventually bringing him/her into the world and raising him/her. Look at is as a calling with a limited time frame. Unlike some jobs we might do for the Lord, having a baby involves all 3 parts of you...body, mind, and spirit to bring it to pass. Just like jobs in the workplace have a set system in order to accomplish the work at hand, you too can set goals and make sure daily pregnancy chores are taken care of. You're the CEO of this small enterprise called Motherhood. You were "hired" by the Lord to do this. Let's ask the Lord to grant us grace, diligence, and fervor in this new era you're entering.

Lord,
Thank You for this task You have given me. Although my job during pregnancy will not last long, I want to approach every day with gladness, boldness, and fervor. I want to do it heartily as unto You. Help me to appreciate each day as you are fashioning a little person inside of me. Help me to seek You at all times concerning all kinds of matters that will come into my sphere of influence during my pregnancy. Help me to set goals, manage chores, consider my health as a high job priority, prepare my home for my baby, and plan for the future of this child. May this child be blessed in part because of the way I am doing my job as an expectant mother. In Your name I pray, Amen.

Journal Tip: Now that you are nearing the end of pregnancy, do you feel the time has passed quickly or slowly? Have you realized that for the limited time of your gestation that this is a job you can do unto the Lord? What kinds of things can you take care of daily to ensure you are doing your job as an expectant mother?

Notes:

_____

_____

_____

_____

_____

_____

_____

_____

_____

THE WAY OF THE LORD

"There is a way that seems right to a man, but in the end it leads to death."
Proverbs 16:25

When it comes to pregnancy, there is a process that must be completed that we don't really have control over, nor should we. The baby grows in a way that God has ordained it. Each cell does its work and divides, just as God made it to. Our uterus grows, our bones soften, our hormones change, our placenta is formed… all these things without instructions from us. Can you imagine having to help in the process? You wouldn't even know where to begin. Too often we take the drivers seat in life when God is simply asking us to let Him take the wheel. There are many times that we think that we can figure it all out in life. God needs our cooperation to see His plans succeed, but that doesn't mean that we should have the ultimate control. Is there something in your spiritual life today that God is telling you to let go of and let Him take care of it?

Dear Lord,
Thank You for having order and authority when it comes to my life and also in my household. I praise Your name for fashioning this baby entirely by Your plan. You made the blueprint. I acknowledge Your wisdom and authority not only in this pregnancy, but also in my spiritual life. Wherever I have decided to take control where You need control, show me. I place all things back into Your hands. I want whatever You have designed for my life. I know whatever You have for me is much greater than anything I can imagine. Your dreams are bigger. Your creativity is endless. Wherever I have struggles with wanting to control my life, show me where to correct. I ask that my will would line up with Your will. I want to parent in the way you intend for me to parent. Help me to teach my little one that we are dependent upon You in life, but also that it takes our cooperation in submission to Your plans to see them through. Thank You, Lord for this precious little baby. Watch over him/her today. Open a door for me to learn or do something fun and exciting about maternity today. I ask it in Your name. Amen.

Journal Tip: What do you have planned to do today? In life, how do feel God's plans are meshing with Your plans? Do you have struggles with letting God move in areas where you would like to take control? If so where? What can you do to allow God's best in your life?

Notes:

_____

_____

_____

_____

_____

_____

_____

TAKE IT TO MOUNT MORIAH

"Then God said, 'Take your son, your only son, Isaac, whom you love, and go to the region of Moriah.'" Genesis 22:2a

Most of us remember this story in the Old Testament where God tested Abraham by asking him to take his only son and sacrifice him on Mt. Moriah. The point of this was not that God was asking Abraham to do wrong, but pushing the limits of Abraham's commitment to him. God doesn't ask for human sacrifice, but for the sacrifice of our own heart by being obedient to do what He asks. Abraham waited a long time for his son and bore him in old age. Think about what that would have meant to Abraham to have to give him up. This story is also a foreshadowing of God's sacrifice of Jesus on the cross to pay for our sins. He gave His one and only Son to die for us that we might live. I take this story as a challenge to us all as parents. Are we willing to be obedient to the Lord in every area of our child's life? Will we seek Him diligently about the raising of our children and in leading them in His ways? We also must remember that God has entrusted our children to us, but they are not ours to keep. They are ours to raise. They are ours to also let go. At the end of this story on Mt. Moriah, God tells Abraham that He is going to make his descendants as numerous as the sand on the seashore and that all nations of the earth would be blessed because he was obedient. Can you see other ways this concept applies to life? What do you hold most dear today? Perhaps you need to take it Mt. Moriah today and turn it over to God.

Heavenly Father,
I thank You, Lord for this lesson of taking what is most important in my life and turning it over to You. I ask that You would assist me in being an obedient servant. Help me be obedient to You when it comes to my child. Teach me how to guide him/her in life and teach me to let go of possessiveness, control, or anything else that might hinder him/her in his/her walk with You. As I am obedient in parenting, I pray that You would bless my descendants as well. Let godly principles, precepts, and promises cling to our minds and hearts.
If there is anything in my life that I need to turn over to You so that You can bless it, please do it today. I ask for forgiveness where I have taken matters into my own hands instead of entrusting them to You. This may go for my job, my finances, my self esteem, my family, my possessions, even my baby. Touch my baby in a special way today and bless him/her through my obedience. I ask it in Your name, amen.

Journal Tip: Have you committed in your heart to be obedient to God in the area of parenting? What are your thoughts as you read the account of Abraham? Has God shaped your sense of values? How so? How will that be a blessing to your child?

Notes:

_____

_____

_____

_____

Week 34

JOY DURING PREGNANCY

"May the God of hope fill you with all joy and peace as you trust in Him, so that you may overflow with hope by the power of the Holy Spirit." Romans 15:13

Pregnancy can be a time of unsurpassed joy. What a wonderful thing God is doing within you! It's often said that the Labor and Delivery Unit is the happiest floor in the hospital. God wants to give us joy overflowing. He wants to fill us with joy. This much needed fruit of the Spirit is something that problems can't overtake. Let Him fill your entire being with His joy today.

God,
I ask for Your joy to flood every inch of me today. I want my earthen vessel to be so filled with Your joy that this baby will be filled with it, too. I ask that You rejuvenate my spirit and refresh me with Your joy. Let others see the overflowing of Your joy radiate from me. Amen.

Journal Tip: What do you think of when you consider God's joy? What things have caused joy during your pregnancy?

Notes:

_____

_____

_____

_____

_____

_____

_____

_____

_____

_____

_____

_____

_____

_____

_____

HE HAS ORDAINED OUR DAYS

"All the days ordained for me were written in Your book before one of them came to be."
Psalm 139:16b

To say that God knows everything about us is somewhat of an understatement! God knew of us before we were even conceived and knows every day that will be granted to us on this earth. I have often used this verse in speaking peace to moms (including myself) who have lost children. God's plans may not always be ours, but there is one thing for certain. He has our life's entire book written before we were born! He knows how long each person will live. Two weeks from conception, forty days, or one hundred years, He has ordered our days. If he has ordained each day, then He knows what will occur in every one! We may be shocked about things that happen in life, but God is never surprised.

God,
I thank You for being all knowing. I ask that You take away any grief or sense of loss that may be overwhelming me today and replace it with Your perfect peace. I do not blame You, Lord, for the bad things that happen in life, but I understand that You had knowledge that this would occur. So, Lord, I ask that I would be in the center of Your will in this day and hour. Settle down my physical and emotional system and help me to get over any shock I may be feeling. Set my feet on a path to healing. I come against fear of any kind that is associated with loss. Help me to see You in all of this and to see Your hand. I place my child in Your hands for all the days if his/her life. You already see the days written for him/her in Your book. Keep my eyes focused on You and not the situations around me. Settle and calm my spirit today, Lord. Bring comfort that only the Holy Spirit can bring me. My days and hours are in Your hands. Mend any areas where I may have had unrealistic expectations. In Your name I pray, Amen.

Journal Tip: Have you experienced loss of some kind or do you fear loss? Has God spoken anything into your spirit from what you read? How does this make you feel about your child's life?

Notes:

_____

_____

_____

_____

_____

_____

_____

_____

Week 34

BABY'S CRY

"The eyes of the LORD are on the righteous and His ears are attentive to their cry."
Psalm 34:15

Have you ever heard that dogs bark, ducks quack, pigs oink, and babies cry? That's the truth. Babies cry. They cry a lot. Crying is caused by a variety of reasons including, hunger, tiredness, needing changed, too hot, too cold, etc. Crying is how your baby communicates. Knowing this, however, doesn't make it any more enjoyable when you're awakened at two in the morning to an ear piercing wail for a feeding. The truth is that crying (especially for babies who cry constantly) can wear on a person's nerves, especially if you're a first time parent. God can help you in this area. Take comfort! This stage doesn't last forever! Someday you'll probably miss hearing it!

God,
I ask that You go before me and my baby in this area of crying. I ask that You would help my baby not to be colic ridden or inconsolable. Give me discernment and knowledge to quickly understand what my baby is trying to communicate and to fulfill that need. I pray that You would bless me with an abundance of patience and love for my child. Help me not to become short fused, especially at times when the baby's crying is inconvenient. Show me ways that would help my baby not be a constant crier. In times of need, help me to remember to listen to Your voice for instruction. Teach me how to respond to my baby when he/she cries. Help me to always remember the joy of my baby's first cry! Amen.

Journal Tip: What are some ways you would cope with crying? What would you do if the baby wouldn't stop crying (as in colic)?

Notes:

_____

_____

_____

_____

_____

_____

_____

_____

_____

_____

_____

260

Week 35

LOVE OF GOD

"But from everlasting to everlasting, the LORD'S love is with those who fear him, and His righteousness with their children's children." Psalm 103:17

Can you imagine it? The God of the Universe, the Creator of all things loves you deeply. If you fear Him and have a relationship with Him, that relationship will continue for all eternity. Before we were even formed He loved us, knew we were going to be born, where we were going to be born, and what we were going to do with our lives. He's known every struggle you would face, every trial (large or small), and has blessed you with His righteousness. If you walk with Him, then He gives a promise to your children and their children, that His righteousness would be theirs as well. Not a bad deal if you ask me!

Dear Lord,
Thank You for Your unfailing love today. People may fail me or change their minds, but You do not. You are forever the same. Regardless of what I do or where I am in my life, You love me just the same. I want to fear You, honor You, and serve You in all I do. I want Your love to be with me and to shine through me. As I am being used right now to house this baby You have given to me, help me to honor You and become the best mother that I am capable of becoming. Touch my baby today and let him/her be reassured by the rocking movements of my walking, the touch of my hand, or the soft muffled sound of my voice. I love this little one and I want him/her to know it. Thank You, Lord for Your continual promises to me and the generations that will be blessed through me. In Your name, amen.

Journal Tip: Do you sense God's love throughout your pregnancy? Has He spoken through His spirit to you today to let you know you are the apple of His eye? Is it comforting to know that His righteousness will follow after you and be available to not only your children, but if He tarries, your grandchildren as well?

Notes:

_____

_____

_____

_____

_____

_____

_____

_____

Week 35

<u>ANNOUNCEMENTS</u>

"But the angel said to them 'Do not be afraid. I bring you good news of great joy, which shall be for all the people. Today in the town of David a Savior has been born to you; He is Christ the Lord'; Suddenly a great company of the heavenly host appeared with the angel, praising God and saying, 'Glory to God in the highest, and on earth peace to men on whom his favor rests.'" Luke 2:10,13-14

When God announced the birth of His Son, He did it in a big way! Can you imagine the scene that night over a field near Bethlehem? I don't imagine that you will announce the birth of your child in such a grand way, but perhaps there will be singing in the heavens when your baby enters the world. All of God's ways are unknown to us. Have you considered what you are going to do to announce the arrival of your little one? With technology available today, it's possible that all your friends and loved ones will be able to see him/her shortly after birth. Don't forget to pack your cameras, etc. when you are planning for your birth. It might be a good time to consider what type of announcements you would like to have, too.

Dear God,
I know that announcements are important to You. You always do things top notch. I pray that You will show me the way to announce the arrival of my little one. Give me the knowledge that I need to decide among all the hundreds of choices I have. Open the resources I need. Make available to me what I need. I pray that You would also give me wisdom to spend wisely. Have Your way in this area. I want to honor this special time in my life and bring You glory as well. In Your name, amen.

Journal Tip: What kinds of things are you considering for baby announcements?   Have you made a list of people you want to contact after baby is born?

Notes:

_____

_____

_____

_____

_____

_____

_____

_____

_____

_____

WHEN YOU WANT TO GIVE UP

"I can do everything through Him who gives me strength." Philippians 4:13

Sometimes during pregnancy, it seems like you want to give up. It takes so long for your little one to arrive (or at least it feels that way). If any negative circumstances: financial, relational, physical, etc. have added to your woes, just remember what Paul said in Philippians. He said he had learned the secret of living in every kind of situation, which is relying on the strength of the Lord to see you thorough it. We have dependence on God continually, but it can mean the most to us when we are at our weakest and most vulnerable. Pregnancy is one of those times. We are not "ourselves". We don't feel like our normal former self, nor do we appear that way. So, some of the best Biblical advise can be learned from Paul, who was an expert in trials... do all things through Christ, who gives us the strength.

Lord,
I ask for the resolve to do all things through You. You, in turn, will give me the strength I need to do whatever it is today that I need to do. You are my source and I depend completely on You. I ask that in the days ahead You will continually lead me to a place of resting in You. I want my mind to rest, my body to rest, and my emotions to rest. I know that placing my thoughts and cares on You will lessen my burden and create a better environment for my baby to grow. Remove the turmoil and strife from me and help me to understand that with You in control, nothing is impossible. Take charge today and give me the strength for the days ahead. In Your name I ask all these things, amen.

Journal Tip: What kinds of things are you facing today that you could turn over to God?

Notes:

_____

_____

_____

_____

_____

_____

_____

_____

_____

_____

Week 35

BABY'S BATH & THE WASHING OF THE WORD

"Cleansing her by the washing with water through the Word..." Ephesians 5:26

I've never heard anyone pick up a baby and say, "Oh, how dirty and stinky you are!" On the contrary! Most of the time babies smell of baby bath soap and powder! We tend to be extra sensitive to the cleanliness of our babies. And we enjoy it. They coo and giggle as they splash around in the water. Becoming clean isn't a worry or task, it's a pleasure! When do we begin disliking cleanliness? Just as in life, as we grow and mature, it becomes harder and harder to stay clean from the things of the world. Cleanliness should be a daily habit for our bodies, minds, and spirits. In this passage in Ephesians, God is talking about the church being washed clean so that we can be presented to the Lord as a radiant church, without stain, wrinkle, or any other blemish. What a picture of cleanliness. What are we to wash with? The Word! It makes us clean through and through. So, as you prepare to give your baby his/her first bath after birth, think about how important the routine of daily washing and cleaning will be... especially when he/she starts eating solid foods. Remember that we need to be cleaned up and refreshed by the washing of the Word daily as well.

God,
Thank You for the cleansing that comes when we wash in the water of your Word. I pray that You would remind me as I clean my child that You, my Father want to cleanse me as well. You wash away all the dirt and slime of the world before it gets encrusted on me. Thank You, Lord. I am looking forward to bathing my baby. Keep him/her safe from harm (drowning, slipping/falls, scalding, etc.) during bath time. I know that it will be a fun experience and an important one, too. Help me to not just emphasize the cleanliness of the outward appearance, but of the heart as well. In Your name I ask it. Amen.

Journal Tip: Do you have supplies ready for that first bath? Are you looking forward to it? Try to get a Bible for your baby before birth. Write a note in it and underline scriptures that have meant something to you!

Notes:

_____

_____

_____

_____

_____

_____

_____

_____

Week 35

NURSERY AND PREPARATIONS

"However, as it is written: 'No eye has seen, no ear has heard, no mind has conceived what God has prepared for those who love Him.'" 1 Corinthians 2:9

When we think of our heavenly home, the Word assures us that He is preparing a place for us. In expectancy, you are busy preparing your home for the arrival of your little one. You are busy thinking about the nursery, what he/she will sleep in, what kind of mobile to hang, what colors the room should be, what kind of baby monitor to buy, what kind of bedding you will use, and what kind of accent furniture you will have. You want everything to be just right! This is an exciting time and should be a joyous one.

Dear Lord,
Thank You for being a God of preparation. I know that You are preparing me in this time to be a godly mother to my child and teaching me all kinds of new things about parenting. I thank You that You are preparing me spiritually for this ministry of motherhood. I pray that even as I prepare my home for my baby's arrival that You would put everything in order. Help us to have all that we have need of. You know the desires of my heart and I know You see everything as already done. Show me what I am to purchase and what will not be needed. I want my preparations to be done in a way that would honor You and bless my baby as well. Bring about all things for Your good. Thank You, Lord. Amen.

Journal Tip: What kinds of things have you done to your home in order to prepare for baby? Do have a nursery or crib in your room set up and ready to use when baby comes? Describe your preparations and describe the nursery/sleeping area you have created for your baby. If you are an adoptive mother, what would you like the nursery to look like?

Notes:

_____

_____

_____

_____

_____

_____

_____

_____

_____

_____

Week 35

NEED HELP FROM GOD TODAY

"My help comes from the Lord." Psalm 121:2a

Do you need something today? Perhaps you need help with housework or childbirth classes or meal preparation. Perhaps it's finances or a baby bed. Maybe it's strength or courage. When we are out of resources, isn't it comforting to know that we can go to the one whose resources are limitless? Whatever you may have need of today, I know that God can provide you with a practical, applicable answer. Take your needs to Him today. No need is too great for Him. Stand back and see what He can do!

Lord,
You know what I have need of today and that without Your help, I am powerless. I ask that You meet this need in a real, practical, and tangible way. Help me to wait patiently on You as You bring it to pass.
May peace guard my mind and heart to know that You have heard me and will answer. My hope and my confidence are in You. Amen.

Journal Tip: Are you in need of anything today? Big or small, God is over all. Write down what you need and why it is important to you. When God provides, be sure to come back to this journal entry to tell how He answered. Has He met any of your needs in the past? Can you count on Him this time?

Notes:

_____

_____

_____

_____

_____

_____

_____

_____

_____

_____

_____

PLEASANTNESS

"Perfume and incense bring joy to the heart, and the pleasantness of one's friend springs from his earnest counsel." Proverbs 27:9

We all like things that are pleasant. Needless to say that there will be days in pregnancy that we don't feel so joyous in heart. Occasionally, you'll just need to look for those things that are pleasant. Perhaps that means treating yourself to something like a bottle of perfume or maybe it's spending an hour or two with a friend. One is good for the body; one is good for the soul! God gives good things for our encouragement. Once and awhile it's good to remind ourselves of that fact. May God bless you with joy of heart and pleasant things today! Be encouraged!

Dear God,
I thank You that You care about the most basic of needs that I may have. Every day isn't trimmed with a silver lining, but You can give a joy to my heart that no one or nothing else can bring. Bring into my path today things that are pleasant and encouraging. I know You will guide me to exactly what that is today. I pray for a pleasantness to replace any and all negativity, discouragement, or wrong thoughts or attitudes. Help me to gain a godly focus today on my situations and surroundings today. Let Your peace and grace rest on me today. In Your name, amen.

Journal Tip: Think of something pleasant from your day and write it down. Then list at least three more things that you are thankful for today.

Notes:

_____

_____

_____

_____

_____

_____

_____

_____

_____

_____

_____

Week 36

BLESSED BY THE LORD

"They will not toil in vain or bear children doomed to misfortune, for they will be a people blessed by the LORD." Isaiah 65:23

May the blessing of the Lord rest on your household today. Even if this verse isn't a clad iron guarantee that your children will prosper in material ways, it is a promise that they will blessed spiritually by the Lord. God is in control of your life and He will never leave you or forsake you. Your children will not be doomed to misfortune. They will not work without anything to show for it. He does want to give His children increase and make them people of greatness. Isn't that a blessing from the Lord?

Dear Lord,
I know that whatever I do in life or whatever my children will do in life is blessed by You. You honor those who fear You and walk in Your ways. Bless the work of my child's hands, whether it be learning in school, fund raising, or whatever efforts they will make as a little one. May he/she never be called a person of misfortune. Bless him/her in material ways as well as spiritual ways. I ask that he/she would testify to others of your goodness and give an account of their blessing. We are all fortunate people who are blessed to have You as our God. Praise Your name, Lord. Amen.

Journal Tip: Where is your blessing? Can you describe some of the ways your child is already being born into blessing?

Notes:

_____

_____

_____

_____

_____

_____

_____

_____

_____

_____

_____

_____

SWELLING

"For forty years you sustained them in the desert, they lacked nothing, their clothes did not wear out nor did their feet become swollen." Nehemiah 9:21

Thank heavens pregnancy doesn't last forty years! Your forty weeks of pregnancy may seem like it, though! These verses in the book of Nehemiah provide a historical view into the care of the Lord on behalf of the children of Israel during the time of desert wandering. He sustained them, they lacked nothing. Their clothes didn't wear out, and their feet didn't become swollen. What a blessing to impart on a pregnant woman. Have you experienced any swelling so far? If you do, be sure to report it to your doctor. Some swelling is normal, especially during your last trimester. If you notice it in your feet, you can elevate them and rest more. Be sure you're drinking plenty of water, too. That will help flush out your system.

Dear God,
Thank You for Your provision today. I ask that You would watch over me and care for all the needs I may have today, physical, spiritual, or emotional. I pray that You would keep me from drastic swelling during my time of pregnancy. Keep me alert to changes in my body so that I can be diligent about my health. Grant me times of rest in the day where I can get off my feet and relax, uninterrupted. I know that You are keeping me during this time and raising up a blessing within me. Watch over us during these forty weeks, Lord. Amen.

Journal Tip: Have you experienced any swelling so far during your pregnancy? Do you have a good report to give how God has sustained you during these weeks you have been expecting?

Notes:

_____

_____

_____

_____

_____

_____

_____

_____

_____

_____

_____

_____

Week 36

WAITING

"Wait for the Lord; be strong and take heart and wait for the Lord." Psalm 27:14

Waiting, waiting, waiting. Does it seem like your pregnancy will ever end? Sometimes, the hardest thing in life to do is wait. But, the word tells us that in our waiting, we should be strong and take heart. God will bring your pregnancy to an end in time. Waiting can also be made more difficult when we are faced with pressures or circumstances that make every second of the clock seem to tick by slowly. Physician ordered bed rest can be one of those times. If you have been put on bed rest or are having limited physical activities due to swelling, toxemia, hypertension, sciatic nerve trouble, or just because of fatigue... be strong in the Lord. Ask Him to show you how you can be used during this time of waiting. Waiting can also be a time where we can talk and listen to the Lord more effectively. Perhaps He wants to use you to reach out to others by phone, letter, or e-mail. Others are facing difficulties, too. Perhaps you can be used as a light! Waiting is just the period of time right before action!

Heavenly Father,
I acknowledge You in all the events in my life today and thank You that You are sitting with me while I wait. Show me what I can do for You in these days of waiting. I can be productive as well as reproductive! Settle my heart and my mind to be strong. I want my life to please You, even when You have called me to rest. Let all be for Your glory. Sometimes You don't remove obstacles from our path because You're trying to teach us something in the process. Open my mind and heart to receive what You are showing me this day. Keep my baby well rested and safe today. As I get extra rest, supply the baby peace and contentment. In Your name, amen.

Journal Tip: What is God showing you about pregnancy so far? What have you been doing while you have been waiting for your baby to be born? Have you enjoyed aspects of pregnancy? Is God speaking to you to do anything for Him while you wait?

Notes:

_____

_____

_____

_____

_____

_____

_____

_____

_____

Week 36

FINDING A PEDIATRICIAN

"It is not the healthy who need a doctor, but the sick." Luke 5:31b

As you approach delivery, it will be important to select a pediatrician for your baby. The doctor will probably come to the hospital to see the baby when he/she is born and will care for the baby and will likely give the circumcision to your baby if it is a boy. The professional medical care for your child starts the day he/she enters the world. In the first year of life, baby will see the doctor every few months for a checkup and immunizations. After that, routine care and having someone available if you child should get sick or injured is essential. Finding a good pediatrician that you will like and is close to where you live is important. Perhaps you have friends that can recommend someone. Let's ask God to help you in this decision.

Dear Lord,
I thank You God that I can bring all things to You and You are there to hear me. I know that You have someone in mind to care for my little one once he/she is born. I pray that You would make the connections needed in order to help us locate our doctor. I ask that even today You would give me peace and direction. I ask that You would give my child a doctor that will be around this area in the years to come so that I don't have to change doctors. I ask for stability in the pediatrics office and friendly, skillful nurses, DO's, aids, technicians, and appointment takers. I ask that my child will like the doctor and feel comfortable around him/her. Help me find a place that is convenient and that will work with any health plans I may have. I place all these things in Your hands. In Your name, amen.

Journal Tip: Have you been searching for pediatricians? Write down a few names you are considering or the one that you have chosen. Remember to pray for your pediatrician often, as his/her care will be needed often in the life of your family.

Notes:

_____

_____

_____

_____

_____

_____

_____

_____

_____

Week 36

GENTLE COMFORT

"As a mother comforts her child, so will I comfort you; and you will be comforted over Jerusalem." Isaiah 66:13

Usually a trait that comes to mind when we think of the word "mother" is comfort. There will be many times in the life of your child where he/she is hurt physically or emotionally and will come to you for comfort. There is nothing like a mother's gentle touch and soothing voice to calm her child. Even at birth we see mothers holding their little ones close and soothing their cries. Just as our mothers are comforts to us, God has promised to be there. He sent His Holy Spirit to be a comforter in ways that we cannot imagine. He is able to touch the deepest needs that no one else can see. As a mother, you will not only be able to comfort your child, but you can also pray for him/her allowing God to meet the needs we cannot soothe.

Dear Lord,
I thank You for Your comfort that is available to me and my baby. I ask that I would be a gentle, comforting mother who would be attentive and compassionate to the needs of my child. If I need growth in this area, I pray that You would do it. I pray that You would shine through me at those times and allow my little one to see a reflection of You in me. Give me the words and the actions that I need to take. I pray for guidance and Your leading in comforting my baby. Freely You have given Your Spirit to all of Your children and I ask that Your Spirit be in operation in and through me. Thank You, Lord, for soothing me today. In Your name, amen.

Journal Tip:
Do you see yourself as a soothing mother? Why or why not? Why is comforting necessary to your relationship with your child?

Notes:

_____

_____

_____

_____

_____

_____

_____

_____

_____

_____

Week 36

PROTECTING BODY, SOUL, AND SPIRIT

"Then we will no longer be infants, tossed back and forth by the waves, and blown here and there by every wind of teaching and by the cunning and craftiness of men in their deceitful scheming." Ephesians 4:14

You can never be too careful about your child's protection. That goes for their physical well being as well as emotional and spiritual. Little children are not grounded and rooted in the things of the Lord. They can be swayed by harmful advice, bad company, bad doctrine, etc. As they grow and become stronger in the things of the Lord, they will be less likely to fall into such traps and snares of the enemy. These are simply signs of the times and we as parents must rise up in protection of our children. Passive parenting will not do! Parents are to watch over their children; their activities, friends, and influences. You must have the boldness to stand against things that would threaten their well being. Too many parents ignore the still small voice of the Holy Spirit speaking warning in situations, yet we cater to fear of what might happen to our kids and entertain it. Stop being fearful and start confidently praying over your child. Let's pray that the Lord would open up our ears and eyes as parents, to be sensitive to the urging of the Holy Spirit and to proclaim boldly the things of the Lord over our children.

God,
Even though I cannot shelter my children from all harm, I am thankful that Your ever watchful eye is open to them at all times. You see his/her future already. I pray that my ears and eyes would be open as a parent. Warn me about things that would potentially harm my child in any area. I pray that I would walk so close to You that there wouldn't be anything that slips by my radar when raising my baby. Help me to guard over his influences of television, friends, magazines, books, the internet, etc. Guardianship does not mean control. Lord, I do not want to control my child. I pray that there would be balance. When there are areas that deal with others, help me to be forthright and bold with my stance when it comes to my child. Give me the words that I would say in that hour and to not stand back silent while others dictate what will happen to my son/daughter. I pray that I will have an active roll in shaping and forming my child and his/her character through prayer and communication with him/her and You. Even if something what I perceive as bad happens to my child, I know that You can turn anything the enemy has sent for harm into something good. I pray these things for my baby as he/she is in utero as well. I am his/her guardian in this hour. I pray that if something is coming against me that would harm my child that You would give me wisdom in how to deal with the situation. Thank You, Lord. Amen.

Journal Tip: Can you think of an instance in life where your parents stepped in and provided you helpful assistance or wisdom? What do you think are the worst evil influences on kids today? How will you combat these things?

Notes:

_____

_____

_____

A JOB WITH BENEFITS

"Praise the LORD, O my soul, and forget not all His benefits." Psalm 103:2

The most sought after jobs in the marketplace are those which pay well and have benefits. Do you feel like motherhood is a job with benefits? If you are living a Christ, the Word tells us that you already are blessed with benefits. The verses that immediately follow our focus verse give insight to what some of these may include; forgiveness of sins, healing, redemption, crowned us with love and compassion, our desires are satisfied with good things, and renewal us. Read on in chapter 103 to discover more benefits.

What kinds of benefits will motherhood bring? Years of love and fellowship with your child are two benefits that instantly come to mind. Over the years you will discover more and more positive attributes through motherhood. No, it doesn't usually pay in a monetary way, but it will pay in others. Your rewards will be priceless.

Dear God,
Thank You for all the benefits that You have given to me simply through living a life in You. I ask that You would show me the benefits of motherhood, especially when I feel like my job is unappreciated or unnoticed. Even carrying a baby during pregnancy is hard work with seemingly little reward. I ask that I would have Your vision to see what great gain there is in being a Christian parent. Remind me of the purpose You have in me and what I am called to do in regard to my child. Thank You for my job with benefits. Amen.

Journal Tip: What rewards come to mind when you think of Christian parenting? How is mothering a benefit to you? Do you see your job as a mother a task or is it a blessing?

Notes:

_____

_____

_____

_____

_____

_____

_____

_____

_____

_____

_____

LABOR IS COMING SOON

"Come unto Me, all you who are weary and burdened, and I will give you rest."
Matthew 11:28

Have you been experiencing pre-labor pains or soon to be? God wants us to come to Him, draw near, and rest in Him. Perhaps that can apply to you physically, but most importantly, spiritually. Don't worry about what lies ahead. Allow God to bring rest to your spirit. Going into labor and delivery will be much easier if you are prepared mentally and spiritually for it. Childbirth classes are a good way to prepare for delivery. They typically begin around weeks 36-37.

Father,
I come unto You right now. You said that if I come unto You, You would give me rest. I ask for this in all areas of my life; physical, mental, emotional, and spiritual. I ask that You would divinely prepare me for delivery. Help my spirit to rest in You at all times. Let there be a quietness about me that will permeate every fiber of my being. Help me to focus on You and trust in You in these final days and hours. I ask for a sweet anointing to saturate me and for Your Spirit to fill me and lift me up. Sustain me in these last few days. In Your name I pray, Amen.

Journal Tip: How are you feeling as these final days approach? What do you think your biggest challenge will be? What are you most confident about? Are you scheduled for childbirth classes? If so, what method or technique will you study (Lamaze, Infant/Childhood CPR, etc.)? Where will the classes be located?

Notes:

_____

_____

_____

_____

_____

_____

_____

_____

_____

_____

_____

Week 37

BURDENS CARRIED

"Take My toke upon you and learn from Me, for I am gentle and humble in heart, and you will find rest for your souls. For My yoke is easy and My burden is light."
Matthew 11:29-30

Carrying a heavy burden these days? As your pregnancy progresses, you may not only feel the strain of the physical weight you are carrying around, but you may also feel heavier in heart. It's not uncommon to feel overwhelmed or emotional at times. Let me encourage you today that no matter what you are feeling in this hour, God is able to handle it. If you are weary in body or in soul, come unto the Lord. He says in His Word that His yoke is easy and His burden is light. This is also a time to remind you that we all carry things in life, but we're not meant to keep them. Your pregnancy won't last forever. There will be a delivery some day in the near future. Whether it's in body or soul, God will deliver You if You allow Him to be in charge of your burden.

Dear God,
Thank You for seeing me in my most difficult times and loving me just the same. You are My God and I trust in You. You see the depths of my heart and the thoughts of my mind and You're not shocked one bit. I ask that You release me from any burdens that might be weighing heavy on my soul today. I give it over to You and ask that You grant me rest. I declare that the things that are burdening me will no longer affect me because I am turning them over to You. Your Word says that You are gentle and humble in heart. I know you deal with me in such sweet ways. Help me to find rest in You in this hour. I praise You, Lord. Watch over my baby today and his/her development. I pray that everything is progressing smoothly and flawlessly. Let Your will be done in my baby today. Amen.

Journal Tip: Are you carrying any burden today that needs turned over to the Lord? This would also be a good time to check the progress of your weight. Don't forget that it's normal and healthy to gain 25-35 pounds during pregnancy!

Notes:

_____

_____

_____

_____

_____

_____

_____

_____

Week 37

JESUS FORMED IN YOUR CHILD

"My dear children, for whom I am again in the pains of childbirth until Christ is formed in you." Galatians 4:19

Parenting is often referred to as a labor of love. There is no doubt when we physically give birth to children that there is a lot of pain involved. The same can be likened to spiritual or emotional births and growths. In this passage of scripture, Paul is concerned for the Galatians. He uses this phrase to express the anguish he is going through while praying that Christ and His likeness would be formed in them. He uses this analogy of the pains of childbirth often throughout his writings. He feels the stretching of his faith, the anticipation of expectancy, and the pain of waiting as the birthing processes in the Galatians are unfolding. We, too, may experience some of these pains in seeing Christ formed in our children. Sometimes, we'll feel like Paul who described his plight as, "<u>again</u> in the pains of childbirth (over them)…". We may go through this spiritual process more than once as God brings our children to new places in Him.

Dear God,
Thank You for forming Christ in my life. I know that my walk has been a process and will continue to be until the day I shed this earthly body and spend eternity in heaven with You. I thank You that You are birthing new things in me, especially motherhood. Thank You for my little one today. As I am growing in expectancy, prepare the heart of my son/daughter to receive You. Cultivate a spirit that is teachable and workable. I ask that as I parent him/her and see him growing physically, spiritually, and emotionally, that I would labor in love for them. Help me to intercede in prayer for them and stand in the gap when it is needed. Birth new things in them continually, from the time he/she is born. Help me not to see birth pains (in the spiritual or physical) in a negative fashion, but in acceptance of that the process will bring forth good. Touch this baby in a special way today. Thank You, Lord. Amen.

Journal Tip: Is God birthing anything within you today? What do you think may be one of the first spiritual birthing processes when it comes to your child? Do you think your laboring in what you just described will be quick and easy or long and hard?

Notes:

_____

_____

_____

_____

_____

_____

_____

_____

BABY SHOWER

"I will send down showers in season; there will be showers of blessing."
Ezekiel 34:26b

Baby showers can be one of the most exciting times during pregnancy. You get to share your joy with your friends and family and enjoy fellowship and refreshments. Motherhood and pregnancy are things worthy of honoring, but in reality not every mother has a scheduled baby shower. I've often thought about the similarity between rain showers and how God just showers us with blessings. The Word says He rains on the just and the unjust. I watch as the media displays important people of society having babies and telling about their extravagant gifts, but many not even knowing the Creator of their precious little one. It could make someone who is not as financially fortunate feel horrible if they aren't able to celebrate in that overt manner. But take heart today! Not all the blessings you receive during pregnancy come in the form of wrapped up gifts. In fact, the best gifts are the ones that are not material. You are showering your baby with blessings and prayers every day! God sends His many blessings on mothers during pregnancy and has a special heart for moms! So, whether you have a baby shower or not... enjoy each day as a celebration of the life you have and the one that exists within you. You are honored today!

Heavenly Father,
I thank You that You don't just have one special day to shower us with Your blessings and love, but that every day is an opportunity to receive blessings from You. In this season of expecting, help me to remember that it is Your acknowledgment of me that counts and not the approval of others. Whether I have a baby shower or not, I choose to celebrate my life and the life of my baby every day! You love me so much that You sent Your son to die for my sins. I know that You are going to send blessings my way not just in material ways, but in other ways as well. You'll supply everything that I have need of. I thank You for my family and friends who care about me and this baby You have blessed me with. Raise up people around me that would be a good support system for me, even after the baby is born. Link me up with people who can not only help me in a physical way, but mentoring as well. Help me to walk in thankfulness and gratitude. Thank You, Lord. Amen.

Journal Tip: Write down how you plan to celebrate your baby and who will help you celebrate!

Notes:

_____

_____

_____

_____

_____

_____

Week 37

TIME ALONE AND REFLECTION

"Then Jesus went with His disciples to a place called Gethsemane, and He said to them, 'Sit here while I go over there and pray.'" Matthew 26:36

Before Jesus went to do His greatest spiritual act for mankind (dying on the cross for our sins), he went to the Garden of Gethsemane to be alone and to pray. Although your act of childbearing can not equally be compared to what Jesus went through, there are some common threads… it's a spiritual act as well as a physical one. Even your mind is involved! Before you go into childbirth, take some time to get alone for prayer and reflection. Some couples are even taking short vacations (of course close to home or even at home) just before the baby comes. This gives you time to connect for one last time before your family changes forever. It also allows for you to get on the same page, so to speak. This is an important key to your final preparations for childbirth and motherhood. Prepare yourself for the task ahead.

Dear Lord,
Thank You for Your times of refreshing and strength that You have given to me so often during my pregnancy. I praise You for seeing me through to the completion. As the time draws near for me to deliver, I ask that You would open a door for me to get alone for prayer and reflection. Prepare me for the task ahead. Strengthen my mind, body, and spirit. Under gird me with Your power and help me to focus on the purpose of my journey… to bring a fresh little soul into the world. Thank You, Lord. Amen.

Journal Tip: Do you have plans to get alone for prayer and reflection before giving birth? If so, where will you go? Who will go with you?

Notes:

_____

_____

_____

_____

_____

_____

_____

_____

_____

_____

_____

Week 37

GOD GOES BEYOND OUR DREAMS

"Now to Him who is able to do immeasurably more than all we ask or imagine."
Ephesians 3:20a

No matter how much you imagine or dream about your baby and what he or she will be like, nothing will compare to the first rapturous moments following his/her birth. Not only will you have just undergone one of the most miraculous events in mankind, but you will see God's mighty handiwork firsthand. You will not believe the beauty you behold, nor can you anticipate the feelings of love and pride that will well up within you. He really does go beyond all we can hope and imagine in the birth of our children.

Dear Lord,
I anticipate the arrival of my baby with overwhelming joy! Thank You for all You have done to create this little one within my womb. Your handiwork is marvelous. Your perfect plan for creation has been experienced by me personally and I am forever changed! Help me to enjoy every moment of labor, delivery, and postpartum and to capture precious thoughts and memories to cherish in my heart. I pray that those who are there to assist me with childbirth will also help me in taking pictures or gathering memorabilia. Thank You for going above and beyond what I could ask or imagine. Amen.

Journal Tip: Be sure to make a list of what items to take to the hospital that goes beyond the normal clothes for you and the baby. You may want to include cameras, your journal, a phone card or cell phone, change for the vending machine (for your husband), etc.

Notes:

_____

_____

_____

_____

_____

_____

_____

_____

_____

_____

ENVIRONMENT FOR DELIVERY

"Do not be terrified; do not be discouraged, for the LORD your God will be with you wherever you go." Joshua 1:9

There are many environment options to deliver your baby in. Many hospitals offer Labor, Delivery, Recovery Rooms or even Labor, Delivery, Postpartum, Recovery Rooms. Perhaps you're planning on having your child at a birthing center or at home. Some may even choose birthing in water! Regardless of where you are, the Lord will be with you! There are no limits in the Spirit.

God,

I pray that You will be with me in my room during my delivery. You know where I will be at the moment this baby is born. I pray that everything that is needed for my delivery would be available to me. I pray that it is sanitary, clean, fresh, and inviting. I ask that the medical staff, attendants, technicians, interns, and doctor(s) or midwife would be ordered of You. Don't let anyone who is not supposed to assist in the delivery of my baby be allowed into my room. Nothing will happen to me that is not ordered by or allowed of You specifically. I ask that I will feel Your presence surrounding me at all times. May there be a peace in my room and a confidence in You. Help me to put my trust in You. I pray that I will be comfortable and find it easy to relax. I pray for privacy when I need it and help when I need it. Let there be something in that place that reminds me of You, Lord. Amen.

Journal Tip: Where do you plan on delivering? If it is in a hospital, have you taken a tour of the facility? Write down a brief description of what you anticipate your delivery room to be like.

Notes:

_____

_____

_____

_____

_____

_____

_____

_____

_____

_____

_____

COURAGE FOR THE DAYS AHEAD

"Be strong and courageous." Deuteronomy 31:6a

What is the definition of courage? Courage is bravery; moral or mental strength to venture, persevere, and withstand danger, fear, or difficulty. You may think you need an extra dose of courage for the days ahead. Having courage doesn't mean that you don't have any fear or difficulty. Those are the very elements that make courage arise within us. It's also important to note that God gives us the strength we need in the very moment of trouble. In our weakness, He becomes strong. So, don't look upon your current situation without hope. Have courage!

Dear Lord,
I thank You for the strength that You give and the courage that You impart on those who follow You. No matter what lies ahead in the days to come, I will not fear because You are with me. I know that courage does not mean that there isn't fear, but through courage, I can stand strong in You. Whatever I am facing today, I place it in Your hands and ask You to rule and reign in that area. I pray that You would raise up a spirit of courage in me today and lift up my countenance. Amen.

Journal Tip: What are you dealing with today that requires courage? Write it down and speak God's courage into that situation!

Notes:

_____

_____

_____

_____

_____

_____

_____

_____

_____

_____

_____

_____

_____

HOPE AND HEALING

"Then he went up and touched the coffin, and those carrying it stood still. He said, 'Young man, I say to you, gets up!' The dead man sat up and began to talk, and Jesus gave him back to his mother." Luke 7:14

Are you in heed of hope or healing today? No matter what the situation looks like in your eyes, it is never too late for God to step in and intervene. Our focus verse tells us that even the constraints of death are of no power when it comes to God…He has defeated death, hell, and the grave! He will heal in His time and His way, no matter what our perspective. Do you trust Him to be Lord in all areas of your life? Pregnancy is a time of self examination and growth, both spiritually and emotionally. Things you may not have thought about in years that have been lying dormant within you can resurface during pregnancy. Take care of those issues as they arise. Pregnancy is also a time where we can feel more pressures than we are used to. It's all in how you will handle thing. Is there something that you are struggling with lately? Perhaps a physical condition has you discouraged. Perhaps you have an emotional need? Trust God to bring life back into that area. There is always hope.

Dear Lord,
Thank You for the hope that You have placed in my heart today. Even if the situations around me seem to be at their worst, things can change when You come on the scene. I place this pregnancy, my baby, our health, my finances, my relationships, my work, my physical limitations… everything into Your hands today. I ask that You would give me peace and assurance that all things are going to work out for the good. Nothing constrains You or keeps You from working in situations. You are all powerful. Touch my baby as he/she is growing today. I pray that nothing I face in this world would have an adverse affect on my pregnancy or my baby. I praise your name, Lord. Amen.

Journal Tip: Is there an area where You want God to heal today in you or your baby? Have you seen God bring life back to any area of your life that you previously thought was dead? How have you grown spiritually or emotionally in the past few months?

Notes:

_____

_____

_____

_____

_____

_____

_____

Week 38

<u>REST ON EVERY SIDE</u>

"He said to them, 'Is not the LORD your God with you? And has He not granted you rest on every side?" 1 Chronicles 22:18a

Rest is an important aspect of pregnancy. It not only does your body good, but it benefits baby as well. It decreases your heart rate, increases your energy and stamina, not to mention what it does for your mental well being. Try to get off of your feet today and relax as much as you can. You may be trying to tie up lose ends before the baby comes, but don't neglect the rest. Too often mothers make that mistake of overdoing right before delivery and end up depleting their energy levels. Delivery will take a lot out of you. May God grant you rest on every side today in every aspect of your life.

Dear God,
I speak peace into this home today and into my hectic life. I thank You for being with my during this challenging journey. I pray that I would have comfort in my body today and rest. Give me opportunities during the day to rest and relax not only my body, but my spirit and mind as well. When I lie down to sleep, I ask that you would grant me peaceful slumber. Help my body to relax and my baby to relax so that I can sleep undisturbed. Grant rest on every side this day. In Your name, amen.

Journal Tip: How are you sleeping at night? Do you get enough rest during your day? Is there a scheduled time that you rest or when do you catch a break? Is your baby active at certain times of the day?

Notes:

_____

_____

_____

_____

_____

_____

_____

_____

_____

_____

Week 38

DAY OF DELIVERY

"... about the times and dates, we do not need to write you... will come on them suddenly as labor pains on a pregnant woman..." 1 Thessalonians 5:1-3

This passage talks about the hour that Jesus will return. No man knows the times and dates, but only the Heavenly Father. In the same way, God already knows the time and date that your baby will be born. Perhaps that day will hold significance for many. Have you ever thought about that? Even if there seems to be nothing special about the date your child will enter the world, it is special to you and special to God. He has fashioned it to be so. No other day will ring as sweetly in your ears in the years to come as birthdays will be remembered and celebrated. Enjoy the time you have now during your last few days or weeks.

Dear Heavenly Father,
Thank You for the final days I have during my pregnancy. I pray that You will make them joyous. Help me to enjoy each moment. I want to trust You to keep me and my baby until the day that I am to deliver him/her into the world. I will not fear the laboring process, for it is what You designed in order to give birth to my baby. Help me in that hour to deal with the pain and pressure. Speak to me words of encouragement that will build up my spirit. I will hold fast to Your hand. In Your name, amen.

Journal Tip: As you approach your due date, are you enjoying your days and finding something special or encouraging in each one? How many days do have left until your due date? How does it make you feel knowing that the Lord has selected a time and day for your baby to come into this world?

Notes:

_____

_____

_____

_____

_____

_____

_____

_____

_____

_____

Week 38

THE TIME TO DELIVER IS IN HIS HANDS

"My times are in Your hands." Psalm 31:15a

It's getting closer and closer to the time to deliver. You should take the time you have left to relax and only engage in light exercise (if you even feel like it). Save your energy. You'll need it for delivery. Your baby will probably drop 2-4 weeks before delivery. When that happens you will begin to breath a bit easier, but walking becomes a little more difficult as baby's head engages. Let's pray for the Lord's will to be done today and to keep you in His care.

God,
Thank You for being with me today. My times are in Your hands. Only You know the time, day, and hour that my baby will be born. Help me during these times to conserve my energy. Give me peaceful times of rest and relaxation. I know it won't be long now and I ask that You keep me safe in Your hands today. Help me to time contractions when they come, but not to be alarmed. I ask for peace in those times and that I would remain level-headed. Bring to memory everything I have learned and to apply it when needed during labor and delivery. Place everyone who will need to assist me where they are to be. I ask for favor during labor that it would be quick and that you would lubricate everything that needs lubricating. Help me to efface at a good pace and for dilation to progress at a steady rate. Keep my heart rate beating evenly and my stomach from becoming nauseous. Be with me every minute, Lord, so that I can feel your presence. Amen.

Journal Tip: Have you been having contractions? Have you timed any? When is your next doctor's appointment?

Notes:

_____

_____

_____

_____

_____

_____

_____

_____

_____

_____

FEAR AS DELIVERY APPROACHES

"What time I am afraid I will trust in thee." Psalm 56:5

It's normal as delivery day approaches to be anxious about the whole thing, especially if you've never had a baby before. No amount of planning can fully prepare you for the actual events. Fears and worry can weigh heavily on your mind. To have trust in the Lord means that you are going to put your faith in Him to see you through. Guess what! God created the birthing process! He fashioned your body to do just what it needs to deliver a baby! Trust in Him and His ways.

God,
I will put my trust in You to keep me and my baby safe during delivery. I know that You fashioned the birthing process and that everything is going to go according to Your will. Help me to stay focused on You today and during the birthing process. You know what my fears are. Your Word says that You are not the author of fear. I bind the enemy who would like to cause me to lack faith in You and Your Word. I pray that everything will work in my body according to Your will.

Journal Tip: Write down some of the ways you have prepared for birth or what you have learned about the birthing process that have helped you. Have you read any books, magazines, watched DVD's or television shows that have helped?

Notes:

_____

_____

_____

_____

_____

_____

_____

_____

_____

_____

_____

_____

Week 38

NEWBORN APPEARANCE

"Naked I came from my mother's womb..." Job 1:21a

If you've never seen a newborn baby before, one "fresh out of the womb", you may be in for a bit of a surprise! Not only are they covered with blood and other material, but sometimes their heads can be misshapen if they took awhile coming through the birth canal. Not to worry. This is all very normal. Baby will look much better once he/she has been cleaned. They will cut the umbilical cord (or allow your spouse to do it), assess their condition, clean them up, and usually hand them back to you within a matter of minutes. If you have questions about anything you observe in your baby, be sure to ask questions of your nurses and doctor. That's what they are there for. If you need any type of stitches, they will usually do that while baby is getting taken care of. You'll probably hear the baby crying as all of this is going on. Have someone take lots of pictures and enjoy your new bundle of joy!

Lord,
Be with me during my delivery. Send Your angels forth in my room to assist, protect, and minister. Give everyone who will help in the labor and delivery skill, expertise, a good attitude, compassion, and attentiveness. You know my needs before anyone else does. Make provision for those even before I go into labor. I place all things in Your hand and in Your timing. Even though I don't fully know what to expect, I do expect You to be there with me at all times, giving direction, peace, comfort, and assurance. Bless me Lord, with a flawless delivery. In Your name, amen.

Journal Tip: What kinds of things are you planning for delivery? Do you want an epidural? Do you want to go totally natural? Are you planning a C-Section? Has God prepared your heart for delivery? How so?

Notes:

_____

_____

_____

_____

_____

_____

_____

_____

_____

_____

TIME TO DELIVER

"And surely I am with you always, even to the very end of the age." Matthew 28:20b

The time is here to deliver! When you begin laboring, sometimes it's hard to keep focused on the task before you. You may seem overwhelmed at the process that may seem to have control of you. In that very hour, God will be right there with you, through every contraction, every pain, every high, and every low. He will be there at the very moment that you deliver your little one and welcome him/her into the world. Whether your room is filled with doctors, nurses, or just a midwife... always remember the heavenly guest who is standing beside you, anxiously waiting to behold His newest creation!

Heavenly Father,
I place this delivery in Your hands right now. I ask that everything will go as You have planned it to go. I cast all my fear, anxiety, and burden on You. I know that You are here with me through all of this. You are my rock, my strength, and my sustainer. I pray that You will deliver this baby in the exact fashion, time, and way You have ordained for him/her to enter this world. Set the doctors, nurses, equipment, people and angels in charge over this delivery. Give them knowledge and skill as they deliver my baby. Most of all, I pray for your presence and anointing in the room, Lord. Let me feel you near at all times.
May this baby enter this world with joy! Thank You, Lord, for this little life. I commit all these things into Your hands. Amen.

Journal Tip: How does it make you feel to know that God will be with you during your delivery? What has made you anxious about delivery? How can your faith in God help you overcome your fears?

Notes:

_____

_____

_____

_____

_____

_____

_____

_____

_____

_____

Week 39

PAIN IN CHILD BIRTH

"Will not pain grip you like that of a woman in labor?" Jeremiah 13:21b

Perhaps pain doesn't have to grip us as terribly as it once did to our mothers before us. Modern technological advances have made great strides in reducing the pain during labor and delivery. Nonetheless, pain is a part of delivering your baby. Try to look at it as a positive. Pain is your body's way of telling you that something is going on that needs attention. Certainly you can appreciate when it comes time for baby to be born that he/she needs attention! The birthing process is one that God designed and created. Even though there is pain, it will not be more than you can bear. God can give you wisdom in what kinds (if any) of medication you should have and be with you in the process of labor and delivery. Many women have found comfort in Christian music or scriptures while laboring! God has resources for you. Perhaps you are having a Cesarean Section. You may avoid labor, but there will still be surgical pain. Let's ask the Lord to go before you.

Heavenly Father,
Even though pain is a part of labor and delivery, I ask that You go before me into the labor and delivery phase of my pregnancy. I ask that You give me wisdom in what medications to seek and what methods to use to help calm me. Help me to relax as I contract. I pray that Your Spirit would saturate the room I am in at that moment. May your angels surround me and may You protect me at all times. Help the pain not become more than I can bear. Give me strength and endurance. Calm my spirit within me. Touch the baby and let this process be as painless as possible for him/her. May the process go smoothly and according to Your will. I ask for an anointing to come upon me and stillness to envelope all witnessing this birth and that they would be amazed! Let this birth somehow bring You glory, Lord. In Your precious name, Amen!

Journal Tip: What kinds of things will you use to help reduce pain or relax you during labor and delivery? Who do you plan to be in the room with you?

Notes:

_____

_____

_____

_____

_____

_____

_____

_____

FORGETTING THE PAST

"Forgetting what is behind and straining toward what is ahead..." Philippians 3:13

I am always amazed at how I have felt after the birth of a baby. All the pain you had endured seems to fade away and you suddenly realize it was all worth it. That's what has made women over the centuries willing to face it all over again to have more children. What is in the past is in the past. It doesn't affect our future unless we allow it to. Clinging on to the negative things will keep us from moving forward. That goes for parenting or anything else in life. God also births things in our emotions and spirits and the process is not always pleasant. Often newness must come through a birthing process. What is Christ bringing forth in you today (besides your baby)?

Dear God,
I thank You that I can leave what is behind and press toward what is ahead of me. All the pain in life, friends that have come and gone, job changes, geological changes, and pregnancy all push me toward something greater. I ask that whatever it is that You are birthing in my emotions or healing will come forth today. I ask for Your will to be done completely and totally in me. I know that You are with me during these times of newness. May I receive a new hope and a great joy because of what You are doing. I ask that You would grant me peace today. Rise up new life in me. I know that when the birthing process is over that You will help me to move on in a new realm. Amen.

Journal Tip: What do you think God is doing in you today? How do you feel in this stage of your pregnancy?

Notes:

_____

_____

_____

_____

_____

_____

_____

_____

_____

_____

_____

MATURITY

"But solid food is for the mature, who by constant use have trained themselves to distinguish good from evil." Hebrews 5:14

As your baby grows, you will eventually wean him/her off breast milk/formula and put him/her on solid food. When a baby is born, his/her body is not mature enough to digest solid foods. The child needs milk for sustenance. Over time, the physical growth and use will demand more nutrients to keep their bodies running, so we add solids. God doesn't want any of us to stay babies! Spiritually, He expects us to grow and mature in Him. He wants us to move on to deeper truths and not stay in the elementary truths. The author says in this verse, "who by constant use have trained themselves to distinguish good from evil." Constant use means that we are not only hearing the Word, but putting it into practice in our daily lives. The distinguishing comes in because we are to be people of discernment, not just operating in a basic understanding of the truth. God wants growth and fruit in our lives. His children are our children and He wants that for them as well.

Dear God,
Thank You for this beautiful day, regardless of how I am feeling. I thank You for the process of pregnancy and Your Spirit that sustains me all day long. Thank You for this little one, whom I can feel moving and growing. I ask today that you would bring maturity in my spiritual life and eventually into the life of my baby. Help us to grow up in You. I want to constantly use what I have learned in Your Word in my daily life. As maturity comes, bring discernment and not just an understanding of basic truth. I pray that I would have a fruitful life and that my child would as well. Thank You for Your constant care. Amen.

Journal Tip: How does maturity come to your spirit? Why is it important for babies to grow and mature spiritually, physically, and emotionally? How have you matured during your pregnancy?

Notes:

_____

_____

_____

_____

_____

_____

_____

_____

Week 39

MERCY DURING BIRTH

"When it came time for Elizabeth to have her baby, she gave birth to a son. Her neighbors and relatives heard that the Lord had shown her great mercy, and they shared her joy."
Luke 1:57-58

Delivery time is close at hand. This verse gives us great hope that God will grant you mercy during labor and delivery. When it came time for Elizabeth to deliver, all her neighbors and relatives heard that the Lord had shown her great mercy. What a testimony to God! It causes us to praise Him name. I delivered a child on the morning of 9/11/01 right when the planes were crashing into the Twin Towers. God was with us the entire time and we were able to minister to the nurses and doctors. There was such peace in the room. I can testify that God showed me and everyone in the room such grace and mercy on that day! Even the hospital chaplain could hardly believe the peace that was in our room. He asked us how this could be and said it didn't even appear that I had delivered a child. I was able to say without a doubt... it was God! May God grant you mercy during your delivery.

Dear Heavenly Father,
My request is simple today Lord, that You would show me favor and mercy during my labor and delivery. I ask that all things will go according to Your will. As I call on You during that time, let it be a testimony to You and bring glory to Your name. I ask that all who hear about my delivery will be full of joy and excitement. Thank You, Lord, for being with me every step of this journey. Amen.

Journal Tip: How long now until your due date? Do you trust in God to show you mercy during your pregnancy? Have you heard of other deliveries that have caused you hope and joy?

Notes:

_____

_____

_____

_____

_____

_____

_____

_____

_____

_____

Week 39

APART FROM BABY

"It was also called Mizpah, because he said, "May the LORD keep watch between you and me when we are away from each other." Genesis 31:49

You've been pregnant so long that it's probably unimaginable that you will one day soon be apart from your baby. You may long for that day to hold your baby and for others to also be able to hold him/her, but it's normal to feel a little sad as well. You've been home to your baby for nine months (ten lunar months) and you've been used to having baby with you at all times. Most hospitals are very gracious these days and allow mother and baby to room together, but there will still be times when baby will be taken away to the nursery to check his/her vital signs, etc. The physical separation, along with hormones that come to a screeching halt when your body realizes that the baby production has shut down, can set the stage for maternal anxiety. Post-partum blues can set in a few days after delivery. These cases can be mild or severe. I have known people that have had both. But, the day of delivery is fast approaching. I love this verse in Genesis 31, which tells us that the LORD is going to keep watch between you and your baby when you are away from each other. There is a special bond that will never be broken. No matter age your child is (a newborn or to the time when he or she goes away to college or to get married), God will continue to watch between you and your baby while you are away from each other. Let's ask God to be with you during this time.

Heavenly Father,
I know the birth of my baby is going to be such a joyous time, but it will have some sorrow as well. Knowing that this phase of our lives has passed from one era to the next can be a bit much to handle. I pray that my emotions, my hormones, and my body will all line up with Your will. I ask that You would keep me from severe post partum depression. If at any time I begin to experience these things, give me the wisdom and discernment to call out to you. If I need assistance, help me to acquire that and to not feel guilty about doing so. I place my post-partum time into Your hands. I am comforted by the fact that You are going to keep watch over me and my baby while we are apart from each other. Help me during this time. In Your name, amen.

Journal Tip: What are your thoughts about life after delivery? What are you looking forward to? What are you not looking forward to?

Notes:

_____

_____

_____

_____

_____

_____

_____

FINAL PREPARATIONS

"We will shout for joy when you are victorious and will lift up our banners in the name of our God. May the LORD grant all your requests." Psalm 20:5

Pregnancy is almost over for you. It is time to shout! God is so good. I know you can look back and say with confidence that the Lord was with you all the way. He is Jehovah Nissi, the Lord Our Banner! When I think of a banner, I think of it being raised high in the air as before a troop in battle. It signifies who the group is or their leader. God is our banner who has gone before us in the battle and struggle of bringing a new little life into the world. A banner is what is also waved after the victory. The banner shows everyone who is to be glorified for the victory. God is our banner! He is glorified!

As you read over your journal in the years to come, you will know and see that God has led you through an awesome time in your life and that you are stronger for it. You will have proof in the pages. Your child will be able to see exactly what you prayed and thought each day of their life before they entered the world. What a special gift and legacy you have given to him/her.

We have walked this journey for quite some time. Much prayer has gone up on behalf of you and your baby. I am sure as you have read this book and written in your journal that God has brought many other things to mind to pray for your baby. Keep it up in the years to come. You will never regret it!

I am honored to have walked beside you during your pregnancy. My friend let me close by saying; **MAY THE LORD GRANT ALL YOUR REQUESTS!** Bless you!

Dear God,
I thank You for keeping me safe and protected during my pregnancy. I pray that this discipline of praying for my child will continue even after delivery. Watch over me as I deliver and help all to go smoothly with no complications. I pray that everyone who is to be in the room with me will feel Your guidance, presence, and direction as we bring our new little one into the world. Bless him/her from the moment he/she arrives. Watch over us and give us success in our family. In Your name, amen.

Journal Tip: What do you have left to do in order to prepare for baby's arrival? Is everything ready? What are you looking forward to on delivery day? Write a final prayer for baby.

Notes:

_____

_____

_____

_____

_____

_____

PART 4
Week 40 and Beyond

Congratulations! You've made it to your 40th week! Take this time to relax and prepare yourself for delivery. Don't neglect your prayer time during these final days, however! Read back through the pages of your journal and reflect on what God has done in your life. Use the following blank pages for journaling!

FINAL JOURNAL TIPS:

Write down some final thoughts and prayers for your baby.

What has this journey meant to you?

How have you changed since you first found out that you were expecting?

Ask family members to write an entry about your baby or thoughts on your pregnancy.

Make a list of the things you will be determined to keep in prayer for your child as he/she grows. Include at least 5-10 items that are very important to you (e.g. education, spouse, development, etc.)

Write down your favorite verses you have about your pregnancy or baby.

Write down your first thoughts about your baby after delivery and a description of him/her.

Notes:

Notes:

298

Notes:

_____

_____

_____

_____

_____

_____

_____

_____

_____

_____

_____

_____

_____

_____

_____

_____

_____

_____

_____

_____

_____

_____

_____

_____

Notes:

300

Notes:

PART 5
If Something Unexpected Happens

If Something Unexpected Happens

There is nothing that can describe the feelings that the unexpected can bring, but we are not without hope. Human words seem so inadequate, but the presence of the Lord is priceless. In the midst of our trials, He brings comfort and security. His presence is what will make the difference in the days ahead.

Whether you have lost a baby to miscarriage or perhaps discovered that something is wrong with the baby or your pregnancy, God is STILL in control. I reminded of the three Hebrew children in the fiery furnace from the book of Daniel (chapter 3). The Word tells us that God didn't stop the fire from burning, nor did He turn down the heat. He was, however, in the midst of them and they were not harmed. That's exactly what happens when we go through a trial. The trial probably won't instantly disappear, but there He'll be... in the middle of all our pain and suffering...with us and you will not be utterly destroyed! When we go through trial, it refines us and really brings out what's inside our hearts. It's important to run to HIM and cling to HIS Word. Our lips can still praise Him and testify that He is able to calm our storm today! "We testify to what we know and what we have seen." The Lord can do a work in you right this minute. You are NOT alone. I wanted to lead you in a prayer and share with you some verses the Lord gave to me through my difficult times of miscarriage.

Lord,
I pray that You would work Your perfect peace my spirit today (and the hearts and minds of all those in my family). Let it be a peace that passes all understanding. May Your Word bring strength and comfort to me. When I am weak, You are strong. There is nothing I can do at this moment to take away the pain that I am feeling. It's hard to rise above the anguish and see clearly. Help me in my grief. God I need You. Fight for me. I need to sense Your presence in a real way in this hour. I lean heavily upon Your mighty arm. Your Word says that Your yolk is easy and Your burden is light. I am asking You to bear this burden. Help me to trust in You and to rely on Your strength to uphold me. This situation feels bigger than my faith right now, and I ask that you give me rest. Hold me up, Lord. As I am grieving, I pray that You will be in every step. I want a godly, healthy process to unfold in my/our mental, physical, emotional, and spiritual areas of life. When I am afraid, I will trust in You. Help me, Lord. Let Your Word be ingrained into every fiber of my being. Let Your will be done. Amen.

Journal Tip: You may or may not feel like writing now. If you do, express your emotions and feelings as best you can. This will aid in helping you cope during this time. Write down references to scriptures that you find the most helpful. Has God spoken anything to your heart during this time? Who has come to help you in your time of need?

*** If you have suffered a miscarriage, you will need time to grieve. There are many resources available to assist you in the process and stages of grief. Talk with your Pastor or perhaps a friend or family member who can be there for support. Make sure that you have a network of prayer partners who can intercede for you. ***

304

Notes:

_____
_____
_____
_____
_____
_____
_____
_____
_____
_____
_____
_____
_____
_____
_____
_____
_____
_____
_____
_____
_____
_____
_____

VERSES TO HELP YOU IF SOMETHING UNEXPECTED HAS HAPPENED:

"Do not be afraid, for I am with you..." Isaiah 43:5a

"When I am afraid, I will trust in You." Psalm 56:3

"But He said to me, "My grace is sufficient for you, for my power is made perfect in weakness."
2 Corinthians 12:9a

"In this you greatly rejoice, though now for a little while you may have had to suffer grief in all kinds if trials. These have come so that your faith- of greater worth than gold, which perishes even though refined by fire-may be proved genuine and may result in praise, glory, and honor when Jesus Christ is revealed."
1 Peter 1:6-7

"You intended to harm me, but God intended it for good to accomplish what is now being done..."
Genesis 50:20a

"All things are Yours, whether... the world or life or death, or things present or the future- all are Yours."
1 Corinthians 3:21-22

"All this is for your benefit, so that the grace that is reaching more and more people may cause thanksgiving to overflow to the glory of God. Therefore we do not lose heart. Thought outwardly we are wasting away, yet inwardly we are being renewed day by day. Four our light and momentary troubles are achieving for us an eternal glory that far outweighs them all." 2 Corinthians 4:15-17

"Consider it pure joy, my brothers whenever you face trials of many kinds, because you know that the testing of your faith develops perseverance. Perseverance must finish its work so that you may be mature and complete, not lacking anything." James 1:2-4

"Hear my cry, O God; listen to my prayer. From the end of the earth I call to You. I call as my heart grows faint; lead me to the rock that is higher than I." Psalm 61:1-2

"I will lift up my eyes to the hills- where does my help come from? MY HELP COMES FROM THE LORD, the maker of heaven and earth. He will not let your foot slip; He who watches over you will not slumber. The LORD watches over you - the LORD is your shade at your right hand; the sun will not harm you by day, nor the moon by night. The LORD will keep you from all harm-He will watch over your life; the LORD will watch over your coming and going both now and forevermore." Psalm 121:1-8

"From birth I have relied on You; Your brought me forth from my mother's womb. I will ever praise You." Psalm 71:6

"As long as we are at home in the body, we are away from the Lord." 2 Corinthians 5:6b

"Trust in the Lord with all your heart, and lean not upon your own understanding; in all your ways acknowledge Him, and He will make your paths straight." Proverbs 3:5-6

"Finally, brethren, whatever is true, whatever is noble, whatever is right, whatever is pure, whatever is lovely, whatever is admirable- if anything is excellent or praiseworthy- think about such things." Philippians 4:8

"(God said) Behold, I will create new heavens and a new earth. The former things will not be remembered, nor will they come to mind... the sound of weeping and of crying will be heard in it no more. Never again will there be in it an infant who lives but a few days..." Isaiah 65:17, 19b, 20

"For He does not willingly bring affliction or grief to the children of men." Lamentations 3:33

"Now we know that if the earthly tent we live in is destroyed, we have a building from God, an eternal house in heaven, not built by human hands." 2 Corinthians 5:1